Sacramental Whine:
Chronicling
the
Independent Sacramental
Movement

Volume II

Bishop David Oliver Kling

ISBN 9798522515966

Table of Contents

Foreword

Rev. Timothy Olivieri

Nearly every episode of Sacramental Whine begins with the same charge to the guest; "What is your elevator speech for the Independent Sacramental Movement?" There is, however, no greater elevator speech than refer to Sacramental Whine itself. The elevator speech exercise illustrates the diversity of the movement and the ideas therein. Any one elevator speech may satisfy the casual inquirer and answer the question, who is cleric the cleric before me? This podcast answers the broader question of what the Independent Sacramental Movement is truly about and where they, too, might fit in.

Traditionalist or Gnostic and every degree in between and every imaginable combination of the same can find a home among their fellow seekers in a community centered around creating the churches we all wish we had growing up. These voices and their differing purposes, contexts, backgrounds, and missions come together in a uniform format for listeners of all varieties.

What was once an anomaly of severely splintered minority groups largely unknown by the public has become a thriving spiritual movement with professional chaplains, pastors, and administrators. Sacramental Whine, as a podcast and in this printed form, carries on the movement's academic tradition following in the footsteps of the works of Bishop John Plummer. As Plummer's *Many Paths* gave voice to the micro-denominations of that time and the private devotions of wandering bishops, now Bishop Oliver gives voice to the jurisdictions which have matured from there.

Sacramental Whine comes at a point of cultural shift for the Independent Sacramental Movement. It is a time when some, myself included, begin shying away from the use of the word "independent" and begin focusing on the role of the sacraments in the spiritual and social life of its jurisdictions. No longer are we merely dissatisfied Catholics who can be written off as pretenders playing church in their home chapels. We are sacramental Christians with our own traditions and practices. No longer does the typical person stand at a metaphorical crossroads looking only to Anglican, Roman Catholic, or Orthodox

Churches to fulfill their sacramental needs. Now we stand as another option with its own history and an outstretched hand welcoming all. There is a sacramental community for everyone.

I have previously advocated the use of the term "United Sacramental Movement" to describe Christians united by sacraments even if not ecclesiastical polity. It is a term I stand by. Though I recognize that it is a term that, ironically, causes nearly as much division as it hopes to heal. Beyond the grace of the sacraments the many jurisdictions of the ISM are united by the emerging media within the movement. Standing at the forefront of this emerging media is Bishop David Oliver Kling and the Sacramental Whine podcast.

As you read the words of the many guests to follow consider how these different voices come together in one truth. Consider also how your voice might also join the chorus.

Rev. Subdeacon Timothy J.M. Olivieri
Administrator
Community of St. George/Liberal Catholic Church – The Young Rite
March 2021
Ithaca, New York

Introduction

Welcome to Volume II of *Sacramental Whine: Chronicling the Independent Sacramental Movement*. This series of books sprang forth from the podcast, *"Sacramental Whine,"* and I hope that through both the podcast and the books the story of the ISM will be told and the best kept secret within Christianity will become less of a secret.

In Volume I, several characteristics of the Independent Sacramental Movement were addressed. Let us look at another characteristic of the ISM, which is fluidity. In looking up the definition of fluidity, the Oxford Dictionary has several definitions that I believe easily show applicability to the ISM. One definition is, "the ability of a substance to flow easily." Another definition is, "Smooth elegance or grace." And the third being, "the state of being unsettled or unstable; changeability." All three of these definitions help to illustrate the fluid nature of the Independent Sacramental Movement which I will break down.

"The ability of a substance to flow easily."

It is not uncommon for clergy within the Independent Sacramental Movement to move between jurisdictions like some people change their socks. Now, I'm only joking; however, the fluid nature of the ISM does foster ease of mobility allowing clergy to move between one jurisdiction to another without too much difficulty. This also includes jurisdictional mergers, schisms, and even "rebranding."

I have witnessed bishops and priests moving between multiple jurisdictions in a short period of time, often with no meaningful probationary period. I have seen several clerics leave a jurisdiction in protest over one thing or another and watch a new jurisdiction form out of the conflict. I have also seen bishops close a jurisdiction only to reappear as presiding bishop of another, rebranded, jurisdiction with a different focus, name, or identity.

In "mainstream" denominations it is often difficult to move from one to another just as it is difficult to get ordained. Even progressive denominations like the Unitarian Universalist Association or the United Church of Christ have long and arduous ordination processes; however, in the ISM it is commonplace to have ordinations without formation or education with clergy floating through several jurisdictions in their lifetime. The positive side of this phenomenon is that ISM clergy have several options in which to "rest their head," while the negative side is a lack of stability or apparent stability.

"Smooth elegance or grace."

There is another aspect of fluidity and that is moving freely through various theological realms or belief systems, resulting in syncretism. I know several ISM clerics who also hold lineage within Buddhist traditions and can freely flow between the worlds of Buddhism and Christianity without any internal conflict. Likewise, with the rise of Christopaganism it is not uncommon to see an ISM priest or bishop also involved in some form of Paganism, either directly such as holding a Wiccan lineage or in the liminal space of Druid Revival Druidry which emphasizes nature spirituality without the polytheism of other forms of Druidry. I have known ISM clergy who practice Hermetic magic and mysticism and are adepts in Kabbalistic spiritual practices. All these examples embrace an identity that includes Independent Catholicism. Historically, Liberal Catholicism of the Wedgwood and Leadbeater variety have embraced Theosophy which holds to Eastern ideas such as reincarnation; however, these Theosophical views are not limited to those within the Liberal Catholic Church tradition but also include a wide swath of clergy in more traditional Independent Catholic jurisdictions. You only need to slightly peel back the onion to discover this about the Independent Sacramental Movement.

Is this a strength within the movement, theological fluidity, and lack of hard orthodoxy? It can be, but it comes at a price. I have mentioned that the ISM is a spectrum of practices and beliefs. There are many within the ISM who would gladly be Roman Catholics if the Church would ordain women or accept gay and lesbian priests. The theological conservatives and "fundamentalists" will likely never accept the theologically fluid within the ISM; however, those in the more fluid camp of the ISM are in the ISM because they want to be and not because they must because of other existential issues. The Roman Catholic Church used to teach, "No salvation outside of the Roman Catholic Church," but this thought has changed to a more ecumenical and interfaith point of view and within the ISM the idea of pluralism, or various ways to reach salvation, has become popular. The popularity of pluralism makes theological fluidity possible.

I also know clergy within the ISM who were once very fluid who find themselves less fluid now and who work to distance themselves from their syncretistic past. I understand this well because I have done the same. As I find myself getting older, and working as a chaplain within hospice, I have less of an interest in spiritual practices outside of the Christian tradition and find myself attracted to Eastern and Oriental Orthodoxy; however, I remain in the ISM because I value pluralism, inclusivity, and equality. I believe the ISM has an opportunity to be the "post-post-modern" church of tomorrow.

"The state of being unsettled or unstable; changeability."

One of the advantages of the ISM is that we are small and able to adapt quickly to change, something that I call "Our Sacred Advantage." If there is a problem that needs fixed the response can often be quick and the problem solved without having to go through numerous meetings and legalistic conferences. This is a strength of the Movement. The changeability within the ISM seems to foster relationship building and networking over bureaucracy and "byzantine" legalisms. Bishops and clergy are starting to network and work together, and jurisdictional lines are starting to blur as bishops become open to working with other jurisdictions and friendships established.

While the ISM is filled with people who live out multi-faith perspectives and syncretize various spiritual practices together this is often seen as a negative by some within the Movement. There are those who cringe at the esoterically inclined and would prefer the Gnostics leave the ISM sandbox. Even I, who delights in my acceptance of diversity, have limits to what I will accept and tolerate within the rich tapestry of ISM theological diversity. The fluid nature of the Independent Sacramental Movement is simultaneously elegant and graceful and unsettling.

Rt. Rev. David Oliver Kling, M.Div.
Co-Presiding Bishop, Community of Saint George/The Young Rite
Affiliated Bishop, The Ascension Alliance
Assisting Bishop, The Convergent Christian Communion
April 2021
Massillon, Ohio

The Elevator Speech

"Do your best to present yourself to God as one approved, a worker who has no need to be ashamed, rightly handling the word of truth." — 2 Timothy 2:15

In this chapter, we will take a closer look at the elevator speech which asks the question, "How would you describe the Independent Sacramental Movement to someone who has no idea what it is?" A nice succinct definition to this question is, "The Independent Sacramental Movement is an incredibly diverse autonomous movement with hundreds of micro-denominations rooted in apostolic succession and celebrating the seven sacraments instituted by Jesus Christ." That's a succinct elevator speech. But don't take my word for it. I have compiled several others such as:

Archbishop Alan Kemp, the founder and first Presiding Bishop of the Ascension Alliance:

When I tell people that I'm an independent Catholic priest, or I'm a bishop or whatever, depending upon who it is that's asking me the question, usually I will say that the Independent Movement is a group of people who have valid ministries that they identify as, Catholic or as Orthodox but are not part of the mainstream Roman Catholic Church and they're not part of the Federation of Orthodox bishops (SCOBA). I would say that the independent movement tends to be a wide diversity of people with different orientations. There are people that are on the liberal side who are very free in terms of what is their focus in terms of being open to all kinds of things. Then there are people on the other end who are extremely conservative and who may be more conservative in their ideology than, for example, the Roman Catholic Church or some of the Orthodox jurisdictions.

Within the independent movement, you have valid ministry by virtue of apostolic succession, the same claim to sacerdotal authority as the Roman Catholic Church or mainstream Orthodox churches but you have the freedom to explore beyond some of the doctrines that had been adopted by the Roman or the Orthodox churches. I like to talk about how the movement is very diverse. Personally, I'm on the progressive or liberal side as opposed to the conservative side, but I certainly recognize that there's a lot of diversity within the independent movement.

Bishop Brian Stanford, with the Gnostic Catholic union:

For me, it's something that I've been actively working on and I find myself having to give an elevator speech frequently because I have a public job. What I try to say is usually too much. I start with, back in the 1700s, there were these people who split off from the Roman Catholic Church. Recently my fiancé described me to someone as being a renegade Catholic priest and what I'm doing as Catholicism probably doesn't sound like anything you have ever heard of as Catholicism. So as an experiment, that's the elevator speech I'm working with right now, which usually makes people laugh and then gives an opening so they can ask more questions. Then I can go into more of the detail that I love.

Bishop Carol Vaccariello, an Independent Catholic Bishop and United Church of Christ pastor:

The best way to describe it is that being a sacramental movement means that we observe the sacraments which most people relate to as the Roman Catholic Church. We've kept the best of the Roman Church in terms of the sacraments and we've let go of the hierarchical structure that is oppressive. It's an observation of the sacraments in a religious system to assist our living. The sacraments people most often think of are baptism, marriage, and communion.

Bishop Chris Carpenter, Presiding Bishop of the Reformed Catholic Church:

It's interesting to me because I came to the Independent Sacramental Movement out of desperation, because I had been a Roman Catholic priest and I was backed into a corner by my then bishop. I had been very critical of the Independent Sacramental Movement. Yet when I had to seek it out and affiliate with it, I realized the diversity of it is tremendous, more than I ever realized. The history of it is longer and more significant than I ever realized. I encourage people to explore other options for Catholicism. It's not all about Rome. Rome and the Roman Catholic Church is not the only Catholic Church and hasn't been the only Catholic Church for centuries. I encourage people to broaden their minds and be adventurous and take a leap. Check out what communities are near you. They might ultimately feed you better than the traditional Catholic churches or the Roman Catholic Church that you're probably more familiar.

Bishop Gregory Godsey, Presiding Bishop of the Old Catholic Churches International:

Independent Sacramental Movement is the anti-mainstream churches or we are a decentralized version of Christianity that spans from all sorts of conservatives, also liberal and very progressive to very much 15th century Tridentine. There's so much variety within the independent movement that if you can't find something that fits you, you're just not looking hard enough. Most of the people in the movement are ministering to people in the world, and they're not concerned about being a huge edifice. They're not concerned about bringing in millions of dollars. They're concerned with helping people become more spiritual, and can heal some of the division, some of the pain, caused by the mainstream jurisdictions and mainstream denominations in the world.

Father Jerry Maynard, with the Apostolic Catholic Church:

I would tell people that the Independent Sacramental Movement is a conglomeration of individuals and communities around the United States but also around the world who identify with the three most prominent Christian traditions of Anglican, Catholic and Orthodox, but who for some reason, whether theological, political or practical divert from the main hierarchies of those traditions.

Bishop Joseph Menna, the Prior General and Bishop of the Augustinians of the Immaculate Heart of Mary:

I've met a lot of people who don't have any idea that we exist. I live here in the northeast in the Philadelphia area where the Roman Catholic Church, is still very strong. People do not generally understand that there are other ways to be Catholic. When we're out at events, we try and schedule ourselves to be at different local fairs and things of that nature with a table and people come up and they ask what is this about? We've used capture phrases before to catch people's attention, things like "Vatican Free Catholics" to try and spark conversations. I usually begin by explaining the history of the Old Catholic Church and their break from Rome over the election of their bishops. I talk about Carlos Duarte Costa and his church in South America to try and get people to understand that these breaks with Roman Catholicism are more about policy and polity rather than theology. That it's the same sacramental worship, the same beliefs, the same devotions, but we have a different quality of how we govern ourselves and see ourselves.

Acolyte Kathleen Ostlie, with the Apostolic Johannite Church:

The Independent Sacramental Movement emphasizes tradition and the sacraments, but doesn't fall in line with churches people are more familiar with like the Roman Catholic or Orthodox Churches. It presents itself in a similar way. It tends to carry deeper doctrines more openly in a lot of Independent Sacramental communities, there's an esoteric undertone to a lot of it, some more than others. It isn't just priests behind closed doors doing things all the time, they tend to involve the congregation, at least in the Apostolic Johannine Church, in what's going on and explaining the deeper meanings to the congregation rather than it being only for the clergy.

Bishop Kenny von Folmar, Presiding Bishop of the Convergent Christian Communion – formerly known as the Anthem Network:

The Independent Sacramental Movement is a collection of diverse expressions of the church, that can be anything from Catholic to Orthodox to Anglican. I tell folks that have maybe left the Roman Catholic Church and have found a home in a place where they can express themselves as they really are, or even Orthodox who have not found a home in the traditional canonical churches have found a home in the independent Packer metal movement.

Father Kevin Daugherty, with the Convergent Christian Communion:

The Independent Sacramental Movement is an incredibly complex network. The Independent Sacramental Movement is a large association of Catholic and apostolic Christians who believe in historical Christianity as expressed in the traditional sacraments and through apostolic succession – but without being under the direct authority of the Vatican or any other traditional metropolitan see. We have independent Catholics, Independent Anglicans, Independent Orthodox, and, even through there's great diversity, the ISM is somewhat cohesive and there's a lot of ecumenism within these different parts of the movement. The different bishops of the movement usually recognize one another. There are common sacraments and common lines of apostolic succession. We bring together the fullness of Christianity as commonly expressed within Catholic, Orthodox, and Anglican churches, be we possess the freedom and the organic movement of the early apostolic Church!

Bishop Lainie Peterson, Presiding Bishop of The Open Rite:

I tell them that the ISM is a movement – not an organization or a denomination – within the broader Christian Church in which individuals who have apostolic succession offer the sacraments within an independent, hyper-individual or congregational context. In this movement, people are ordained to the Holy Orders – as deacons, priests and bishops – who offer the Eucharist and the other sacraments, often within small, local communities, or in some cases, in broader ministries through chaplaincy or charity.

Deacon Michael Holford, with the Ecumenical Catholic Church of Australia:

I begin with the imperfect phrase, "Independent Catholic." Most people know what "Catholic" means. I emphasize that we are a church apart from the Roman Catholic Church, whith bishops in apostolic succession. As an analogy, I point out how the Old Catholic Church and the Anglican Church enjoy apostolic succession but are not tied to the Roman Catholic Church. I emphasize the importance of the sacraments as the central feature that defines us as a movement.

Bishop Nina Paul, Presiding Bishop of the Open Catholic Church:

It's not always an easy conversation, depending on my audience. If I'm with people who are very devout Catholics, very strong Romans, I try to explain to them that we've been around for a long time. I'm a bishop in a church that is not connected to Rome, except by ineage and sacraments, and I'm not under their canon law. They'll say, "You can't be a bishop because of canon 1024!" – which states that only baptized males can be validly ordained in the Roman Catholic Church – and I respond, "I'm not subject to your canon law!"

Father Robert Mitchell, with Ekklesia Epignostika Seminary:

What's important about the Independent Sacramental Movement is that the doors are open to your experience of Christ. We often believe that we have to conform before we enter through the doors, but in the Independent Sacramental Movement, the doors are open, even before we believe, and all people can come in, look around, and experience the sacraments.

Subdeacon Tim Olivieri, with the Community of Saint George (The Young Rite):

I describe the Independent Sacramental Movement as a movement within Christianity that is centered on the sacraments, as they are typically practiced within the Catholic and Orthodox traditions. Unlike those traditions, though, the ISM places greater emphasis on smaller communities that are independent of the larger denominations. At times, I question the "I" in the "ISM" – but our independence is part of who wer are and what whe do!

There you have it, several different elevator speeches. What's your elevator speech?

> *"Cleanse your mind from anger, and your remembrance from evil and shameful thoughts, and then you will find out how Christ dwells in you."*
>
> —St. Maximus the Confessor

Concluding thoughts...

Apologetics is "to speak in defense" of one's faith. The Elevator Speech is a type of apologetics in that it gives the speaker the opportunity to tell the story of the Independent Sacramental Movement to a stranger, a friend, a co-worker, or family member. Through the Elevator Speech we are sharing with another our truth of this Movement and how we share that truth is important.

Schism means to divide; therefore, a schismatic is someone who has divided something. The word schism is used primarily to describe divisions within a religious context and schism as an ecclesiastical phenomenon is common within the Independent Sacramental Movement. It is not uncommon for someone to get ordained by one micro-denomination, or jurisdiction, and then within a year move to another organization.

If the Elevator Speech is a type of apologetics, I wonder about the narrative that is being promoted by the speech itself. A common theme within Elevator Speechs is a defense of "independence," which is essentially a defense of schism. Defending the division within the Body of Christ. I want to ask the question, why? Why be independent of the Roman Catholic Church, the Anglican Communion, or any of the Eastern Orthodox Churches?

I can speak for myself and give voice to my narrative. My initial exposure to Roman Catholicism occurred in the late 1980s when I was 18 or 19 and stationed in Washington, D.C. I was a young sailor. Had never been baptized and while I loosely identified as a Christian, I had started to explore various religions. Not far from the barracks was the base library, with an under-funded collection of books. I discovered a multivolume Catholic Encyclopedia, likely printed in the 50s. What caught my attention was a copy of "This is the Mass," by Bishop Fulton Sheen. Published in the late 1950s the book beautifully presented the Tridentine Mass that existed prior to the Second Vatican Council. At this time in my life, I had attended the generic Protestant service on base, but it didn't touch me. It didn't resonate with me, but when I started reading "This is the Mass," I became enamored with it. I wanted to go to the Catholic service on base, but I was nervous.

Eventually, I found the resolve to attend that Roman Catholic worship service at the base chapel. I was surprised and disappointed in what I discovered. What I witnessed was nothing like Fulton Sheen's depiction of the mass. In fact, I felt there wasn't much difference between the Protestant worship service and the Catholic service, at least in my experience at the base chapel. I was confused.

Eventually, I was baptized. Father Joseph Terry Marks baptized me at Our Lady of Fatima Chapel, a Traditionalist Roman Catholic Parish. Father Marks was an independent Traditionalist Catholic priest affiliated with the Society of Saint Pius X. A year or so later I was confirmed at St. Athanasius Traditionalist Roman Catholic parish near Alexandria, Virginia by Bishop Richard Williamson of the Society of Saint Pius X. Two weeks after my confirmation I was a postulant at Christ the King Monastery in Culman, Alabama. A Traditionalist Roman Catholic Benedictine monastery under the leadership of Father Prior Leonard Giardina, O.S.B.

Traditionalists do not identify as being a part of the Independent Sacramental Movement, even though I place them under the ISM umbrella they emphatically reject being in the ISM. Instead, Traditionalists claim they are the true Church, and the "Novus Ordo" Church are usurpers and the true schismatics. An interesting comparison can be found between the Elevator Speech of a Traditionalist Roman Catholic and someone in the Independent Sacramental Movement. The link is in the defending of the division, or schism, with Rome.

For the Traditionalist the defense is all about how Rome abandoned the magisterium, or deposit of faith, of the Roman Catholic Church. The Traditionalist is pained by the loss of Latin in the liturgy, the priest facing the people instead of "*ad orientem*," communion in the hand, Eucharistic ministers, and an entire litany of other complaints. The Elevator Speech of the Traditionalists always hovers around tradition and their embracing of tradition as the holy of holies juxtaposed against what Rome is promoting now as Roman Catholicism, and their independence of Rome's "shenanigans."

In the Independent Sacramental Movement, the juxtaposition with Rome is usually the opposite. Rome refuses to ordain women, accept various sexual orientations, embrace innovation and experimentation, and so on and so on. The often-spoken ISM narrative is like that of the Traditionalist in that it reinforces the division between "who we are" and "who they are." An US vs. THEM is perpetually reinforced.

In my time with the Traditionalists, I discovered a love for tradition, of liturgy, and of everything "Catholic." I believe there is some truth and wisdom to the lamentations of the Traditionalists; however, their promotion of an US vs. THEM ecclesiology was too much for me to stomach.

I do not feel the same US vs. THEM vigor within the Independent Sacramental Movement, at least my corner of it, as I did as a Traditionalist Roman Catholic. However, it is still present, and I wonder, what would it be like if we started to craft a different narrative of our branch of the Body of Christ? A narrative that doesn't promote division but instead promotes connection. What would that connection look like?

For Reflection, Contemplation, & Prayer:

- What would an apologetic look like that defended sacramental Christianity in all its various forms?
- Is it healthy to promote an US vs. THEM ecclesiology? What is the benefit of promoting "independent" when explaining the Independent Sacramental Movement?
- What is your Elevator Speech? After reading this chapter has your speech changed?

"Belonging, Becoming & Believing"
A Conversation with Bishop David Strong

"I have been crucified with Christ and I no longer live but Christ lives in me the life I now live in the body I live by faith in the Son of God who loved me in gave himself for me." — Galatians 2:20

Bishop David Strong is the Presiding Bishop of the Apostolic Catholic Church in America (ACCA), a multiracial, inclusive, spirit-filled church committed to making disciples in the Independent Catholic tradition. Bishop Strong is the founding pastor of Spirit of Christ Independent Catholic Church in Tacoma, Washington. He is a passionate advocate for civil rights in the community and has extensive experience in non-profit leadership. He was ordained in 1992 and consecrated a bishop in 1994.

KLING: Can you talk a little bit about your local community, Spirit of Christ Community Church?

STRONG: Spirit of Christ was founded in 2012, and it started out of the need to support LGBT issues. I was with a local United Methodist pastor at the time, and he said, "Well, David, what are you gonna do about this?" and he then said, "You can rent the chapel in our church and get started." It was prompted by a United Methodist minister, and one of the things that in the initial part of that was that I realized there was no open and affirming experience in this community that also recognized an African American way of worship. Yet, I knew I was sacramental and Catholic in my expression, having been raised in the Black Church and the Catholic Church together, I thought, "How do I bring these two together?" That was how Spirit of Christ started.

I had a friend who said, "We want to let it grow organically," and as I looked around, I began to tell people what we were doing and getting out in the community. A variety of people came. Now, our congregation has folks from Korea, Guatemala, Ukraine, Mexico, with African American and white people. We still use music of the African American tradition and praise tradition, and that worship has allowed us to create a Catholic presence. This is not something that I made up in terms of understanding worship, but my experience. My Roman Catholic Church experience was with amazing black priests and nuns and folks who embrace black culture and Catholic worship. For example, I spent a weekend with the late Archbishop James Lyke and Sister Thea Bowman at St. Joseph's church in St. Louis and they have had a profound impact on me and how I embrace being black and Catholic.

KLING: In your jurisdiction, the Apostolic Catholic Church in America, you talk about being sacramental and sanctified. Can you talk about what you mean by the sanctified tradition?

STRONG: Sure. Sanctified is a term that is used often in the African American community for the idea of holiness or charismatic expressions. Within the ACCA, before we became the ACCA we were called the Orthodox Catholic Church of the Moors. There were three African American priests, two others besides me, and a white priest that was pastor of a black congregation in Saginaw, Michigan. We came together because of that sanctified expression. Almost all African American worship tends to be charismatic. What I thought of as we talk about this are three traditions, we worship sacramentally, we take social justice, and we live sanctified and that leads us to focus on holiness. Too often in a lot of our movements we will focus on the holiness aspect of it and not on the social justice or the social justice aspect and not the sanctified or holiness part. It really is about embracing a way of living, and for some folks that is the charismatic expression within our Church. In our case, through the Spirit of Christ, you will see people who raise their hands. Sometimes in worship, we may go beyond the words written on the liturgy. It really is about a way of living out our faith.

KLING: Can you talk about the creation of local faith communities? I know, in the past, you have spoken heavily on the need within the Independent Sacramental Movement to form local congregations. Can you talk a little about that?

STRONG: I believe very passionately in this movement, and I believe that we want to get it in beyond this, and still the most common way that people gather is in local faith communities. We traditionally call those parishes and often we look at that and get overwhelmed, all the structures that come with it. I'm not sure that we must repeat all of that, but I do believe to make more Independent Catholic disciples, we need to create more faith communities. There is a lot of literature about church planting out there, but obviously not from our perspective. There is a lot of literature on renewing churches and one person that is making a lot of news right now is probably Father Michael White and his book, *"Rebuilt: Awakening the Faithful, Reaching the Lost, and Making Church Matter."* It was written from a more established Roman Catholic perspective, but he has some principles that I think works for us. In the Independent Movement we are creating, we're not rebuilding, we are creating from ground zero, from scratch. So, we need to create more communities and those communities may meet on Sunday morning. They may meet in a rented church space; they may meet in a coffee shop; or a laundromat but creating more communities so that the people know and embrace Independent Catholicism, as a way of living Independent Old Catholicism. I try to encourage people across our Movement to create faith communities.

KLING: It would seem like this impetus to create local faith communities is linked to evangelism. Can you share a little bit of your thoughts on evangelism?

STRONG: For me evangelism is sharing with people your faith in a way that is non-corrosive, that is not intended to scare people into church, but to welcome them and to use the words of Jesus, "Come and see." While the clergy can be the impetus for that it's your lay people that are going to be the ones who will say say, "Wow, you go to church, tell me more about that." It's about invitation, and for most of us, as Father Michael White says, "Because, it's the weekend, stupid." The weekend experience matters, and most people are going to encounter us as a faith community on the weekend. Individually, people are going to encounter us through their social network, and our people need to be able to articulate what it means to be Independent Catholic, or Old Catholic. If our people can share their faith in a way that invites people, then that's the first step of evangelism.

KLING: It seems like your concept of evangelism is linked to sanctification. That is, living a holy life and being committed to social justice. When you combine the two you present an example that other people can look at and go, "I want to be like that," or "I want to be a part of that," and it's different than beating people up with the Bible and saying, "You need to come here otherwise you're gonna go to hell." Or saying, "If you don't come here, you're not in the in crowd," instead, it's a polite way of inviting people to the faith. To experience Jesus in a local context with a group of people that are open and inclusive, and just good people.

STRONG: Yeah, and then of course, what do you invite them to? To worship, and you try to make the mass (Eucharist) the most excellent thing that you're able to offer with the gifts you have. I understand that in our Movement we often don't have choirs, and music teams and all that. Therefore, community building is key. When people come to worship, they should experience reverence and connection and a call to live out for Christ. Discipleship, that that's how we do it. There are techniques we use along the way, but once we get people in the door our goal is to help them become disciples of Christ. One of the important points from the book *Rebuilt* is the idea of building discipleship paths. One day there was a Roman Catholic priest who visited our church and he said to me, "You know, David, I heard you mention in your sermon that often people belong before they believe." I had heard that from somewhere else, and when I think about it, the process for us is that the first step is people finding a sense of belonging in our community. As they begin to make friends and connect to the community spiritually, then we move into a process of becoming. Now, they are embracing the sacraments and are active in ministry in the local congregation. At some point, the believing happens after listening to the gospel and worshiping and participating in the Eucharist. It's a three-step process. We believe it's a gradual process of growing into discipleship and in community.

KLING: I like that belonging, becoming, and believing!

STRONG: Because something's gonna come with belief, right? Then they are trying to find belonging because they haven't found a way of belonging within other communities for a variety of reasons. When we invite people, we need to bring them into something to help them continue to grow, we don't just meet you where you are and say, "Okay, well here, this is our development that you need to do as a spiritual person." My dad was a Pentecostal minister, and he often talks about holiness and sanctification. Sanctification is a very Catholic term, and what we're trying to do is help people live the holiness that Christ invited us to.

KLING: Thank you for sharing that perspective! One thing I wanted to talk to you about is you have stated that we, meaning "we" the Independent Sacramental Movement, need to own the term

"Independent Catholic" as a term to identify ourselves. Can you elaborate on what you mean by that and share your thoughts?

STRONG: Sure. I recognize that we have different terms, but often when you say, "Independent Catholic," some people respond with, "I don't really like that term, and seems like it's attached to being independent of Rome." But I think that we need to own it. It's a different way of being church, and not just about being independent of Rome or the Anglican Church. It's about a way of being church. When I look over the history of this Movement, there's the Old Catholic movement and its ecclesiology, which I think is lovely. It's something we all should embrace, of bishop, priests, and deacons being the fullness of church gathered at the Eucharist and those wonderful things. When I look at people who have embraced Independent Catholicism or its history, I look at the Philippine Independent Church which has full communion with the Old Catholic Church and the Episcopal Church. I think about the movement in Brazil, Bishop Carlos Duarte Costa, and the African Orthodox Church which came out of the Episcopal Church, and all three of those Independent movements came out of a need for folks to not just keep a spiritual connection, but out of some struggle. With the Philippine Independent Church, there was colonization from the Spanish and American churches. The Apostolic Church in Brazil, a concern about the church embracing Nazis, and then the African Orthodox Church, because the black folks in the church did not have the right to vote their convictions. They were independent, not because of a rebellion against theology, but because they were claiming self-determination. They wanted to hold on to their liturgical, and sacramental faith and they wanted to speak social justice. What I'm saying is that we shouldn't be embarrassed by the term Independent Catholic. It doesn't have to be defined as independent of something else, and we can embrace the theology of the early church in the midst of it.

KLING: Are you familiar with the term "Independent Church Movement?" I think it's predominantly associated with churches in Africa that rebelled against colonialism and established independent churches, mainly independent of the Anglican Church because there were a lot of English colonies in Africa. I recently discovered this movement, the Independent Church Movement. There's no known to me link to the Independent Sacramental Movement, but it shows an ecclesiology that wants to disassociate itself from European colonialism.

Even though our situation here in the United States is very different, then the church in Africa, there could be a similar mindset as we navigate through our own sense of self and identity and our own ecclesiology. Being independent of spiritual colonialism, from the authority of the Vatican or the Anglican Communion or even Eastern Orthodoxy. I think there's something there, but I can't quite grasp it yet. I think it feeds into what you're saying.

STRONG: I am familiar with that movement, but I don't know of any connection. I want to share with you an English missiologist, named Roland Allen. Roland Allen went to China to grow the church. He wrote about three things that make the church progress; the church needs to be self propagating. It needs to be self sufficient, and then the clergy needs to reflect with the people. He was a white British missionary that went to build churches, and he wrote a few books on missiology around that idea. I think that's what most churches are getting at is that we embrace the theology of the church, but not the cultural captivity of the church that is often imposed. I've heard of the "Independent Church Movement," and if you read Peter-Ben Smit's book, "Old Catholic and Philippine Independent Ecclesiologies in History," you would see some of those ideas too. That colonization became a problem for them because of Roman Catholicism became associated with Eurocentrism and I can see that happening today in America. People not being comfortable with African American expressions of worship. It's not a Eurocentric Catholic expression, but that doesn't mean it's not Catholic. We are often too caught up in this captivity of a Eurocentric way of understanding and doing things. I'll give you an example, applause in church and dance in church is constantly looked upon as not being part of the liturgy, and yet there are cultures in which that's part of how they express themselves.

KLING: Cultural expression in worship is important. I'm a big fan of watching YouTube videos and I enjoy looking at videos of Ethiopian Orthodox liturgy, Coptic Orthodox liturgy, and similar liturgies. There's a lot of stuff out there, and I'm just fascinated by the cultural expressions such as how the Ethiopians and the Copts worship differently from a Roman Catholic Church. The European centric mindset tends to be "this is how we need to mirror," and I agree with you that we do not need to do that. We can look at other cultural expressions as valid and uplifting, often more so than the Eurocentric.

STRONG: It's not that the liturgy stays the same, it just gets shaped by a cultural expression of a particular faith community. So not everyone would do what Spirit of Christ Community does. We have tambourines and certain hymns we use, some of which come from the South Carolina Gulf Coast. So, the ways the tambourine is played in our church is probably different than in a predominately white church that uses a tambourine, but it's still for the glory of God. That's the focus of our worship, the glory of God, and is how we come to glorify God is in our expressions, and the shape of the liturgy is still followed and honored.

KLING: Thank you for sharing all the things that you've shared. Is there anything that you that you feel called to talk about that you'd like to to discuss?

STRONG: Well, I believe that having had some of my own struggles in ministry and within the Independent Sacramental Movement that I understand this is not easy work. It is not easy trying to create a parish and bring people together, and to get out of your own social network to invite people. Your friends may be loving and supportive, but they may not be interested in your church. I've had to move beyond my semi-introverted personality to build relationships with people. I think that's the key to our Movement, creating face-to-face moments. There are a lot of people out there who are seeking spiritual connection, and I think it is a tremendous gift when we call ourselves Independent Old Catholic or Independent Sacramental Christians. This is a tremendous gift to offer, and as we see expressions of Christianity that seem to be negative and exclusive that we need to be one of those groups that are letting folks know we exist. We may be small micro-denominations, but we are not insignificant.

KLING: Exactly, and I've said it before, the Independent Sacramental Movement is one of the best kept secrets within Christianity. We have a lot to offer. People need to know that we're here.

STRONG: We need to invite people no matter how small we are. We need to invite people to worship with us and to build a relationship with us, and to grow together.

KLING: Letting people know we are here is important and inviting people to worship with us is essential. I love this Movement. I've been a part of it in different aspects since 1991. We need to own who we are, because there have been times when I've thought about try out ministry with the Unitarian Universalists or with the Methodists or with the UCC, and every time God calls me back to the Independent Sacramental Movement. "Sacramental Whine" was created because I need to own it, my involvement and calling to Independent Sacramental Christianity. This is where I am at and this is where I need to be because this is where God is calling me. I need to own that and and invest myself 100% into it instead of trying to chase a paycheck by going to this denomination or that denomination. I need to own it; we need to own it. It's been a blessing since I since I made that choice. We need to get the word out!

> *"God doesn't want his church to fail. And he's assured us it won't not even the gates of hell will prevail against it. That's the movement we want to be a part of. So how do we do it? How do we make our parish church grow? wrong question. We don't make it grow. Only God does that."* —Michael White, *Rebuilt*

"Concluding Thoughts"

Belonging is important. Feeling like you are where you are supposed to be is important too, and many of us have felt marginalized in churches and it is essential for long term spiritual fulfillment to feel like you belong and have an opportunity to grow and mature in your faith. This discussion with Bishop David Strong reminds me of class I took as part of my Doctor of Ministry program at Methodist Theological School in Ohio.

The class I was taking, *Transforming Mission*, was being taught through Zoom. One of the books we had to read for the course is by Stephanie Spellers and is titled, *"Radical Welcome: Embracing God, The Other, and the Spirit of Transformation."* A key element of the text is for communities to become "radically welcoming." This is not just tolerance, but an embracing and accepting of differences. It's about saying, "We accept you for who you are, and we love you for being you."

The paradox is what I experienced within this course which occurred during a class discussion. We were talking about doing parish work during the pandemic and someone brought up the celebration of the Eucharist on Sunday celebrated via Zoom to their congregation. Several participants within the class shared that it was their practice to mail the elements of bread and juice to members of their congregation. The elements would be "consecrated" during the Zoom worship service by the minister, and the parishioners would partake of the elements at the proper time.

I shared my theological perspective of the Sacrament of the Eucharist and talked about matter, form, and intention. I mentioned transubstantiation and the real presence of Christ. I shared my views on the pandemic and the benefit of "spiritual communion," of watching the Eucharist celebrated by a priest but being unable to partake of it because you are not in the same proximity as the celebration.

I was reminded by the professor, "You know you're attending a Protestant seminary?" I remember being silent the rest of that day. I attended that seminary for my Master of Divinity. That seminary was my home, place of employment, and school for four years of my life. Of course, I was aware it was a Protestant seminary. I did not feel "radically welcomed," by either the professor or most of the students.

I have been labeled by several of my peers as the "ex-Roman Catholic." Throughout the Doctor of Ministry Program there have been comments made by peers, likely in good faith, such as, "You used to be Catholic, what do you think about..." It has been a challenge for me to education them on what is an Independent Catholic and what is the Independent Sacramental Movement. Full acceptance has been a challenge.

Sadly, I have never felt fully welcomed within the Doctor of Ministry program. During my four years as a Master of Divinity student I often felt marginalized too, but I found a small cadre of folks to call "family." Belonging is important. I can dwell on the marginalization or I can use it as a source for transformation. I can use the experiences I have to inform how I develop and evolve as a chaplain and as a bishop within our Movement. If you cannot find a place that is radically welcoming, then create one that will be radically welcoming to others and to yourself.

For Reflection, Contemplation, & Prayer:

- What are some examples where you have felt marginalized? How did you overcome these feelings?
- What are some cultural expressions within Christianity that you find helpful or inspiring?
- What are some ways that we in the Independent Sacramental Movement can let people know that "we are here?"

"Looking for the Real Deal"
A Conversation with Brian Stanford

"Through these, he has given us his very great and precious promises, so that through them you may participate in the divine nature, having escaped the corruption in the world caused by evil desires. For this very reason, make every effort to add to your faith, goodness; and to goodness, knowledge; and to knowledge, self-control; and to self-control, perseverance; and to perseverance, godliness; and to godliness, mutual affection; and to mutual affection, love." — 2 Peter 1:4-7

Father Brian Stanford of the Liberal Catholic Union said to me, "I grew up in a Christian-ish household. My mother is a Christian and my father is an atheist. I never had religion foisted upon me and was encouraged to question and search. At the age of 14 I consciously entered the spiritual path when I discovered a copy of Donald Michael Kraig's book "Modern Magick" and the Dammapada. I began experimenting with ceremonial magick and meditation."

Over the following years Brian spent time with Hare Krishnas, lived in a Zen temple, got addicted to heroin, went to prison, came out transformed. He continued his spiritual Quest through chaos magick, Gnosticism and Vajrayana Buddhism. Years of Buddhist meditation and Vajrayana practice resulted in an epiphany which ultimately led him into Christianity, the Divine Feminine through Mary, and the Independent Sacramental Movement. After two years a Christian he found the Liberal Catholic Union and was recently ordained to the priesthood, having previously been ordained a deacon.

His focus is investigating and practicing esoteric strands of Christianity, learning various aspects of Independent Catholic practice and training in the martial arts. He lives in Ashville NC and is currently working to build a community of people who are interested in engaging with Christianity in new and alive ways.

Brian Stanford is now a bishop and the Liberal Catholilc Union is now known as the Gnostic Catholic Union.

KLING: What are some of the things that you wanted to talk about? Father Brian?

STANFORD: I was curious to know about some of the esoteric or Gnostic things that have formed your theology. One of the things that you have talked about was that you've moved away from this over time. I'm interested in your thoughts about this and discussing it.

KLING: Well, sure. Where do I want to start? When I first entered the Independent Sacramental Movement, it was back in the early 1990s and it was through the Traditionalist Movement. I was at a Traditionalist Benedictine monastery, Christ the King Monastery in Cullman, Alabama. I spent some time as a monk, but before that I was baptized by an Independent Traditionalist Roman Catholic priest, Father Joseph Terry Marks, who was not a member of, but loosely affiliated with, the Society of St. Pius X. The SSPX is a religious order, a priestly fraternity within the Roman Catholic Church. That half the time they're excommunicated the other time they're reconciled with Rome. I think currently they're reconciled with Rome, but some of the bishops and priests who were involved with the SSPX, have left, and continue to be schismatic Traditionalists.

I was initially involved in that aspect of the Independent Sacramental Movement, and at the time they were in a phase where they were not in communion with Rome. I was baptized in 1991 and then 1992, I was confirmed by Bishop Richard Williamson, who was at the time still with the SSPX. Now, Richard Williamson is ex-communicated by Rome after at least one reconciliation with Rome. To my knowledge, he's currently ex-communicated and living in exile somewhere in South America. Likely, training Traditionalist Roman Catholic priests. He's an interesting story, and he's cuckoo-for-cocoa-puffs. Still, a fascinating character, who is way on the far-right deep end of the spectrum who has crashed and burned several times over.

The reason why I bring all that up is because the monastery that I was at did everything pre-Vatican II. The liturgy was in Latin, the Tridentine Mass. We would wake up at 4:00 AM and be in chapel by 4:20 and the superior of the monastery, he was a prior when I was there, but later becoming an Abbott. His name was Father Leonard Giardina, O.S.B. He would sometimes start the morning chapel services by letting us know that he received a phone call in the middle of the night. It was somebody with a specific prayer intention and he would light a candle on the altar and asked us to focus our prayers on that candle and on a particular prayer intention. That's a form of sympathetic magic for anybody who studies the Western Mystery Traditions within Western Esotericism.

My entry into the Independent Sacramental Movement, and Catholicism was through the Traditionalist movement, which is rooted in orthodox (pre-Vatican II) theology. It also seemed mystical to my young 20-something mind. When I formerly entered the movement through ordination and consecration, I was in my 30s and was at a festival called Elysium Gathering, a festival that I organized and promoted. I organized the festival early that back in 2004, it was there that I was ordained and consecrated. I was later sub-conditionally consecrated by Bishop John Plumber, who I still know and consider a friend many years later. Initially, it was through a Gnostic stream, which was, in apostolic succession. It wasn't some sort of rogue Gnostic church that didn't have an apostolic succession. Gnosticism was part of my identity early on and I ran with it. In exploring what is Gnosticism, I realized that I'm not that. I was more in love with the romantic idea of Gnostic and Gnosis, but after really reading, for example, the Gospel of Philip or some of the other Gnostics streams of thought, I discovered that I really don't subscribe to this idea of a demiurge and the dualism of Gnosticism.

I think one of the reasons for that was when I was in college, I had opportunities to study all sorts of religions. I spent time studying Judaism and in studying Judaism, the idea of the God of the Hebrew Bible (Old Testament) and the New Testament, being the Demiurge and there being this actual God beyond the Demiurge that Gnostics venerated started to bother me because it just smacked of this idea that the God that the Jews worship was the Demiurge. I didn't subscribe to that. Then I tried to rationalize it in a different way, and then it just got to a point where I thought, "If I'm not subscribing to these ancient forms of Gnosticism, do I really feel like I need to use that label?" And I thought, "Well, maybe not."

Then in certain parts of my spiritual journey, I found myself, working at a Unitarian Universalist Fellowship, two different Unitarian Universalist congregations. One as the Director of Religious Education and another, as the Consulting Minister. While serving in these roles subjects like Gnosticism just didn't come up because I was in either college or seminary, and I was being inundated with all sorts of new ideas and concepts. When I was in seminary, I think took probably 9, 10, or 11 theology courses, that's a lot of theology courses. I took a lot of other courses that would be considered practical theology, like church leadership and homiletics, but I'm talking strict theology, such as, Doctrine of God, Doctrine of Christ, and others. I realized that one can be orthodox in their theology, but also esoteric in their approach to Christianity.

So, what do I mean by that? If you look at certain strands of mysticism, within the church, you have Julian of Norwich, you have Saint Gregory Palamas and the whole idea of the Jesus prayer and getting your soul into this state of *theosis* by practicing repetitive prayers, we see that practice done within Eastern Religions with mantras. I know, if you talk to an Orthodox monk, they will scream at the idea of the Jesus Prayer being the equivalent to a mantra, but coming from a religious studies point of view, it's very similar. I learned that you can be Orthodox and still, look at Christianity from an esoteric point of view, simply as an alternative to fundamentalism. I'm certainly not a fundamentalist. I fall on the esoteric side, because I'm going to look at things scripturally and at tradition and try to peel back layers because that's what esoteric means, hidden.

I think that's where I'm at now, but I don't want to do violence to where I was. So, I'm not going to be an evangelist that opposes Gnosticism or Gnostic strains of thought, because that gets me nowhere. I can appreciate, for example, the awesome story that's in the Hymn of the Pearl, a Gnostic text. I can look at that and say, "That was a great read 14 years ago, and it's a great read now." I can still pull-out things from reading the Hymn of the Pearl that I may not have gotten, years ago and say, "Ah, that's really cool," and I can appreciate that, but I'm not going to look at that from a fundamentalist point of view and say, "Oh, you must believe that because you're a Gnostic Christian," If that makes sense.

STANFORD: Totally, and like someone who had reached out to me on social media after we last talked and asked me a question and had pointed out that you and I hadn't talked about dualism and ancient Gnosticism and how that manifests, and coming from my perspective as a modern Gnostic, it has really made me think about this. I've been reading some Bede Griffiths lately, and I'm really fascinated in the way that he contrasts Gnosis and Yana. If someone's practicing Jnana Yoga like the yoga of having direct experience with the divine, then you call them a Jnana Yogi, right? That's what they are. But it's weird because I think of Gnosticism in that sense. I love reading the Gnostic Gospels, but what I've realized is I see them as two different maps of something.

I'm curious because I feel like I read things in the New Testament that refer to the Ruler or Rulers of this world, and there's definitely a sense in which orthodox theology seems to view these Rulers as a negative. A view of the material world as a fallen condition. Which seems to be proto myth that's underlying both. What do you think of the things in the New Testament that speak of the Ruler of this world in relation to something like the idea of the Demiurge?

KLING: I reject this idea of the Demiurge. I reject the idea of there being Archons manipulating things, but I'm a little bit more open to that, I suppose. I haven't given it much thought. What I will say about the dualism encapsulated in classical Gnosticism is that I reject it because I like creation. I think God created the heavens and the earth. He looked on it and said, "it's good." It's not the source of all evil. I think there are a lot of things that can be evil in the material world, but I think that we create that, we create this sense of materialism that isn't good for society. If we look back on our historical record, there was a time when CEOs of companies didn't make hundreds of times more than their average employee, that's a new thing.

The idea of dualism I think comes out of Zoroastrianism and perhaps Gnosticism is an evolution of Zoroastrian ideas. I look at the Hindu tradition and the Buddhist tradition, many of them tend to be non-dualist, and I appreciate that about them. I think oftentimes Christianity gets turned into dualism when looked at through a fundamentalist lens. There's this idea of God being all good, or the classical definition of the all-powerful omnipotent all-knowing God, and in some sort of Ultimate Evil that's not as powerful as God but has a major influence on what goes on. I think if we look at, and I'm not the biblical scholar that I wish I was, but my understanding is that a lot of the Gnostic tendencies in the New Testament come from the Epistles, whereas, the Gospels are not written with Gnostic ideas, except for maybe the Gospel of John. I don't really feel the need to have all this extra stuff, such as the Demiurge and the Monad. Then all the emanations and the idea of Sophia. Then we've got Sophia did this, this, and this, and that's how we have the Demiurge. That would be a wonderful play or an opera or something to tell that story, but to look at the classical Gnostic narrative, the cosmology, I'm not sure I buy it. I look at the Christian tradition and I look at the Doctrine of the Trinity and I'm more comfortable with that view. I look at the creeds and having been forced parse them apart in seminary and look at all the different parts I can look at the creeds now and understand what these words mean and be okay with it. I can look at the deeper meanings behind the creeds, and I don't feel the need to go outside of the canonical tradition to find something hidden, if that makes sense.

STANFORD: Sure. You are "like" a Gnostic, like Gnostics in all traditions, and it's interesting that you mentioned Zoroastrianism because I'm in the midst of reading a book about that. I've been thinking a lot lately about the question of the condition of the material world. We just had a tragic death in my family, and you mentioned CEO's making, billions and billions of dollars or something as ancient as murder. I feel like the Gnostics and the Zoroastrians and Orthodox Christianity, so many of these, especially the religions that came out of that general area are very concerned with why is there suffering and evil, right? How it's at least being experienced for me now, theologically is that I resonate with both. What I was thinking about was it was like having more than one map to vast territory. When I read the about the fall of Sophia, to me, it is a great play. It's mythic, it's a fabulous story, but I don't read it in a way that I think of it as literal. I don't think of any of them as literal descriptions of anything. I think of all of them as the souls and the spirits striving to have Gnosis. Trying to have a direct experience with the Divine and the dualism is interesting because I feel like I am not completely convinced that I wouldn't describe myself as a dualist and I wouldn't describe myself as a non-dualist. Although, I've had profound non-dual experiences, but I see them as a both and situation. It's interesting because I think a lot of times talking to people in the ISM, using these terms, I think maybe we're not all talking about the same thing.

KLING: I agree. One thing I was thinking, as you were talking, is that there's a lot within the Christian tradition that a lot of people simply just do not know. I'm talking about the orthodox tradition. About Roman

Catholic tradition, as well as Eastern Orthodox tradition, non-heretical and for example, the book, "The Cloud of Unknowing," or "The Triads" by Gregory Palamas, these are esoteric texts, but they're part of the tradition. I think many people within the Independent Sacramental Movement who are on the esoteric side will go towards Gnostic texts when there are a lot of texts that are part of the tradition that they could be digesting. You don't need to go outside of the tradition, and I would put most of the classical Gnostic texts outside of the tradition.

STANFORD: Oh yeah. It's a fascinating thing for me in two directions. I live in Asheville, North Carolina. I've been involved in esoteric things for most of my life. This is a town that has a lot of that kind of stuff going on. I interact with people all the time who know all the reasons to reject Christianity. They understand all the problems with Christianity, but they've never heard that there are other sides of Christianity. If you grow up as an American Christian, or that's what you're exposed to, I wonder. Gnosticism is one of those hidden in plain sight sort of things that's always amazing to see and know it has been there all along. Gnosticism wasn't my experience of Christianity growing up and I've yet to encounter anyone who it was their experience of Christianity growing up. I think it's something people end up discovering, but I agree with you.

KLING: One of the things that I try to do if I'm talking to somebody and they bring up a reference to the book of Revelation or the book of Daniel is that I make it a point to try to educate them. The book of Daniel is considered the least inspired book of the Hebrew Bible by the Jewish community and the book of Revelation almost didn't make it into the Bible. There was a movement within early Christianity to not to accept it as Biblical canon. I like to point out to people that most Christian denominations that are kind of nutty usually get their theology from either the book of Daniel or the book of Revelation. The hidden knowledge that I try to share with them is that for example, these texts were written at a certain time, are very contextual in what they say they are about and what they are not about. For example, in the book of Revelation, it looks like it's a prophecy of things to come. In reality, and many scholars agree with this, the beast from the sea, the beast from the land, et cetera, were references to the Roman empire, the Roman merchant class, and the Roman military, and it was a warning to Christians at the time to be aware, to not take certain things for granted.

It wasn't prophetic as people might think, as in this is going to happen a thousand years from now. It was written to say, "Look, we're living in a system of things which is going really great, but don't get too comfortable because it could change, and it did." When the book of Revelation was written, it was written in a time when there wasn't persecution, but not too long after it was written the persecutions started.

It was written as a propaganda piece or as a sort of op-ed to the people who listened to it. It was all oral tradition back then. A lot of people couldn't read. As people would hear it, they would get the connections and be like, "ah, I get it." It would be like when we watch Saturday Night Live, we get the jokes. But if you were to watch Saturday Night Live a hundred years from now, you might be thinking, "I don't get it. What's this? Why is this funny?" It is contextual, and part of my mission in addressing esotericism is to look at things with a different light and go deeper and take the things that scholars are coming up with and being able to shed some light on things. I think that's where I have evolved into from where I was 14 years ago. Does that make sense?

STANFORD: It totally does. I never know how to say whether it's my conversion to Christianity or my reconversion to Christianity, because I was baptized in a Presbyterian Church when I was 10 years old and from a very early age, I rejected Christianity as it was presented to me. It just didn't make sense to me that there was a cosmic creator God that was angry and judgmental. The whole story just didn't make sense to me, and I rejected it and went down a spiritual path. Then I had a conversion or reconversion experience, and a big part of that, was that the circumstances just started to hit where I started seeing that there was and is a living esoteric tradition in Christianity. That is exactly like what you're saying that it is Orthodox.

Even books like "Meditations on the Tarot," the author [anonymous] is an orthodox Roman Catholic but was pursuing an esoteric path. I think for a lot of people that kind of thing exists in Christianity, and I think it's a critical discovery for any reinvigoration of the Christian tradition. I think that's a crucial piece of it. It is for me and the people in my community. I agree with you. It's a place where people should look.

KLING: I want to add something on this topic before we move on to something else. My sense of non-dualism and my approach to Christianity is such that while I may be comfortable spiritually in my role as a Bishop within the Independent Sacramental Movement and as one rooted in non-dualistic Christianity, I can also go to a Hindu temple and get something out of it spiritually. I can go to a mosque and get something out of it spiritually. I can go to a synagogue, et cetera. I can go anywhere there is faith and a connection with the Divine and find connection. I think that this is what separates me from the folks who are in the fundamentalist camp. I think you could use the term esoteric Christian as a contrast against a fundamentalist approach to Christianity. Having attended a United Methodist seminary, I have a lot of friends who are, of course, United Methodists. I also have a lot of friends who are ordained in the United Church of Christ, and most of them are mainstream. They're not into any of what we would call esoteric studies, but they're certainly not fundamentalists. I think that they would be interested in some of the things that we call esoteric, if they were more aware that these things existed. For example, when I took a course in church history, we had a list of books that we had read and write about, and none of them really interested me. They seemed very typical to me and were books I had already digested. One was The Rule of Saint Francis and similar books. I wanted to read Gregory Palamas, but the professor had never read the book I wanted to read, "The Triads." He agreed to allowing me to read Palamas instead of what was on the list, and he had to read it too so he could grade my paper. That was my way of spreading some of this stuff. I hope that answers your question about Gnosticism and my own experience.

I want to turn our attention to another topic. I've been interested in what is known as imposter syndrome, and there is an interesting coincidence that occurred recently. Last night, I was watching the final season of "The Big Bang Theory," and it was the 18th episode of the 12th and final season where one of the characters Amy used the term imposter syndrome in the episode. It was funny and she used it correctly. I thought it was ironic since I knew I wanted to talk about imposter syndrome with you today. I think imposter syndrome permeates the Independent Sacramental Movement and it permeates it in such a way that clergy, which includes priests and bishops, often feel that they're just not good enough and that deep within themselves, they feel like imposters. Sometimes that means they jump from jurisdiction to jurisdiction, and it manifests in many ways. I'm interested in what you think about imposter syndrome.

STANFORD: Yeah, it's a curious thing to me too. I guess I have a question to ask you first, because I think that there's maybe two levels to imposter syndrome. I experienced it at times in my life. I am thinking, "Who am I to be a priest? What am I talk talking about? What am I doing?" I think there's that level of imposter syndrome where you question your own self-worth, and your mission. Then I think there's the imposter syndrome of feeling weird wearing a shirt with a collar because "I'm not actually a real priest, and the people in the church wouldn't accept what I do as legitimate." Are you talking about both things? Are you talking about one or the other?

KLING: Both.

STANFORD: Both?

KLING: However, it manifests, because it manifests in different ways.

STANFORD: I think the one where I sit and think, "who am I to be a priest?" I think that's good. I think it would be a weird thing if I didn't feel that way, because I'm such a work in progress and I fall all the time and I'm not qualified. I'm not qualified to represent anything, and by grace, and by things I don't understand, here I am and I'm doing it. I must do the best I can, but I think that kind of imposter syndrome is healthy. I don't think it's good to sit there and dwell in it, and if I tell my fiancé about it, I get sage wisdom about why I am qualified. That's true too, both of those things are true and it's part of the mystery of grace and it's part of the dualism that we were talking about earlier. In a certain sense, I am a corrupted, fallen, and sinful person. I would just be a liar to say that I'm not, so how am I qualified to be a priest; but, on another level creation rings with the vibration of the Divine, and I am qualified to be a priest. I think that kind of imposter syndrome is legitimate. I think the other one is also legitimate. I don't feel a lot of imposter syndrome in that regard because I haven't had any formal connection with Christianity until I started in the direction that I'm involved. When I was about to be ordained, I have a friend who's an Episcopal priest, a mainstream Episcopal priest, and I was talking to her about this very thing. I was saying, "You probably think, I'm not legitimate." It was like I was confessing to her that I was becoming a priest in the ISM, and that she was a real priest. She said to me, "What are you talking about? What I do is legitimate in the stream of what I do, and what you do is legitimate in the stream of what you do. Do what you do. You are in this Independent Sacramental thing. It's just as legitimate." We have to be like Bishop John Plumber who was talking to me, his advice was, "When you're moving forward and being public in the world about this don't pretend to be something that you're not. Be very clear about what it is you're doing and what it means. Be very, very upfront about it."

To me, what I'm doing is legitimate. It's legitimate in the sense that it has papers and signatures going back, blah, blah, blah. That's not important to me. What's important to me is that it's transmitting the Holy Spirit and if that's happening, it's legitimate. I don't feel any less real than the Roman Catholic priest; although, they know a lot more than I do about things and can celebrate mass in a beautiful, magnificent way while I'm still learning. I see myself as a representative of a different stream of Christianity and I'm just as legitimate as them. I think something to actively cultivate is to focus on what it is we do, and then doing that with conviction. I'm part of the Liberal Catholic Union (Note: now the Gnostic Catholic Union). We have people who subscribe to orthodox theology and we have Gnostic freaks, it's what we do. I don't pretend to be anything different than that, and I feel that it's legitimate. It's why I'm doing it.

KLING: When you talked about not feeling worthy, I don't know if that's imposter syndrome. I think humility is a good thing, and I think having humility, especially for example, when you say mass and you're approaching the altar, it's a good thing to feel "I'm not worthy to do this," but you do it anyways because you've been commissioned through your ordination to do it, to be an *alter-Christus* or another Christ. I think that's good to reflect on and see in relation to our Lord, and to God, our insignificance. That's humility. It's not necessarily imposter syndrome. Imposter syndrome is something that affects a lot of people within the movement, and I'll give you an example of my own struggle with it. I'm a fan of personality type indicators like Myers-Briggs or the Enneagram and within the Myers-Briggs, I'm an INTJ. I'm an introvert, I'm an intuitive, I'm a thinker and I'm a judger. On the Enneagram, which I also love, I am a Type 5, which in some interpretations is the thinker, and in some interpretations I'm the seeker, either way the Type 5 is a cerebral or thinking type. Within the Enneagram you also have wings. I'm a Type 4 wing, which is the individualist. If you read the Enneagram, I'm definitely a Type 5, but I'm also an INTJ on the Myers-Briggs. Part of my predisposition in both my Myers-Briggs personality type and my Enneagram type is that I try to show my worth by being an expert, by showing how much I know about a particular topic.

One of my greatest fears is that I will be seen as incompetent, that I don't know what I'm doing, that I'm completely ignorant, that I'm just a fool. The imposter syndrome really goes to the core of my personality as my greatest fear. I think some personalities, if you look at both the Myers-Briggs, which comes out of Carl Jung's writings, and then the Enneagram, are predisposed to being susceptible to falling into imposter syndrome. I'm sure there are some personality types that are more "I don't care, I am what I am and just accept me for who I am," but mine is different, at least that is how I perceive it.

I remember back when I was at an event, and this was an event that I went to year after, and they had a meet and greet referred to as a scholar meet and greet. I didn't realize it was people who all had academic degrees. I thought it was just people who were well read and liked to read and were knowledgeable. I went to the meet and greet and during the meeting, several people kept dropping terms that I had never heard of before. I remember them using the term phenomenology repeatedly, and I was thinking, "What the heck is phenomenology?" So, I went and got a philosophy degree and I learned about phenomenology. I remember going back years later to the scholars meet and greet, and I was talking about how I'm was finishing up my bachelor's education and getting ready to go to graduate school. I was fully accepted. I was one of them; however, for years I felt like a complete fool because I had a high school diploma, and I didn't have a college degree when I first started going. Then when I started formal education and I knew all the vocabulary, I didn't care to be a part of the meet and greet anymore. It was my own struggle with, "am I good enough?" It's something that has been there. Going back into my childhood I was and still am dyslexic. Dyslexic in the 1970s, it was different back in the 1970s.

There were about ten of us in the LD (learning disability) class at the school I attended, and other kids know when you're in one of those classes, that you're different. It was brutal, but I survived. I grew up with this idea that I, as a kid, I thought, "Am I retarded?" I'm in the same classes as the severely handicapped and I thought that I must be retarded too. Retarded is not a term we use now, but in the 1970s it was thrown around a lot.

This idea of imposter syndrome has been there in the background, my entire life. I remember when I left the Benedictine monastery that I had been a member of and afterwards was living with a Byzantine Romanian Catholic priest. He once said to me, "You need to go to college if you ever want to be a priest in Catholic church." In the canonical Catholic Church, you need an undergraduate degree and Master of Divinity degree to become a priest. I responded to Father John Michael, who I was living with, "People like me, we don't go to college." It took a lot of convincing to get me to go to college. I thought that I couldn't go, that people like me did not have college as an option. Once I got into college, I did very well. There's always been something there telling me, "You're not good enough or you need to work extra hard." It's something that I have struggled with and because I've struggled with it, I see it in others.

STANFORD: I totally get that. I was a heroin addict and went to prison. I have a felony conviction. Any sense of social legitimacy has just imploded, and I feel like an imposter all the time. I work at a grocery store, and I have multiple friends who are therapists and people with college degrees and I never went to college. I know I'm a smart guy, but it's because I've studied on my own. I know what you're talking about. I have struggled with the fact that I did things in the past that have hobbled me regarding mainstream society. It's very difficult. I totally understand that. These kinds of things are difficult and they're also juicy alchemical opportunities. Like everything I said before, "I am, whatever it is that I am." When you're dealing with personal things like that it's a different level. I thought most of the references that I've heard spoken of in regard to imposter syndrome, at least within the ISM, is people's idea about the legitimacy of what you were talking about. Such as jumping from jurisdiction to jurisdiction because you're looking for "just the right thing" or "the real deal" or whatever. The personal sense of the kind of thing regarding society that you're talking about, that's a whole other level, but like I said, "that's the juicy alchemical material."

KLING: I was talking to Bishop John Plumber about education and training. He mentioned that years ago the discussion going on was, "What is your apostolic succession lineage?" The main narrative was who consecrated you and who consecrated them, and is your lineage valid? So, let's sub-conditionally consecrate each other to make sure it's all valid. That was what was in vogue years ago. You don't hear that anymore. I never hear anybody ask, "Who consecrated you and who consecrated them and what lineage are they?" It hasn't come up and It's not a big topic anymore. What he did mention that is in vogue now is, "Do you have an M.Div, or do you have a master's or what is your background?" I don't think that a graduate degree is necessary. John and I agree that you don't need a degree to be a good priest or a good bishop. I would never recommend to anyone to go and get the massive amount of student loan debt that I have, unless it is to go into chaplaincy and become a professional chaplain. You need to have an education if you want to go into chaplaincy, but I don't know if I would recommend it to become a priest. I have a daughter that's about 19 months and the joke is, I'm going to encourage her to go and become a plumber. When have you ever heard of a plumber not having work? As a professional chaplain, it's often difficult finding a job. I have a good job now, but if something were to happen to that job, finding another chaplaincy job could be difficult; however, you never see plumbers who are struggling to find work. If they're a good plumber, then you have plenty of work. So, the joke is, we're going to push her towards being a plumber or maybe an electrician, but I'd rather have a good plumber in the family.

I value my education, and I love it and how it molded me into who I am today, but the things that I learned in seminary and in college I could have learned with a book and a mentor. I think mentorship is the preferred model within the Independent Sacramental Movement to mold and build clergy. If I had somebody that lived local to me and they said, "I want to be a deacon, or I want to be a priest. Can you teach me?" I would say, "I'll teach you how to be a priest. I'll teach you how to serve at the altar. I'll teach you how to listen to people and to be with them when they're dying or when they're in trauma or they need somebody. I can teach you pastoral care. I can teach you how to preach. I can teach you how to offer the sacraments. You don't need to go and spend a lot of money to do that."

STANFORD: Yeah. I think that's the model that we're attempting to develop and work with in the Liberal Catholic Union, the mentorship and apprenticeship kind of thing. I agree with you. I don't know how it compares to college. I'm sure it has similarities and differences. In ways it's better and in ways it's not, but I think it's a really great way of formation. It seems to be something that different jurisdictions are trying to figure out, how do you do this thing? How do you create people who are qualified to move into the role? I saw this within Buddhism. There's a lot of people, I'm one of them, who get consecrated, get ordained quickly and then must get the education as they're moving along. That's not optimal.

I'm not interested in going to a seminary. I love studying. I study all the time, but I'm not interested in going to college. I think there's ways to do mentorship that could really create powerful people who are coming into the thing, knowing what to do. I think that's one of the ways experienced, I don't know that I want to call it imposter syndrome, but I experienced this thing where it's like, "I'm a priest and I'm learning every single day, what that means and how to do it." I'm not someone who's had seminary or college and I think a lot of us are like that, and then we do the work ourselves. We have to do the work ourselves and find people to help us and serve that mentoring role. We are consciously working with that or consciously creating with that and doing that with people. It's the way that I'm interested in doing things.

KLING: I think imposter syndrome is an important topic for us to be aware of because it comes up in conversation frequently. For example, bishops who have been extremely controlling of the people within their jurisdiction. I think part of their insecurity is their own imposter syndrome because they're afraid that if the people in their jurisdiction get exposed to other things, then they might want to go off and join another jurisdiction and then they'll lose people. It's the idea that "I have to maintain power because if they go off and see something else, they might realize that I'm a fraud and they don't want to be associated with a fraud. So, they go off and join another jurisdiction." I think that is another aspect of imposter syndrome, and it permeates the movement. If we keep having this conversation, we can expose it. You know those bad bishops out there but be mindful that there may be some things that are affecting the decisions and the behaviors that we see. Some of those things might be mitigated with just discussion on this topic and awareness of this topic and allowing us to wrestle with it. As I have wrestled with it.

STANFORD: Absolutely.

KLING: I've struggled. I struggle with imposter syndrome and it's okay. When is education going to be enough? When am I going to have enough degrees that I can be, "Okay, I'm legit!" I feel I'm legit, but my point is within my sub-conscience, it's never going to be enough. I'm never going to read enough. I'm never going to know enough. I'm never going to be good enough, and I must be able to say, "Wait a minute, subconscious, I am good enough. I accept myself for who I am, and I am good. I'm not an imposter." Then I can counsel others and say, "Look, you are good enough. You are a good priest. You don't need to have all these credentials. You're fine, the way you are."

"A pearl is a beautiful thing that is produced by an injured life. It is the tear [that results] from the injury of the oyster. The treasure of our being in this world is also produced by an injured life. If we had not been wounded, if we had not been injured, then we will not produce the pearl." —Stephan Hoeller

"Concluding Thoughts"

We deal with labels all the time, and many within the Independent Sacramental Movement struggle with identity and identity related issues. Is this why it is so common for new clerics to jump around from one micro-denomination, or jurisdiction, to another? If explaining what it means to be a Christian isn't enough, add additional labels such as Gnostic Christian or Esoteric Christian? Or mystic? Or contemplative? Or any other label or descriptor that feeds a sense of identity. It can be exhausting trying to come up with an elevator speech for every single label that one struggles to maintain.

I remember a time back in 2005. I was at Elysium Gathering, a weekend Druid festival near Clifton, Ohio. I was sitting at a picnic table talking with occultist John Michael Greer and Bishop John Plumber. We were talking about an idea that never fully came to fruition and that was, "The Church of the Triune Gnosis." We mapped out the idea of forming a religious community that combined three spiritual elements: Hermeticism, Christianity of a Gnostic and Kabbalistic variety, and Nature Spirituality. These three elements were woven together to produce the Church of the Triune Gnosis. While this project never fully developed, I wonder what the elevator speech would look like if it had.

Since that time in 2005 my sense of spirituality has changed. Even though I was highly influenced by my sojourns into Roman Catholic Traditionalism and Byzantine Rite spirituality I fashioned myself a "Christo-Pagan" for a time. I wrestled a lot with, "what does it mean to fully live into a synchretistic way of spiritual expression?" I struggled with identity and labels.

Years later I am a bishop within the Young Rite, and founder of the Community of Saint George a jurisdiction within the Young Rite. While the Young Rite identifies as "esoteric," I have found ways to interpret the esoteric mindset differently, then what I would have in 2005. I'm not going to shout that, "I'm free of all known heresies!" However, I have moved closer to an orthodox expression Christianity and can say unapologetically that I love Jesus.

Instead of pouring myself over Gnostic scriptures trying to find some hidden truths I now find myself with an increasing love of patristics, or the wisdom of the Church found in the early fathers and mothers of the Church especially those who were desert monastics. Labels and identity are still important, but very different now than when I was younger.

For Reflection, Contemplation, & Prayer:

- What are some of the labels that you use to define your spiritual self?
- What defines you as a person? What are all the descriptors that help make up who you are as a person?
- Do you have a mentor, or spiritual director, or someone who helps you on your spiritual journey? Do you see the value in mentorship or spiritual direction?

"Saving Evangelism"
A Conversation with Father Kevin Daugherty

"I wish that all of you were as I am. But each of you has your own gift from God; one has this gift, another has that." — 1 Corinthians 7:7

Father Kevin Daugherty of Lincoln, Pennsylvania, is the co founder, and priest of Kindling fires: A New Monastic order within the Convergent Christian Communion (formerly known as the Anthem Network). Kevin was ordained to Christian ministry in April 2013, became an ordained elder within the Convergent Christian Communion in October 2017, and was commissioned an abbot in June 2018.

KLING: Let's talk about evangelical Christianity. When I hear the term evangelical, I am reminded of a course that I took in seminary simply titled Evangelism. It was a great course; however, a lot of people equate Evangelical with Fundamentalism. What is your take on that term and how do you identify with it?

DAUGHERTY: The term evangelical is always one that I've had a love/hate relationship with, and, like everybody else in the current Western world, I've been acquainted with the conservative Evangelical Movement where they take our faith, and they couple it heavily with a particular type of partisan politics. Then that gets coupled with fundamentalism. Honestly, historical fundamentalism is a very different beast than what we have today. When you read like the writings of Benjamin Warfield or any of the other Princeton theologians, they're of a completely different level than what you see with the Falwells or the Grahams, though I do like Billy Graham quite a bit. I think we do ourselves a disservice when we lump the word evangelical in with that category.

When we take the word evangelical and we just pass it off onto that type of conservative Protestantism, because really the term evangelical was something that belongs to the whole church. Of course, originally it didn't even belong to the church. Originally, it belonged to the pagan world, where it was a term referring to the "good news" of a military victory. Later, the Christian Church, co-opted the term, and we use it to refer to the "good news" of Christ's victory over the principalities and powers and over death and destruction in hell.

It's a word I think is far too holy and far too historically useful and viable and valuable to just surrender to a modern political movement. It's kind of like the word Catholic, far too many people will lump the word Catholic in with the Roman Catholic Church. So, anything outside the institution of the Roman Catholic Church isn't considered Catholic by them, and any of the issues of the Roman Catholic Church, they also associate with the word Catholic. We often have the same with the word evangelical. We take the word evangelical; we give it to organizations like the Southern Baptist Convention and we just leave it there. There are a lot of negative connotations and stereotypes which we associate with the word evangelical, and I really think we need to find a way to save the word from the stereotypes.

KLING: You think it's important that we reclaim it?

DAUGHERTY: Absolutely. One thing, it's a biblical word. It's the term that the Bible passes down to us to describe the victory we have in Christ. I think we just surrender that it's a far too important word to surrender.

KLING: So how would you reshape this concept of evangelism?

DAUGHERTY: Well, I think the first thing we have to do is look at the word evangelical with its full historical context by going back to the New Testament, what does it mean to be evangelical? Well, it means to simply be somebody who is a Christian and who believes in sharing the good news and living out the values that the gospels teach. That's the same message. That's the same use of the term evangelical we see in the middle ages where within medieval monasticism we have the concept of evangelical councils, which is poverty, chastity, and obedience. All the way up through most of church history, the word evangelical has always meant to live like Jesus lived or to aspire to do so, and to share the gospel in an evangelistic way.

Then even as the term evangelical starts to shift with the reformation, because of course originally the Protestants, especially the Lutheran branch, insisted they weren't Protestant, they were evangelical. I mean, they were hoping to return the Roman Catholic Church back to gospel values, and, even as the word evangelical started to have a different meaning with the reformation and the Counter-Reformation, the original historical values, especially the ones that we see in the New Testament they're still there. They're still there and they're still being expressed. We see that with the rise of Evangelicalism within the Great Awakenings, which evangelical mostly got its start within the Anglican Communion with people like John Wesley, Charles Wesley, and George Whitefield.

In their expression of what it meant to be evangelical it is closely tied to the monastic expression. John Wesley, for example, heavily drew from Christian mystics from the Catholic Church and from various monastic traditions. He also drew from Pietistic traditions, and Lutheranism. Once again, the word evangelical is strongly meant to live like Jesus lived. So, when Jesus gives a great commission saying, "Go, therefore make disciples of all nations, baptizing them in the name of the Father, the Son and the Holy Spirit," that's what it meant to be evangelical. That's why the Methodists, especially the Methodists, started pushing missionary movements. It's all the same thing with the Moravians before them, and Wesley was a big friend of the Moravian Church.

What tends to happen is we have 2000 years of history of the word evangelical, and it has several different meanings and several different associations, but there's a common theme of trying to live as the gospel tells us to live. Then we have, within the last 40 years, the rise of the moral majority within the religious right. They start insisting that they were the "Evangelical Church," and then for some reason, everyone else decided to surrender the word to them. At least that's how it seems to me, and it's far too valuable to surrender.

KLING: You mentioned United Methodists. I went to a United Methodist seminary, and I have talked to you about that before, but when I took this course in seminary on Evangelism, it was a required course for those students who were seeking ordination in the United Methodist church. I wasn't United Methodist. I was serving a Unitarian Universalist congregation at the time, and had been ordained in the independent sacramental movement, and the interesting takeaway from the course was the emphasis on congruence, practicing what you preach, being a living witness of the gospel. The takeaway was practice what you preach. I've tried to live by that maxim. An interesting phenomenon within the course was that those students who were required to take it, the United Methodist seminarians, they seemed to absolutely despise and hate the course.

They would secretly make fun of the professor behind his back. I created a Facebook group specifically around the course. So, during class we could chat with one another because we all had laptops we used during the course. I set up the Facebook group because I wanted to learn more about this topic of Evangelism, because it was shrouded in a sort of fundamentalist mystique. I wanted to unpack that and thought, "how can I learn about evangelism in a non-fundamentalist way?"

I created the Facebook group for all of us to communicate and what it turned out to be was all the United Methodist students using the Facebook group to be snarky about the professor and make fun of the readings and the videos that we had to watch. I thought that was an interesting phenomenon that the one student who was serving a Unitarian Universalist congregation, which is not Christian by definition, embraced the course and the United Methodist students resented taking it.

I find that interesting, and I think that's representative of some aspects of progressive Christianity, in that a lot of us seem to lose sight of our spiritual roots that you talked about earlier. Evangelism is not something that we should run away from, but something that we should embrace. It's not something that we should make fun of and say, "Oh, we're not like that. We're not pushy. We're not obnoxious. We're not this, or we're not that," but instead, to look at evangelism as an expression of how we live our faith in congruence with the doctrines of the church, the traditions, et cetera, in such a way that we are practicing what we preach. I thought that was an interesting phenomenon, going to a United Methodist seminary, it seems like a lot of United Methodists have forgotten who John Wesley is and who John Wesley was!

DAUGHERTY: I love how you used that phrase, "practicing what you preach," because that's really what being evangelical or being evangelistic has always been about historically. It's always been about going back to the gospel values and living them. It's interesting that you talk about people being snarky about the concept within the United Methodist church, and your claim about the Unitarian Universalist Church, having nothing to do with that anymore. What's funny about all that to me is from a historical standpoint, first of all, that's what made

Methodists Methodists. They were called the Methodists because they followed a method. They followed a method of holiness of evangelism. They really drew from monasticism, where they wanted to have a rule of life or a method that they followed. It's the same thing with Pietism on continental Europe.

It's also interesting when you look at Universalism, because you could say that historically they were evangelicals as well. We often forget that the Unitarian tradition has its roots within the congregational churches and the congregational churches, especially under the supervision of people like Jonathan Edwards were heavily evangelical and for some weird reason and just a couple of generations, they lost it. Then they started debating the doctrine of the Trinity and then it was gone. The Universalist Church, which of course merged into the Unitarian Church, come directly from Methodism. You had George Whitefield, he was a colleague of John Wesley and an Anglican. One of his students, James Relly got in trouble with Whitefield, for preaching universal salvation, and then one of Relly's students was another Methodist preacher named John Murray.

John Murray is the pioneering preacher who came over to the United States, after the collapse of his ministry back in Britain. He came to the United States and founded what would become the Universalist Church in America. All three traditions, United Methodism, Unitarianism, and Universalism, all three of them have lost that evangelical impulse at some point in their history. Unfortunately, that's been the case with a lot of moderate and progressive churches. You can include many in the Independent Sacramental Movement within that same category. They originally had the evangelical impulse and that's what caused the initial growth and the initial vision and allowed for outreach and charity. Then at some point it just evaporated. At some point, these churches decided that they wanted to not seem pushy. They wanted to seem polite and proper, and they wanted to have their nice Victorian values, with of course liberal theology. It causes the decline usually.

I've seen that personally in the community where I live. All of the mainline Protestant and Catholic churches, and there's even some ISM churches here, like the Polish National Catholic Churches, all of them have declined. All of them have gotten to the point where they have few people, and they can't support themselves. In fact, most recently the church I was baptized in as a child closed; meanwhile, there have been three new church plants. Two are Independent and Charismatic, and one is Assemblies of God.

KLING: All of them are evangelical churches!

DAUGHERTY: Not only identify as evangelical but the problem is that they couple evangelicalism specifically with a political party and simply with a Fundamentalist viewpoint. On the one hand, they're bringing people into the pews, which is essentially a good thing, and they're doing it by being passionate about their faith and sharing their faith and living their faith. At the same time, it's concerning because there's been a rise of Fundamentalism. There's also been a decrease of people coming to the sacraments because these churches are very contemporary in their approach. So, when you go to these churches, you're getting a rock concert, not the Eucharist.

KLING: Right. Well, one thing I've noticed is when churches, such as the United Methodist, were simple and they applied, for example, Wesley's method, which was evangelical, they were everywhere. New churches starting up everywhere, and now, since they've divorced themselves from their original simplicity, they have become so byzantine like, a lowercase B, not to be confused with Eastern Orthodox, but just with overlay on overlay of bureaucracy, upon bureaucracy, upon bureaucracy. It becomes mind boggling, trying to read and decipher the Book of Discipline, which is their book of regulations. I know a lot of United Methodist pastors and licensed local pastors and many of them are frustrated with how the United Methodist system is structured; however, it's their paycheck so they keep their mouth shut and don't rock the boat too much. I think as we're looking at reclaiming terms like evangelical and evangelism, that they are tied to other things. It's all woven together, and the reason why progressive Christianity has distanced itself from this concept of evangelical and evangelism. When we look at one thing, it unlocks other things. Does that make sense?

DAUGHERTY: I think so. You're right about the United Methodist churches, which is definitely the largest and most well-established group of them, they have definitely become very bureaucratic. They've become established, but also, if you look at the original Wesleyan vision, it was thoroughly Anglican, right? They took the entirety of Christian tradition. They had a very Catholic approach and they boiled it all down through the Book of Common Prayer and the original Wesleyans were very much based upon the, Book of Common Prayer. The original Wesleyan tradition was from my reading of it, very diversified. They were interested in reaching out to everybody which goes back to the evangelical vision that they had. That's why you had people from all walks of life. I mean, Bishop Francis Asbury, who was the founding Bishop of what would become the Methodist Episcopal Church, and later the United Methodist church, from what I understand, he never went to university or seminary. He was a blacksmith by trade and originally, he trained as a blacksmith then became a licensed lay preacher. Then from there just worked his way up. The original Wesleyan vision was about people like that, the average person being able to have holiness and faithfulness and sanctity in their lives. I know John Wesley himself, I mean he open air preached just for that reason. He often reached out to people who were coal miners and the people who were rough, rough and rowdy, and that has evaporated in a lot of churches. We've become very polite.

KLING: I know originally, Methodism was not designed to be a separate church. It was designed to be an overlay in whatever church you found yourself a member. If you were going to an Anglican church, then you could, subscribe to Wesley's method and groups would form within those individual congregations. Eventually, probably due to the revolutionary war, Methodism developed as its own separate church. I know when Asbury came over to the United States, he had a meeting, an organizational meeting, and he was wearing an Anglican bishop's cassock and he was not well-received wearing that Anglican bishop's cassock because a lot of Baptist churches were also using Wesley's method.

To my understanding, how Methodism evolved in the USA was you had a lot of Anglicans/Episcopalians and you had a lot of Baptists intermingling. What you got was an amalgamation of low church Episcopalians and Baptists. Put the two together and you have the Methodist Episcopal Church which would eventually become the United Methodist Church, you certainly had a moving away from the Anglican tradition.

DAUGHERTY: I think part of it too is also we baptized the American frontier culture. Why wouldn't we have communion every week, within a lot of Protestant churches in this country?

KLING: In the United Methodist system, the reason why they didn't have communion every week is because they had mostly lay preachers going out and preaching. Then they had the circuit riders who were often elders and they didn't have cars, so it took them a while to travel through the circuit and provide communion.

DAUGHERTY: Exactly. And the same is true within other denominations, such as Lutheran and so on. They all ran on those circuits, there's a frontier and there's low population, and they have communion irregularly.

KLING: And the weird mind-set was, "Oh, we're Methodists. We only have communion once a month or once a quarter." And they think that that's part of the tradition but it's not, it was because of practicality. You only had someone who could come and provide communion, once a month, because there weren't enough elders to supply every congregation. That's how it ended up, but I think it would have been done, weekly, if there was someone present within each congregation that could do it weekly.

DAUGHERTY: Absolutely. I mean, once again, the original Wesleyan spirit was thoroughly Anglican, and fairly Catholic. John and Charles Wesley didn't want to divorce themselves from the sacraments. I've no doubt about that.

KLING: I think once you get to a point where you have people saying, "Well, we've always done it this way," then you have a problem.

DAUGHERTY: Of course, that also goes into the later decline of the term evangelical, where it starts leaving its original roots through Catholicism. Protestantism leaves the original roots and becomes more of a political expression that we see today. Just as we often baptized that American frontier culture, a lot of what we see with evangelicalism today it really boils down to an American civic religion. That decline, I think it's all connected, where we've taken our faith, and we've saturated it with America.

KLING: Can you talk a little bit more about this concept of civil religion because I think we've lost that too?

DAUGHERTY: There's no realistic way to separate religion and politics. You can separate church and state as institutions, but you can never separate religion and politics. They share a moral philosophy, they always overlap. Historically of course, we saw that expressed in theocracies or in cases like the Roman Empire that was previously, the Roman Republic where certain Roman politicians would be considered divine. Julius Caesar made himself a God. Augustus Caesar's adoptive son considered himself the son of God, which of course explains why early Christians got into so much trouble because they took these Roman civic religious terms, as well as Jewish civic religious terms, and applied them to themselves and applied the terminology to Jesus, who became an enemy of the state.

That same concept carries over and you see it within the rise of the papacy in the West, where the Pope becomes more of a political office and elected monarchy. You see it in the East with the, what was called caesaropapism where the ecumenical patriarch of the church was a subsidiary of the Eastern emperor in Constantinople. It carries up through with the rise of the Reformation where King Henry the 8th, creates a national Catholic church, the Church of England, and they later become very Reformed and Protestant and switched back and forth several times.

We saw it with Lutheranism where various princes would adopt Lutheranism within Germany and within Scandinavia. For example, the Church of Sweden, they just directly broke away from the Roman Catholic Church as a national body. There's always this connection between religion and politics and the state was essentially baptized. The state was an expression of the faith. We still have that in the United States. It's in a different form, of course we have the first amendment, but if you go to the Capitol building, you look up to the top of the dome and there's a beautiful painting called the "Apotheosis of Washington," where you see Washington sitting in heaven. That type of mentality has heavily affected the American church, and we don't realize it.

The Church has always been a global body, but we've taken it, and we've really injected a bunch of American values into it. We do have civic religion, and it's often unspoken. We don't have an official state church, but we do have religious values that directly reinforce our political values and vice versa. We do have customs and rituals that do the same thing. For example, you'll go to a church, there's an American flag in the sanctuary, or you have pastors like Frederick Augustus Muhlenberg who was very patriotic or take theological terms and apply them to the founding fathers.

KLING: I think there has been a cross-fertilization within some denominations. For example, you mentioned having a flag within the sanctuary. I think some denominations have embraced this sense of Americanism and have attempted to Christianize it and use it to develop their identity, and I think that's a problem. I think the civic religion that we had in the 1950s was a blend of Judeo-Christian values. You see "In God we trust," you don't see, "In Jesus we trust," but you see, "In God we trust." It was the Judeo-Christian values that permeated our society. Now what you see is something a little bit different, and it's the Evangelical Fundamentalist Christian movement exerting influence on the public discourse and on politics. I think that's the type of civic religion that a lot of people on the progressive Christian side and within non-Christian religions are pushing against when they say separation of church and state. In many cases rightly so, but it does take away from the civic religion that this country had in the 1950s. I'm only looking at a romantic revision of that, so who knows. Does that make sense?

DAUGHERTY: It does. I would add that the civic religion you're talking about from previous decades, it was probably the civic religion of mainline Protestantism. There's a reason it's called mainline, and it's because these are churches that dominated the old power centres of the United States. Principally the in Northeast corridor you had Washington DC, Philadelphia, New York, and Boston. These are the old capitals of the United States, the old economic powerhouses. These are where the mainline Protestant churches had their start and all the power and influence. I mean, pretty much every US president has been a member of one of the mainline Churches except for Kennedy, and Kennedy is the only one.

Mainline Protestantism really had its heyday back in the fifties and sixties, especially with anti-communism. They wanted to really reinforce the fact that we believe in moral decency compared to the communist and fascist ideals.

KLING: That's a good point.

DAUGHERTY: Within the last 40 years or so, especially the late seventies and the eighties, we saw the rise of the Moral Majority. It was originally a convergent movement in church fundamentalist and charismatic Christianity, it was a weird combo. It coupled that with political motivations, and so it did change the conversation quite a bit. We saw the massive decline of mainline churches that changed the conversation quite a bit. We've also seen a change within the Catholic Church on this as well, because a lot of the Catholic social witnesses changed. We don't see many people like Dorothy Day or Fulton Sheen anymore, those Catholics who spoke about politics.

KLING: The Roman Catholic Church used to be well rested within the Democratic Party and was very pro-labour; however, I think Roe v. Wade was the point when the Roman Church switched teams because of the abortion issue. Then suddenly they became not the church that was pro-labour, but the church that was pro-life. That's how the Roman Catholic Church moved into the direction that it became in league with Fundamentalist Protestantism. That's been a while ago, if you go back to the 1960s, Roman Catholicism was tied to pro-labour, the Democratic Party. You had Kennedy then, but today it's very different. It's how politics has gotten into the core of religion and really changed things. That's frustrating.

DAUGHERTY: Be careful, because the other side of the aisle, the Christian Left. I've seen the same exact sins on that side. Frequently, what happens is people look at the Religious Right, and they say, "Okay, they're corrupting the church. They're betraying their values. They're not evangelical anymore. They're tying their faith to political power and they're being hypocritical about it." For example, you know the stereotype of a ultra-conservative politician or pastor who ends up having a same-sex affair, right. That kind of thing; but then there's also the flip side. I've seen so many liberal and progressive churches that are extremely homogenous and unexclusive and unwelcoming and smug, and they will tie their faith directly to the Democratic Party, and when the Democratic Party does something against their values, they don't have a way to respond.

KLING: That's true.

DAUGHERTY: They just have to justify it.

KLING: That's true.

DAUGHERTY: There's a danger on both sides and there's always a danger of losing the original evangelical focus. There's always a danger of letting our faith be co-opted by imperialistic values. It's always a threat.

KLING: I've enjoyed this conversation, and I like the term evangelical more that we've had an opportunity to talk about it. Not that I didn't like it before, but it doesn't come up in conversation very often. So how do we reclaim it? How do you folks in the Anthem network (now the Convergent Christian Communion), how do you reclaim it?

DAUGHERTY: I'm very glad you asked. I've always been involved in groups that identify as evangelical, but they've always been evangelical of differently. Anthem (Convergent Christian Communion) is no exception. I mean, as part of the Convergence Movement, we consider ourselves very broadly evangelical. We believe in blending Sacramental in Catholic thought, Evangelical thought, and Charismatic thought. Trust that they are all part of the whole, that they're all part of the larger Universal Church. When it comes to reclaiming the word, the term evangelical specifically, I think that the thing we really have to do is never surrender it. We can't let other people misuse it. We have to be willing to correct people on this.

When somebody talks about those evil, ignorant evangelicals, we must be willing to have a conversation with them and explain the history of the word, where it's come from, where it's going. So, they can see the bigger picture. The other thing, and the far more important thing, is embracing evangelical values and witness living peacefully, living unmaterialistically, living lovingly, and going to others and sharing the gospel. It's beautiful.

KLING: You mentioned the word Convergence. Can you go into a little bit more in-depth on what you mean by Convergence?

DAUGHERTY: Sure. So simply put, about a hundred years ago out of the Wesleyan Movement emerges the Pentecostal Movement. Pentecostalism is a unique thing in the church. It doesn't really fit into any neat little category. It's often lumped in as Protestantism because it derives from it, and it's certainly not traditionally Roman Catholic or Eastern Orthodox. Pentecostalism as original core was about reclaiming the original vision of the church, in the Book of Acts.

I love to talk about the founding of Pentecostalism because the one thing they told us, it's the term that evangelical has gotten distorted and it's lost, but the original Pentecostals were amazing in the way they would just break apart the social boundaries of the day. They believed in the spirit being back in the church and the gifts of the spirit being back in the church. That's not something that was commonly accepted at the time. They also believed in a church of all nations and of all peoples. The Pentecostal church, the founders, you had African Americans, you had women, and you had poor white people. You had a whole bunch of people who were leading this movement, who were excluded from the mainline churches and they were doing so because they felt like the Spirit of God was telling them to do so.

Some of the earliest LGBT affirming organizations in this country such as the Metropolitan Community Church and the Evangelical Network, both were founded by pastors who were involved in Pentecostalism. I find that interesting, but Pentecostalism spreads out and it infects the mainline churches. So, you have what's called the Charismatic Movement. These are Roman Catholic and mainline Protestant churches that embrace a lot of the Pentecostal fundamentals. They tended to be less rigid than Pentecostals as Pentecostals, believe in certain ethical codes, like modest dress, and you had to speak in tongues. The Charismatic Movement got rid of several of those requirements, but there's a flip side of the movement. There were historically Pentecostal and Charismatic churches that decided they wanted to embrace the sacraments, that they didn't just see the Spirit of God acting through miracles. They saw the Spirit of God acting through the historical rites in ceremony to the church. So, in the 1960s, as a mirror image of the Charismatic Movement, Pentecostal pastors and churches started to embrace liturgy and sacraments and they had good reason to do so. We can go back, and we can read the church fathers and we can see how liturgical and sacramental they were.

If you want to reclaim the apostolic church, the sacraments must be a part of the reclaiming. That's what Pentecostalism originally was about was reclaiming the sacramental church. What the Convergence Movement does is it blends it all together. It takes Charismatic gifts and Charismatic theology and Charismatic values, then you have the belief that the Spirit is still alive and well, it takes all that, and it couples it with historical evangelical thinking. Living the good news, and sharing the good news, and it brings it all together into what is a perfect whole. It brings that all together with a sacramental practice.

You see a lot of these movements embrace a type of Anglicanism in a very true Wesleyan fashion. They start using the Book of Common Prayer and most of these various Convergence churches often have a term resembling that. They'll say, "Episcopal or Anglican," but we're also, seeing Lutherans getting affected. So, for example, Lutheran Charismatic renewal became the Alliance of Renewal Churches and their Convergence Movement organization that's based upon Lutheranism, you start seeing certain Eastern Orthodox groups being affected too.

There was the Evangelical Orthodox Church, which was created from the Convergence Movement, and most of them later joined the Antiochian Orthodox Church. There's also been different Independent Catholic groups that have been affected, and it's what the Convergence Movement does. It puts its fingers in every tradition of the church. This is the whole point, it's a Convergence Movement. It takes all the traditions of the church, Evangelical, Sacramental, and Charismatic. They converge together into a whole and the Convergence Movement, unlike the Ecumenical Movement, where the Ecumenical Movement was based upon having interdenominational cooperation, the Convergence Movement is interest in something far deeper. It wants cross-pollination.

The convergence movement wants to go to every church and minister to every church and to have all the different churches come together into a cohesive whole again. This was expressed a few years ago, very well by Bishop Tony Palmer. I'm not sure if you're familiar with the name, he had 15 minutes of fame because he was a friend of Pope Francis and Pope Francis recorded a video with him that was presented at a Kenneth Copeland Ministry retreat, I think back in 2014 or so. Bishop Tony Palmer was a bishop within the Communion of Evangelical Episcopal Churches, one of the historical Convergence Movement communions. He befriended Catholics and ministered among Pentecostals, and so that right there, really boils it all down to one. That one example shows perfectly what the Convergence Movement is about. It's about going to all people, ministering to all people, taking the best of all Christian traditions, and it embraces that firm Wesleyan spirit. Wesley talks about a Catholic spirit and how the world is his parish, and that's perfectly expressed in the Convergence Movement.

KLING: You mentioned Charismatic and Pentecostal. How would you describe Charismatic worship? Can you paint a picture so I can envision it in my mind?

DAUGHERTY: Have you ever been to an African Methodist Episcopal Church service?

KLING: Oh yeah.

DAUGHERTY: So, my experience, is very similar to that. What you get is on the one hand, you've got a structure and you've got a liturgy and that liturgy originally derives from Anglicanism, like I said, there's exceptions, there's some Catholic and Orthodox expressions, and Lutheran as well, but typically you get a worship service based upon the Book of Common Prayer. Then you throw in spontaneity. So, people may shout or holler, or they may throw their hands up, or they may have a prophecy given to them by the Spirit. The service may be praise filled and energetic and faster paced, or it may express itself in a mystical way, being a historically liturgical service. They strongly believe in the gifts of the Spirit, and there may be a traditional liturgical service on Sunday, but then have faith healing service on Saturday. It's a blending of it all, and it's hard to describe. It's hard to pinpoint.

KLING: That Seems very emotional compared to some of the more stoic expressions of liturgy than what you see in a traditional Roman Catholic liturgy.

DAUGHERTY: It's supposed to be emotional. The Spirit should only be emotional. If you're facing down the face of God, you shouldn't be normal about it. It should be one of the most powerful experiences of your life.

KLING: I would agree, and I recently saw someone make the statement that Eastern Orthodox worship is not emotional. I saw that and I thought, "Nah, that's not my experience." When you are surrounded with beautiful liturgy, it can be very emotional.

DAUGHERTY: It is. I think that is absolutely the case. There are always different expressions and there's always different types of feelings and expression of emotions. Just because something isn't full of popular praise music and complete spontaneity doesn't mean it's also not full of emotion gifts.

KLING: Right. Charismatic liturgy doesn't have to have a praise band and be a concert in order to be Charismatic.

DAUGHERTY: You see that most clearly expressed within the Catholic Charismatic Renewal. Catholic Charismatics, they're everywhere and they are not the type to embrace the stereotype. When you think of Charismatic, people often associate with the likes Joel Osteen or the Joel Osteen like churches where it's very contemporary, very hip, very spontaneous, almost like a rock concert or a motivational speech. You don't see that within many different segments of the Charismatic Movement; especially, the Catholic and Anglican expressions and the Convergence Movement is no different. It blends the liturgy and the sacraments with the gifts of the Spirit.

KLING: The Convergent Movement, the reclaiming of Evangelism, the Charismatic Movement, I find it all fascinating. I appreciate the continued dialogue on these topics.

DAUGHERTY: The Convergence Movement is something I think has been forgotten about. Everyone knows Pentecostalism, everybody knows the Charismatic Movement, everyone knows the Neo-Charismatic movement. They may not know the term Neo-Charismatic, but they know the churches that come from it, such as the Vineyard Fellowships or the Campus Crusade people. Those organizations, but the Convergence Movement is somehow kind of elusive to a lot of people. I think it has been forgotten because they're in their sixties, seventies, and eighties. It was much more commonly placed, and it had a lot of prominent figures behind it, but a lot of these prominent figures have since passed on. Now, we're left with how we remind people of what this is like? Even if you go on the internet and you try to search for it, there's only a couple of articles that are not in-depth and most of the articles that are there have since been deleted or lost because a lot of the organizations that were promoting the Convergence Movement have declined.

I think what happens is a lot of it is just the larger traditional churches within the Charismatic Movement, they absorbed a lot of our members. For example, the Evangelical Orthodox Church. That church is now a fraction of its former self, because most of them joined the Antiochian Orthodox Church, which was open to the Charismatic expressions.

KLING: It sounds like you're not only trying to reclaim the term Evangelical, but you're also working to reclaim the word Convergence and what both of those terms mean.

DAUGHERTY: Absolutely, and that's a vision of Anthem (now the Convergent Christian Communion). That's the vision of our founder, and of course the Independent Sacramental Movement, it's part of that. Like the Charismatic Episcopal Church, the Communion of Evangelical Episcopal Churches, Evangelical Orthodox Church, all these different Convergence Movement Churches have almost always gotten their Apostolic Succession from the ISM. They've always been a part of that, they never openly identify with it, but from a sociological standpoint, they're a part of the Independent Sacramental Movement.

> *"So many today are worshiping in the mountains, big churches, stone and frame buildings. But Jesus teaches that salvation is not in these stone structures, not in the mountains, not in the hills, but in God."* — William J. Seymour

"Concluding Thoughts"

When I was in seminary, I served as consulting minister at the Delaware Unitarian Universalist Fellowship. The congregation was small and comprised a mixture of Secular Humanists, a few Pagan oriented folks, and one retired physician who had been Jewish and his wife who identified as a Christian. The challenge on Sunday was being able to preach a sermon, which was always called a talk or message, that would speak to everyone in attendance.

After every "talk or message" I would conclude with a prayer. The prayer was always addressed to God as "Transcendent Mystery," or "Source of Peace," or "Principle of Justice," or some similar formula for addressing God in a manner that wouldn't incite a riot within the congregation or get me fired for being too "preachy." On one Sunday, a woman within the congregation came up to me and asked me, "Why do you pray after every message? Most don't believe in God here." I responded to her, "If anything it reminds each of us we are not God." She thought about that for a moment, nodded, and never asked again why I pray after each sermon, I mean message.

Evangelism can be subtle. It doesn't have to be aggressive like you see among the Jehovah's Witnesses or by street preachers throwing fire and brimstone at people walking by. It can take several forms and all those forms working together can set the groundwork for God's grace to take hold within the hearts of people.

Ultimately, it is grace that brings people closer to God. A charismatic preacher can help bring about a conversion, but it is the grace of God stirring within a person that brings about the conversion. Good evangelization will plant the seed and start the growing process of faith.

When I was in college, I used to enjoy the debates and discussions that occurred between classes. I become involved in a discussion group that was founded by a few students involved in a conservative Christian campus organization, the name of which escapes me. I had been attending this discussion group, along with my progressive friends, for several months when it was discovered that the founder of this group, Ashley, started it to evangelize the "unchurched." The discussions were usually of a spiritual nature and often controversial or bordering on controversial. I enjoyed participating in the discussions and looked forward to it every week.

On one occasion, Ashley was confronted and was verbally berated for her intention to try to evangelize those of us who were in the progressive camp. The leader of the confrontation, Shane who was an atheist, kept turning to look at me, as if to gain approval from me. Eventually, I felt compassion for Ashley and went and stood next to her and said to Shane, "I don't agree with everything she believes in, but I have more in common with Ashley than I do with you. I believe in God. I believe in Jesus, and the Holy Trinity. I don't care what her intention was in creating this discussion group. I come for the discussion, not for anyone's hidden agenda."

As the oldest within the progressive camp my words shut down the confrontation. After that explosive meeting the discussion group disbanded, but several of us remained friends. The challenge of evangelisation is finding the right cadence, the right melody, the right words to use to stir the soul. To bring people closer to God. To find Jesus. It is a challenge, and the struggle is real, but the rewards are great.

For Reflection, Contemplation, & Prayer:

- Should we embrace the word "evangelical" and claim it, or discard the word in favor of a new paradigm?
- What are some of the ways in which you have encouraged people to seek God?
- Our stories are important. What are some stories of your own that illustrate when you have been evangelized and when you have tried to evangelize others?

"Empowerment through Accountability"
A Conversation with Subdeacon Tim Olivieri

"Let the word of Christ dwell in you richly, teaching and admonishing one another in all wisdom, singing psalms and hymns and spiritual songs, with thankfulness in your hearts to God." — Colossians 3:16

Tim Olivieri is a subdeacon in the Community of Saint George (The Young Rite). He lives in Ithaca, NY. Note: at the time of publication, he is now a deacon and an integral part of the working administration of the Community of Saint George.

KLING: It is good to have you back. What would you like to talk about today?

OLIVIERI: I was thinking about this as you asked me to come back and there was a recent article on CBS about there being priests who were on the sex offender registry, who were finding homes in an ISM jurisdiction. I don't know if you read the article, but it was something that we talked about briefly on the Sacramental Whine Facebook page. It seemed like a relevant topic being in the news right now. The ISM doesn't make it to the news very often, and unfortunately this isn't the best exposure, but I thought that might be a good starting point.

KLING: Well, that sounds like a great topic. I am not familiar with the article. Can you give a summary of it?

OLIVIERI: The article covers several mentions of one particular jurisdiction. This is an article that came out on February 5th of this year (2020) by Lee Cohen. It's available on the CBS website, but it discusses, I believe, two or three registered sex offenders. At least one is a former Roman Catholic priest. These individuals are in active ministry in an ISM jurisdiction, and I'm not going to name them because they happen to have a name that's very similar to some other ISM jurisdictions. They have these individuals in ministry, at a physical location ministering to people. They're not just on a roster. When they interviewed the bishop, the bishop's response was he is aware as is everybody in the jurisdiction of their past, but that in the spirit of forgiveness, of Christian forgiveness, these individuals are welcome to serve in ministry. That's controversial.

KLING: So, we have an article about former Roman Catholic priests who were shown the door by the Roman Catholic Church because of being sex offenders. Those priests are now in an Independent Sacramental Jurisdiction, functioning as priests and dealing with communicants and people. Is that correct?

OLIVIERI: That's correct. These aren't people who were accused of something and then were shown the door. These are individuals who are convicted and are currently on the sex offender registry which makes it disturbing because there's not really any doubt as to what happened.

KLING: What are your thoughts on the article?

OLIVIERI: It's one of those things where it hurts my heart a little bit to read something like that, because on the one hand, the ISM is so diverse. There are so many different jurisdictions, so many different ideas. There are people out there who should not be in ministry that are finding someone to take them in. On the other hand, we have to all feel the brunt of an article like this. The article makes it look like anything that's not under Rome is an "alternative ministry." They keep citing in that this ministry, this church, this issue is not affiliated with the Church of Rome, and it's bad on the level of somebody who should not be in a position of trust, being placed in a position of trust again.

I feel it as a subdeacon in the Community of Saint George. I feel like I'm being coloured with the same brush here and it makes me proud. First, that I know my jurisdiction would not make this decision, of allowing a convicted sex offender to perform ministry. I think it sparks a broader conversation about what we, the ISM, say are our minimum standards or what we will accept. Is there a baseline to what every jurisdiction should be able to sign onto?

KLING: I'm preaching to the choir here because you know it, but one of the things that the Community of Saint George has done is implement a zero-tolerance policy on sex offenders. It's a need not apply policy. We had an incident back in 2015. A bishop tried to incardinate with the Young Rite, and as the only US Young Rite bishop he contacted me. He was a convicted sex offender. I refused to incardinate him. I did not want him to have a spiritual home with us. Moving forward, we have a zero-tolerance policy and the Young Rite used to be known for "we'll ordain anyone" and "we'll accept anyone," and we've moved very, very far away from that original mind-set.

OLIVIERI: I think that's one of the things that we've talked about is my journey to the Community of Saint George and Young Rite. My first encounter, when I was approaching a jurisdiction, to pursue a vocation, the first jurisdiction I approached, one of the bishops it turned out was a registered sex offender who, attempted to conceal his identity. I think this article spoke to me on that level, and it's one of the reasons why I was careful about who I approached going forward, and who I was willing to sign on with. I wanted to make sure that any group that I would be a part of was one where we shared the same values. I felt that in any jurisdiction where I was hoping to be ordained, I needed to feel comfortable that I could receive absolution from any priest or any Bishop in that jurisdiction and be comfortable with that as I would previously walking into any Roman Catholic church and not questioning. I wouldn't have to know the priest at all. I would know, "Hey, if these guys say he's okay then he's okay." I wanted to have that same feeling, but within an ISM jurisdiction. I feel for people who can't have that, and I'm grateful that I feel I have that within the Community of Saint George.

KLING: That's something that we've really worked on, and in the past, we've turned away more people than we've accepted, at least for incardination. Part of that, is raising standards, we are not the jurisdiction for everyone anymore. The European model of the Young Rite, they embraced Bishop Marcus van Alphen's original vision and his original vision was to have as many priests as possible celebrating the Eucharist, and on the surface that sounds like a wonderful idea. In Europe people tend to stay in that status. So, if they're ordained as what we refer to as a "simplex priest," just to say mass, people tend to stay in that status. Those that want to have a public ministry become celebrants. Now, here in the US it doesn't work that way. A lot of people simply do not have the institutional loyalty that they may have in Europe. They will get ordained as a simplex priest, with faculties to just officiate the Eucharist privately, and then they will hop, skip, and jump somewhere else and get incardinated somewhere with full faculties and zero formation or preparation.

In the Community of Saint George, we try to foster community and built a formation program that will hopefully weed out people that have no business being priests. Where the conundrum comes in, taking this back to the original discussion of sex offenders, is if the Roman Catholic Church has tremendous amounts of wealth and can't sufficiently vet their people, and they have people that make it through their system and becomes sex offenders, then how can the ISM successfully vet candidates for holy orders?

It's scary being in leadership, because we don't have the resources to examine people like the Roman Catholic Church does. That becomes a struggle within the leadership role within an Independent Sacramental jurisdiction. How do we put together a formation program that sufficiently trains clergy, but also weeds out would-be sex offenders? It's a challenge. It's a serious challenge.

OLIVIERI: It's also a concern even beyond leadership, for the rank and file. I don't know the jurisdiction that's mentioned in this article. I don't know anyone who's affiliated with it, but it seems like a large group. They do have a physical location for a congregation, that seems like a large group. Was the background of these priests downplayed to them? Did they go through formation? Are they still in formation? Now, their jurisdiction is plastered all over the news, and these priests have probably put this jurisdiction on their LinkedIn and Facebook profiles.

They may have invited family members, to their ordinations, and now they are publicly associated with this group that basically says, "Hey, yeah you're a registered sex offender, but come on in, you can join us." What does that say about your achievement? Right. If you went to a university, you're proud of your degree, and then that university turned around and said, "Hey, anyone who gives us a thousand dollars can have a degree," and you respond with, "Wait a minute, but I did all this work, and now you're just giving it away." Does this have the same meaning? Is this what I thought I was signing on to? Obviously, a university degree is different from an ordination, but that feeling of, "Wait a minute, who am I, who have I signed on with? Who else is in this group that I don't want to put my name next to?"

I think that's a scary thing for anyone, especially for leadership. I can understand those thoughts of keeping you up at night. When I was in a religious order, a Roman Catholic religious order, we had a gentleman come in and he applied to our seminary and he was the nicest guy you had ever met. Everyone who met him, loved him. He was so nice, he was so helpful, and he was the kind of guy who after dinner he would volunteer to do dishes. He applied to join the order and our provincial superior/seminary rector said, "He applied, officially. I think he's good to go. What do you guys think?" We said, "We think he's great. He's going to fit in wonderfully here." He'd been coming for about two months. His background check was clean, everything was good. He applied right before Christmas, and he was supposed to come in on the 15th or so of January. A week before he comes in, there was a robbery at the rectory of one of the parishes that our order served. The priest came in to pull the collection out of the safe so that he could take it to the bank in the morning. The collection was gone from the previous Sunday. Around $8,000 was stolen. There had been a double collection that weekend and the collection was gone. A few days later when this person was supposed to show up, he didn't show up. No one connected the dots on those two things until months later. Several months later, the grocery store we used called because "our purchase order" had some suspicious activity. The grocery store bill from purchases was billed directly to the order, and when they pulled the security footage, it was this guy who had applied and failed to show up, and he was wearing a Roman collar. He was walking through the grocery store and he was loading thousands of dollars' worth of food into a cart and charging it to the church account at the grocery store.

He was charged with that crime when he was arrested. It turned out that he was actively trying to frame a local diocesan priest, and he was trying to get into the rectory to put child abuse photos onto the priest's computer.

KLING: Wow.

OLIVIERI: It was this guy who was the nicest guy, and overnight, it just unravelled. He stole the collection. He was stealing food from us. He was trying to frame a priest because he harboured quite a bit of hatred towards the Roman Catholic Church because of how they handled sex abuse. He was trying to break anything he could, that was affiliated with Rome. We were devastated because we were all fooled. Ever since that happened, it's like you said, "What amount of vetting guarantees that a person is not disturbed or willing to cause harm either to the institution or to another person?" It's an incredibly scary thought that pains me, that it happened to my order then, and the thought pains me that it could happen to an ISM jurisdiction that may not be able to withstand that kind of scandal like we were able to.

KLING: Yeah. Because Roman Catholic Church is massive and truly international. There are millions of people that adhere to the Roman Catholic Church. They're really feeling the pain of these sort of actions, but I have a story that I feel compelled to share also, from my time at Christ the King Monastery in Cullman, Alabama. Full disclaimer, the monastery was a part of the Roman Catholic Traditionalist Movement. When I was there, their status with the Roman Catholic diocese of Birmingham, Alabama was extremely irregular. We were not recognized by the local Bishop, but Father Leonard Giardina, who was the founder of the monastery, had been a monk at St. Bernard's Abbey also in Cullman, Alabama. He founded the monastery without permission but when I was there he had not been officially ex-communicated. He wasn't ex-communicated, by the Roman Catholic Church, until on or about 1996, and I was there in 1992.

We were not recognized, but we had a tremendous amount of support from European benefactors. There was a monastery built with lover 20 plus rooms for monks, monastery church was being built that was large and it had a high altar with several side chapels. It was an extensive compound. They had 78 or 80 acres, so lots of land. Back then, I'm positive, there were no background checks on people wanting to join the monastery because that wasn't Father Leonard's skill set, it wasn't in the Rule of St. Benedict.

People would usually come and visit, and we would meet new potential monks and get to know them. We had a guy come and apply to become a postulant. For those who are unaware, the degrees or levels of monastic membership within a Benedictine monastery starts out with a postulant. Then you become a novice. Then you receive simple vows for three years, and then you go into solemn vows for life.

This man, his name was Santiago Valdez, I'll never forget the name. He came and petitioned to become a postulant. Initially he was fine, and we had no issues with him, but there were some strange experiences that I had with him and they escalated until it became a problem. At first, he was guarded, but pleasant. Then during recreation, which we had for one hour a day right before complin, we were inside and playing cards. We didn't have TV, but occasionally we'd play cards. The whole point of recreation was to do things as a community. You weren't allowed to go off into your cell and read privately, you were expected to be in community with the other monks. When Santiago played cards he would get competitive and aggressive. I went to Father Leonard after a period of time when we were all playing cards. I shared with him my suspicion that something was wrong. I had seen that kind of "glint in the eyes" when I was in the Navy stationed on the USS Dwight D Eisenhower. You were in the Navy too, correct?

OLIVIERI: I know the glint you are talking about.

KLING: Yeah. Well, it's because you're "institutionalized" on a ship, because you're stuck at sea all the time and it brings the crazy out in you. I could see that in him. So, I said something to Father Leonard, "Something doesn't seem right." That was the first incident. The second incident was on a Sunday, and on a Sunday that Father Leonard and Brother Sebastian, the prior and the sub prior (Father Leonard would eventually become an Abbot), were gone. Father Leonard was in Montgomery, Alabama saying mass at a mission parish that the monastery maintained. Because it was Sunday, we were not supposed to do any work, we still prayed the divine office, but we didn't perform work task other than that which was necessary, like cooking meals and doing dishes. Well, Santiago decided to do his laundry. I know this seems trivial to most people, but for monks, this was a major infraction. He was doing his laundry on Sunday, and we were not supposed to do laundry on Sunday. I did what I was supposed to do, I politely told him, "We're not supposed to do laundry on Sunday." He became aggressive and got right up in my face, held his hand back like he was going to punch me. I backed up, I'm 6'3" and a big guy.

I backed up, put my hands up and said, "This isn't proper monk behaviour." I walked away and I reported it as I was supposed to, and nothing was done. A couple of days later, Santiago stands up while we were in chapel, and walks out of chapel. We were in chapel from 4:20 AM in the morning, like every other day, and mass usually ended around 8:30 AM. We had been in chapel for about four hours, and right before mass starts Santiago gets up and walks out of the chapel. Father Leonard leaves to see what was going on with Santiago, it is unusual for someone to just leave chapel. At that point, one of the other monks leaves too and we didn't have mass that day because they took Santiago to the airport. He had said to them, "I want to go to the airport, now. I'm done. I don't want to be a monk anymore."

Santiago leaves, I think he went to Ohio or Indiana. We found out after he left that he had been incarcerated for 10 years or so, and I was right, he had been institutionalized. Having been in the Navy and having been out at sea, I saw the same expressions on Santiago's face that I saw while serving on a ship. You are stuck on a ship, which is similar to what it's like when you're stuck in a prison. He was expressing those same traits that I saw amongst some of the people that I knew from when I was in the military, being part of an institutionalized culture. I knew something was off because I don't think Santiago ever served in the military. Does that make sense?

OLIVIERI: It makes total sense. I've drawn that comparison before and I'm glad to hear that someone else feels the same way. Your experiences when you go through RTC, Recruit Training Command or boot camp, it's hard not to. It has a Shawshank feel to it.

KLING: It Absolutely does. When I was in basic training, it was in Orlando, Florida, family came and took me to Disney World. I thought, "We're going to have a great time." I lasted half a day and said, "I got to get back. I can't handle all the freedom. I need to get back to the regimentation that was, the base." Being in the military and being incarcerated, it messes with your head a little bit. I noticed that in Santiago Valdez. That's one thing we found out, that he had been incarcerated. Of course, he didn't tell us. Another thing that Father Leonard did share with the community was that Santiago was hearing voices from what he claimed was the voices of Jesus and Mary. Maybe he had schizophrenia. I can't diagnose him, but he was claiming to hear voices.

We also found out, after he had left, that he went and lived with an elderly woman, a pious Catholic woman, who was part of the Traditionalist Movement, who wanted to help a "former monk" and would-be priest. She was happy to take him in and help him because he was going to be a Traditionalist Catholic priest. He ended up robbing her and raping her. He went to prison for it, and to my understanding he refused a lawyer claiming that, "God was going to provide." He didn't need an attorney because God was his attorney.

I searched Santiago Valdez on the Internet and found out he had been released from prison, but he "did it again," in 2015 and is serving a 28-year sentence. If Christ the King Monastery had done a background check they would have found out he was a felon. I don't know what crime he had committed before he came to the monastery, but if I had been the vocation director, I doubt I would have allowed him to petition to join after serving a prison sentence.

OLIVIERI: The guy from my story was eventually convicted for stealing the food. They never got him for stealing the collection money. Nobody ever connected the dots until I said it afterward, and nobody wanted to deal with the fallout from it because we had received an insurance pay-out for the stolen collection. I think this is pure speculation, but I think our superior was looking at it as, "If one of our already admitted seminarians was the one who stole the money. The insurance company might have an issue with that." Therefore, I don't think he wanted to chase that one down. Also, some months had passed, and he hadn't done anything at that point, and that's the problem with background checks. It's the same problem with psychological evaluations. Unless you are suffering from some very serious mental illness, you can probably tell people what you think they want to hear.

It's a difficult thing, and going back to something I said earlier, it's a fear that you have when you admit someone into your community. The more serious issue is that when you put on a Roman collar, when you hold yourself out in ministry, whether it's in the sacramental movement or not, you're going to have good and pious people who take you at face value and are willing to show you hospitality and respect. It's incredibly hard to hear something like what happened with the former postulant, you mentioned. Someone took him in and showed kindness, wanting to help as an expression of her faith, she wanted to help this person, and he took advantage of that in horrible ways that doesn't just destroy her trust, but the trust of other people too. Suddenly, anyone who would accommodate any member of clergy now has to think twice about it. That's terrible.

KLING: Yeah. It's the shadow side of the Independent Sacramental Movement, or any aspect of ministry within the Christian tradition, because you and I know that the Roman Catholic Church is not the only church or denomination that has scandal. Scandal happens in every denomination or religious group out there. No organization is completely immune. Even the Amish have issues, but it's scary because the ISM so small. If you added all the jurisdictions together, we're still small, but I've used the phrase before that the Independent Sacramental Movement is the best kept secret within Christianity, and I believe that we have a lot to offer; however, being in leadership, there is that fear factor.

If we get a Santiago Valadez knocking on our door who says all the right things, and we do a background check, and he doesn't show up who's to say that we couldn't potentially have a nightmare on our hands. Or someone like the fellow who tried to join your former order. We must be diligent and there are jurisdictions out there that will take anyone. We need to be diligent and guard the gateway into Holy orders. Keeping the vision of Bishop Marcus van Alphen's which to have as many people celebrate the Eucharist. We are not Donatists, in the sense that we believe that you must be faultless for the sacraments to be valid, but I don't want people who should not be priests celebrating the Eucharist. I wish we lived in a world where it was okay to ordain as many people as possible, and they would all go out and be what our landmarks mandate such as living a "clean life," but the reality of the situation is that it is not guaranteed. We must guard the sacrament of holy orders.

OLIVIERI: I agree. I think that one of the things that strikes me as being a problem are people who ministry hop. This is unique to the Independent Sacramental Movement; although, you do see it in Evangelical circles as well. Even outside of apostolic succession, they're the people who go to the Universal Life Church, and when that doesn't satisfy their need, when they still feel like they're lacking, they go to the First Internet Church of the Web. When that doesn't stick, they go somewhere else and they'll just keep going and going and going, looking for the one that sounds better and always looking for the one that's going to give them the validation they seek. I feel like this happens often within the Independent Sacramental Movement. I've heard of people doing it for different reasons, such as "I didn't like the name of the jurisdiction, this other one has a better sounding name," or "I went to this other jurisdiction because I wanted to introduce Oriental Orthodox lines of succession because I have issues with whatever," and the list goes on.

I think imposter syndrome plays into the often instability within the Independent Sacramental community. I think we all experienced it on some level. I know you've talked about having difficulty getting people to understand, like within your Doctor of Ministry program, how to identify you. There's a certain element of that I think we all face, and I think the scary part is that there are individuals out there who are grabbing all these status symbols. They are putting on vestments and all the outward symbols, and sometimes it's to hide some ugly stuff. Sometimes it's to feed their pride because they are not desirous of Eucharistic celebration. They want to LARP.

KLING: Yeah. I think there are several within the Independent Sacramental Movement who are interested in Live Action Role-Playing!

OLIVIERI: It becomes a religious LARP, and that can get scary. If you think about someone who is doing all of this, just because they want to play dress up, any number of motivations can be hidden, positive or negative. You do this because it feeds your pride. You do this because it feeds your greed, you do this because it feeds your lusts and that's hard to root out. It's just hard to root out.

As I was reading the article today, in anticipation of our discussion, I was thinking, "If I were a priest, I cannot think of a worse thing to happen to me then to be told, "You can never celebrate the Eucharist again." When you think about the Roman Catholic priests for whom that has happened, I cannot imagine that happening to me. I'm not saying that puts me all in the right and that I have no issues. That I never have to worry about vanity or pride, because that is the essence of what we're doing. That's what unites all of us together. That is what unites the very different jurisdictions within this movement. Even though we can't vet people easily, as with a criminal background check, at the end of the day, if you're not focused on the sacramental aspect of what we're doing, really focused on the sacramental life, you're going to wander off anyway, because you're going to get bored.

KLING: You can only own so many vestments.

OLIVIERI: This is true.

KLING: I was thinking of imposter syndrome right before you mentioned it, and I think one of the things within the Independent Sacramental Movement that isn't always emphasized is accountability. When I became the default Young Rite bishop in the United States, I could have easily done everything I could to remain the only Young Rite bishop in the United States. Instead, when I founded the Community of Saint George, I knew that I did not want to be the only bishop governing the Community. So, when I was able to consecrate Kirk Jeffery and then bring Bishop Rob Lamoureux into the fold, I formed a committee of three to govern the Community and this gave me two people that I am now accountable to in addition to being accountable to the entire community.

I think that's important, and that's not saying that jurisdictions that have one presiding bishop on "doing it wrong," I'm not saying that. However, having a group that you're accountable to, I think is important. Yes, there are bishops in Europe that I'm accountable to, the Young Rite Council of Three. That's wonderful, but because they're in Europe they're a long way away and there is a language barrier, even though they speak great English, and I don't speak Slovenian. My point is, being over here in the USA, there was an opportunity to do whatever I wanted. I knew that we needed, as a community moving forward, to have an accountability process. I think that's important when we talk about suitability for ministry and how do we vet people in formation. We can put people through formation, but we also need to be sustainable. Maintaining a good, strong level of accountability and sustainability makes us better prepared to form people for ministry. Does that make sense?

OLIVIERI: I agree, and I think a lot of people, when they hear accountability feel it's a negative thing. I'm struggling with this at work. I work in higher education fundraising and I work on the analysis side to see how we're doing and try to keep good things happening. When you say accountability, people get upset because they think, "Oh, this is, very big brotherish. Someone's watching over my shoulder." I don't want people to feel like they aren't trusted, but at the same time, you should feel accountable to someone.

It should not shock you, in a work environment I think that your boss might come in and say, "Hey, show me what you're working on." It can be tricky in the ISM to do that. When you were in a monastery and I was in a religious order, for us accountability was very simple because we were all in one building, the people who were in charge were there, they could see what we were doing at any given time.

KLING: Whereas you are two states away from me, and what I really enjoy about our Community is that we are all well connected. We interact regularly in any way that we can, and you and I talk on the phone regularly. I regularly correspond with Bishop Rob via email, and all of us are talking on social media. Even though we are not physically close in proximity, we are, still together and keeping each other up to date as to what we're doing and what we're working on.

Recently, somebody online who identifies as a Benedictine monk, and puts O.S.B. behind their name asked a question, and I can't remember the question, but my response was, "Why don't you ask your abbot?" The person responded, "I don't have an Abbot, I'm on my own." The first thing I thought of was the opening chapter of The Rule of St. Benedict that talks about the different kinds of monks and the worst kind of monk, according to Saint Benedict, is the Gyrovague, the monk who does not have an abbot and who does not follow a rule.

It is easy to give yourself a title in the Independent Sacramental Movement. If you're a bishop, you can be an archbishop, you can be a metropolitan, you can be a patriarch and I have seen all these examples. Some are perfectly fine, and I think are appropriate, but then there are some that I see going around as archbishop or metropolitan, and I'm thinking, "Really?" The same is true for people who are members of different religious orders, it goes back to accountability. If you look at The Rule of St. Benedict, it goes back to accountability, and this idea of what Benedict would call "Holy obedience." The idea of obedience would be a negative word in today's usage, but it goes back to accountability, having someone that you answer to and it doesn't mean that they're your boss. They can be a peer such as in the Community of Saint George. There are three presiding bishops, and we're all equal. In our rule, I'm referred to as the first among equals, because I founded the group, but I equally answer to the other presiding bishops and that's important.

I think there are aspects of the Independent Sacramental Movement where people fixate on independent and independence. It's independent from Rome, not independent as in "I'm on my own and I can do whatever I want." That's sloppy ecclesiology.

OLIVIERI: Right. Not long ago, I shared a video about an Orthodox monastery. I really enjoyed watching the video, which is why I shared it with the community. The video starts out with an opening theme where there's a monk who walks down a row of cells very early in the morning, it's three thirty in the morning and he knocks on a door. At each door he would say, "Through the prayers of our holy fathers." He goes from monastic cell to monastic cell, and he knocks on the door and the monks inside each cell responds to him with, "Amen. He goes to the last door and knocks and says his prayer but the monk inside the cell doesn't respond. He stands there for a second and then he knocks again, and finally the monk responds, "Amen." Having lived in religious life, I can absolutely identify with that last monk. You're supposed to get up very early in the morning and a zombie. At the same time, you look at it and you say, "Part of what we do is we get up at three thirty in the morning and recite the divine office, okay."

I can do that on my own. I can set alarms right now this morning, I can get up. I could go through the entire divine office, and that would be fine, except I would do that for a day or two. Then I'd probably fall off. When you're in a religious community you have that accountability. These monks had that accountability of another monk knocking, and it's not that the door remained closed. He didn't come in and check in on you. Someone was knocking on your door and making sure that you were doing what you need to do. This is probably also a check to see if someone's sick or hurt, along the process.

The idea that you're accountable to someone doesn't need to be this scary thing. It should be an empowering thing because it helps you do the thing that you're setting out to do. Those monks wouldn't be able to be as good at monastic life if they were on their own. That's the reason why so few monasteries don't allow a new monk to become a hermit. You have to be a senior monastic before they will let you become a hermit. While learning the discipline you're still accountable. To become a hermit, you are asking for a very long leash as far as monastics go.

KLING: Yes, absolutely. It requires a tremendous amount of discipline to live the life of a hermit and people who are new to monastic life simply do not have the discipline.

OLIVIERI: When you're new to monastic life, when you're new to anything you're learning what you can and cannot do and how things are done. It's like you said, "You went out from boot camp and you couldn't handle all the fun stuff because you needed the rigid lifestyle that you had just learned over a short period." I had a similar experience, when I went to recruit training at Great Lakes, Illinois. I had weekend liberty and I said, "I'm going to go to Chinatown. I'm going to go strut around Chicago in my fresh Navy whites and do whatever." I didn't have a plan. I went out and went to a Chinese restaurant about a mile from base. I was feeling very anxious about being away from base because I was eating a meal at a time when I was not used to eating a meal, and it didn't feel right. I was eating with someone; my mother had come to my graduation, and she wanted to talk to me, and for the last two and a half months I was conditioned not to talk when I was eating.

KLING: And you probably ate the whole meal in five minutes or less.

OLIVIERI: I scarfed down my whole meal, and I had grown up as a slow eater, but I scarfed down the whole meal. My mother didn't know what to do. She was still eating her egg roll and I was done. That's how quickly I adjusted to Navy life and how quickly you adjust to new situations. You and I can go out and enjoy the real world now since we've been away from the Navy for a while. We can go out and do normal stuff now. It's conditioning. You're trained to do the things you need to do. Given the opportunity to veer off and do your own thing, you probably won't. I think it's the same thing with monastic life. If you're used to getting up at three thirty every morning, and you do that every morning with another monk knocking on your door every morning and then you become a hermit 20 or 30 years later, you're going to wake up on your own without the knock.

KLING: You raise a good point when you live a monastic life, you live a structured life. The time that you are in the postulancy and then in the novitiate, those are temporary. Then you have simple vows for a couple years, three years in some orders, and then you're ready for solemn vows in perpetuity. An extensive formation period to prepare you to be a monk, but in the Independent Sacramental Movement, oftentimes what we have for people preparing for the priesthood is, "Oh, you want to be a priest? Great. Well, let's schedule a time to ordain you a priest." No formation, no working through the process, and "poof" someone is a priest.

I believe that with the sacrament of Holy Orders there's an energy transfer. You are transformed by the sacrament, and I think most in the Movement would agree with me. If you go out and ordain someone and you transform the character of their soul, the indelible mark of Holy Orders on their soul, and then you cast them out, "Okay, go be a priest," you're doing them a disservice. That's where problems manifest. The beauty of our system is that we have minor orders and then, the subdiaconate and then diaconate. By the time one becomes a priest you should be ready. You should be prepared and fully formed. Hopefully, that will mediate some of this imposter syndrome that many within the Movement experience, because they're often thrown into the priesthood without preparation. It would be like meeting someone who felt called to be a monk and then them saying, "Okay, we just made you a monk, and now you're a full-fledged, solemn vowed monastic with no time of postulancy, and no novitiate, no time in simple vows. Suddenly you're a solemnly vowed monk. It doesn't work that way, but I think for many people they think it does or they think it should and that's a problem.

OLIVIERI: It takes a while to realize that the journey is just as important, maybe even more important than the destination.

> *"Anyone who receives the name of abbot is to lead his disciples by a twofold teaching: he must point out to them all that is good and holy more by example than by words."* — The Rule of Saint Benedict

"Concluding Thoughts"

The entire concept of "empowerment through accountability" is about how-to live-in community. One of the challenges within the Independent Sacramental Movement, at least within my jurisdiction, the Community of Saint George, is we live a diasporic lifestyle. Often the term diaspora refers to the situation of Judaism after the destruction of the Temple in 70 C.E. Jewish communities were scattered throughout Europe, mainly Eastern Europe, and various places within the Middle East. This phenomenon became known as the Jewish Diaspora; however, the term can be applied to any dispersed people. Those of us in the Independent Sacramental Movement often live a dispersed lifestyle. The Community of Saint George is small, but we have people in Iowa, Ohio, Texas, New York, Michigan, South Carolina, and elsewhere. We can congregate once or twice a year at a synod or convocation; however, we eventually must return home and be dispersed once again.

Living in a monastic community, with every monk living under the same roof makes it easier to sustain accountability. The Internet helps us, in our modern times, to stay connected and for that I am grateful.

Maintaining connection via phone, email, and on-line forums is not the same as being under one roof. It is a substitute that is often lacking, but what other option do we have other than using the technology we have to help sustain our communities?

Due to the diasporic circumstances, we find ourselves within the Independent Sacramental Movement we have two existential predicaments which I will call micro-existence and macro-existence. On a macro level we are members of micro-denominations or jurisdictions that are often scattered throughout the country or the world. On a micro level we struggle to develop local communities in which to practice our ministry, in the case of clergy, and find and build community. My macro-community is the Community of Saint George. As a chaplain I have found opportunities to build local community through my chaplaincy work.

As a hospice chaplain I have several chaplain colleagues who I can fellowship with and to whom I am accountable. My "parish" is my caseload, which usually hovers around fifty to sixty patients and their families and the staff at the nursing homes and assisted living facilities I visit regularly. Likewise, as a chaplain within the Ohio Military Reserve my "parish" there consists of the soldiers I encounter both during drill and outside of it, either through worship I facilitate or when needed to provide pastoral care. Within the Ohio Military Reserve, I answer to the chief chaplain and my chain of command.

One aspect of leadership I discovered when I was eighteen and a young sailor in the US Navy was, "To be a good leader, you need to be a good follower." This is one maxim I think my fellow bishops within the Independent Sacramental Movement should consider and contemplate often. Just because you wear a fuchsia-colored cassock does not mean you are accountable to no one. Accountability need not be considered a negative. Accountability, when done correctly, can and should be empowering. When the burden of leadership is held with pride and vanity then accountability becomes a restraint, but when leadership is embraced with humility and a servant-leadership mindset, then accountability becomes empowering.

For Reflection, Contemplation, & Prayer:

- Who are you accountable to on both a macro and micro level?
- What are some ways you have worked to develop local, sustainable, community?
- How do you view accountability? Have you experienced it as a positive or a negative? How can you make accountability empowering in your life?

"Avenues of Grace"
A Conversation with Father Jerry Maynard

"After the Sabbath, at dawn on the first day of the week, Mary Magdalene and the other Mary went to look at the tomb. There was a violent earthquake, for an angel of the Lord came down from heaven and, going to the tomb, rolled back the stone and sat on it. His appearance was like lightning, and his clothes were white as snow. The guards were so afraid of him that they shook and became like dead men. The angel said to the women, "Do not be afraid, for I know that you are looking for Jesus, who was crucified. He is not here; he has risen, just as he said. Come and see the place where he lay. Then go quickly and tell his disciples: 'He has risen from the dead and is going ahead of you into Galilee. There you will see him.' Now I have told you."– Matthew 28:1-7

Father Jerry Maynard is an Independent Catholic priest formerly with the Order of Mary Magdalene and now under the episcopal protection of Bishop David Strong. Known as "the People's Priest," he leads a ministry of protest, praise and community organizing in Houston, Texas. Father Jerry works on foreign and domestic issues, teaches the spirituality of non-violence, and serves as founding pastor of The People's Church.

KLING: Thank you so much for joining me again, Father Jerry. What would you like to talk about today?

MAYNARD: I would like to talk today about discipleship. I recently attended the Los Angeles Religious Education Congress, which is a yearly gathering of book publishers, artists, theologians, educators, and folks who do religious education full-time. They gather in Anaheim, California under the auspices of the Archdiocese of Los Angeles, within the Roman Catholic Church. There is a large conference on education and there are way too many workshops and keynote speakers and liturgies and worship experiences. I've been wanting to go for years. I finally got the chance to go this year, and I was there to promote Matthew Fox's new book, *"The Tao of Thomas Aquinas: Fierce Wisdom for Hard Times,"* and I wrote the afterword for the book. I was there to advertise the book and get people to buy the book and spread the word around about it.

I had some interesting conversations with people that got me thinking about how the ISM promotes itself and how we in the ISM help to inspire other people to want to be a part of our dynamic Movement. How do we make disciples? People who in their heart and mind have been set on fire for Jesus and for the sacraments but who also have a fire for wanting to live authentically in the world. I want to talk about that a little and hopefully by the end of our discussion, we will have solved all the issues of the world.

KLING: My first question is, when you say discipleship, is discipleship a sub-category of evangelism or are the two terms synonymous?

MAYNARD: I think they're synonymous, but I believe as well that discipleship is something deeper than evangelization. Evangelization is the beginning point. The word literally means to tell good news. Evangelion is "to tell the good news." The good news is that we're all the beloved children of God, that we are all born into a sacred experience that we call this world, and that Jesus came to die so that we might have a chance to live and enjoy this beautiful life. That's the good news. I think that's the starting point, and that's a point that we need to constantly be telling people and proclaiming and embodying because there are a lot of people who still don't know that good news. I think that's necessary, but what I've been talking about is a little bit deeper.

I'm talking about people who already know that they are the beloved of God. They already know they're saved and being saved. People who know that already, but who are learning how to live that out as if it was true. That's a disciple, which is a person who knows that they're loved, who knows in their core that they are put into this world with a mission. That mission is to show other people that they are loved.

I often joke with people, I say, "You know, Jesus died and saved the world already. Now we just have to act like it's true. Like everything's been done for us. Now, let's alert your face that you're happy." Essentially, a lot of people talk about being happy, but their face looks angry.

Let's make it real, let's put our money where our mouth is, and I think that's more of what discipleship is. It's more tangible, it's more bodily, it's more everyday and practical, where the rubber hits the road for people. When you talk about discipleship and you talk about making disciples, what you're really talking about is trying to get people committed to this daily practice of being the beloved, of going into the world telling people we are the beloved, and then going into the broader world and saying, "Hey, we can no longer do this because this violates our first truth, which is that we are the beloved of God." That's where we begin discussing politics and how we organize ourselves and our communities and who we vote for and all these other things. I think discipleship is a lot deeper, but it's related to evangelization.

KLING: There's multiple tiers to this concept of discipleship. Let me break that down a little bit. You have the initial invitation to the gospel and there's a certain skill set for people who can do that, and then once somebody buys into that, then there's another skill set that does what you say by going deeper and building that faith and the rubrics that go along with living a sacramental Christian life. Then there's other related categories like apologetics and defending your faith. Apologetics is not necessarily a part of discipleship, but I see it as somewhat included. We don't have a lot of apologists who can argue in a debating the truths and the perspective of the Independent Sacramental Movement in relation to the Roman Catholic position or the Eastern Orthodox position or various Protestant positions. That's a skill set that I think is needed to take the Movement to another level. I'm just throwing ideas out.

MAYNARD: I think that's good. I agree with you. I don't think we have many people who are spokespeople for the Movement. I think we have some great people like yourselves who represent the Movement, and who get stories out there. More people are familiar with us. So, I think if we were to look at the Movement from these stages, that as, as you enumerated them, I think we are in the evangelization stage, because we deal with people who come from larger traditions that are much older, who have been oftentimes wounded. I think we are in our communities doing the work of trying to reintroduce these wounded individuals to their original, what Matthew Fox calls, their original blessing. That they were born into the belovedness of God, that when God thinks about them, God thinks that they are beautiful, that they are beloved, that they are the apple of God's eye. God doesn't spend time in disappointment of them, but rather that God delights in them. God is not a bogeyman who is always trying to get us, but rather God is a great lover who wants to be with us and hold us and massage us into the truth that we are already born into this great experience of cosmic love.

I think that's for us, we do that a lot because we're dealing with lapsed Catholics or people who were married and divorced. Because they got divorced, they couldn't go to communion anymore, and then they got remarried. Or with LGBT people, or women who've had abortions. People who are addicts. We deal with a lot of very vulnerable people in our Independent communities, partly because we ended up being the ones that they find and will end up being the only ones who are willing to engage with them and say, "No! Your experiences are valid, and you deserve to be a person of faith, just as much as everybody else." I think we do that. I think we do that very well, that evangelization element but for us to grow, we need to go deeper.

That's kind of where I'm constantly contemplating, with the people that we have, and that we're administering with, how do we keep that experience of ministry growing so that it's not transitory. What is your issue? Let's deal with that, but I think we have to go deeper with the populations of people that we have, and I think you would understand this as a chaplain because you have to do this in your space sometimes.

Going deeply with people in experiences and moments where we have to go deeper, and we say, "Okay, yes! You are divorced or you're LGBT, or you're HIV positive. Yes. God loves you." Now, we need to get deeper than that, "Now, you just found out that you have cancer. How are we going to get you to deal with this experience that you're having to deal with now and deal with it without having to constantly have this idea that God is looming over you in judgment." How do we flip that? I think that's where great pastoral care comes in, being able to be present to that person and go deeper with that person.

That's where the seeds get planted of true authentic faith, because people who go through those experiences with a great pastor and with the experience of the sacraments, when they come out of it, they are completely transformed. Once you go deeper, they tell everyone else, and then they become evangelists and express to people the deeper realities of God that they have in their life. I think that's what it means to make a disciple.

KLING: I appreciate that you mentioned the pastoral care model in my role as a chaplain. I meet people where they are and let them set the agenda. Reflecting on that methodology and applying it to the Independent Sacramental Movement along with in this concept of discipleship, looking at the Independent Sacramental Movement in its fullness, there's a lot of marginalized people and often for very different reasons. You have LGBT individuals who are here because they're gay or lesbian or transgender and you have people who are here because they were divorced or for reasons surrounding some of the decisions that they've made. You also have people who are here because they have one foot in Neopaganism, but they're attracted to the gospel message.

MAYNARD: Yea.

KLING: They're marginalized by their faith choices and people who are in that camp are often rejected by the Pagan community, but also rejected by the Christian community and sometimes they feel lost. One of the things that the Independent Sacramental Movement does is it normalizes all these marginalized people. If you look at LGBT issues, for example, it's not that big a deal in the Independent Movement. I mean, we're not struggling over whether we should ordain a gay or lesbian person. We just don't struggle with that, at least most of the jurisdictions I interact with. Most jurisdictions are okay with it, those who are not also part of the Traditionalist Movement. I don't know of any that refuse to ordain someone because they're gay. I couldn't name one jurisdiction that does, because there's hundreds of jurisdictions out there. Those that don't may be jurisdictions of just one or two bishops. Do they really count? Maybe, but still there's plenty of jurisdictions out there that have normalized being part of the LGBT community and active within ISM ministry.

There are some jurisdictions that have no room or no interest in entertaining those who follow an esoteric path, but there are plenty that do. I would say that the movement does tend to normalize those people who feel marginalized. And I think that's a strength of the Movement.

MAYNARD: Yeah, I completely agree. I like that dynamic. I wouldn't say normalize. I think we legitimize. The word is not wrong, we do normalize targeted communities, but I think we also legitimize targeted communities. What I mean by legitimize is that we remind them of their original blessing. We remind them that they are worthy to experience these moments of grace or these avenues of grace that we call the sacraments. They are worthy of them all and these other communities, the Anglicans, the Orthodox, the Roman Catholics, tell people you can't receive communion because you're divorced. We read about that all the time. There are so many bishops and priests who think that they can deny people communion.

I often hear about a Catholic school that has fired a teacher because they're LGBT. I think we normalize targeted communities in our movement, but we also remind them of their legitimacy. I think that's a beautiful sacred act that we do. The experience of God must not be restricted to the few or to the old.

I believe we are all born misfits. What I mean is we all have minds and hearts that want to learn new things, get excited about life, and wonder, and build one's values around a profound experience. I think that's so cool. This idea that, whether we know it or not, in the Movement, we democratize, the Divine, the sacred experience. We certainly democratize the sacraments, which are avenues of grace.

KLING: Can you break down what you mean by democratize?

MAYNARD: Democracy comes from a Greek word, which literally means the people power. When we talk about democratizing mysticism or democratizing the experience of God, whether that's through the sacraments or through Bible study or through meditation or whatever type of spiritual practice you utilize, it keeps it from becoming something that's just on the shelf that you look at and you kind of adore from a far and you can't touch it. It keeps it from becoming distant and disconnected.

Matthew Fox talks about democratizing in his book, *"The Tao of Thomas Aquinas: Fierce Wisdom for Hard Times."* What we're talking about is taking it, the sacraments, off the shelf to get it out of the glass and allowing it to be mobile. That you can experience with your senses, that you can have a deep connection with. I think when we democratize God, when we democratize mysticism, the sacraments, what we are doing is we are forbidding the creation of Divinity as something that's separate from us. What we are trying to do when we democratize the sacraments, or God, or Divinity, or mysticism, or whatever word you want to use, we're affirming the Incarnation. We are trying to dare to say that this is real, that this actually happened, that the God of the universe came down to our time and space and sanctified our experience. So, that every moment has the capacity to be a moment of grace. God is so intimately connected with us that every time we breathe in, we're breathing in the experience of God.

KLING: It sounds like it's moving away from this idea of God being exclusively transcendent and the idea that God is also indwelling within nature and within humanity.

MAYNARD: Absolutely. I think all of us are born with the capacity to experience the sacred. I think all of us are born sacred, but because we are finite beings engaging with the infinite sometimes God is elusive. The divine is elusive, but it doesn't mean that God can't be experiential or personal. That's the whole point of the sacraments is that we are getting an avenue, a little window open that lets the fresh air of God into our lives. Whether that be through baptism, communion, confession, matrimony, holy orders, we're getting a glimpse into what it means to be a child of the living God.

I think it's something that you need, and we need more of in our Movement. We need more people who are going deeper, and I think there are some people who are going deeper. My friend, Bishop David Strong is doing that well in his community, Spirit of Christ Community Church in Tacoma, Washington. I think of my friend, the Reverend Doctor Trish Vanni with her community in Minnesota, Charis Ecumenical Catholic Community. I think they're doing it well or at least trying to, and you certainly as well, as, Jesus says, "You'll know them by their fruit," obviously you're doing something right.

I think we need more conversations about where the rubber hits the road for us when it comes to faith. Otherwise, all we're doing is just playing dress up. Everything is pointless if it doesn't manifest into our lives. So anyway, what do you have to say? I have been talking too much.

KLING: I've been thinking about the idea of discipleship and evangelism. Recently, I've been writing a paper for a course I'm taking in my Doctor of Ministry program and I've been looking at Old Catholic history and the idea of ultramontanism, which is the rise of the papacy, which ultimately led to the doctrine of papal infallibility. It's linked to the Society of Jesus, also known as the Jesuits. I was thinking about the Jesuit Order and I was thinking it would be interesting if there was an Independent Sacramental order like the Jesuits, in that it would advocate for the Movement in general. I know it sounds kind of stupid, but it ties in with this idea of apologetics and what I've said several times, "The Independent Sacramental Movement is one of the best kept secrets within Christianity."

I believe the Movement has a lot to offer, but unfortunately, we're splintered. One of the beauties of the Movement is that there's a lot of diversity, but the downside of that is there's not a lot of communication, or discipleship among the various components of the Movement. There's discipleship when a lay person decides they want to become a Christian, but then there's a type of discipleship when a lay person decides they want to be a priest and that's been a problem within the movement. There's a formation problem. Not a lot of jurisdictions have formation down to a science.

We've created a culture in the Movement where one can email a bishop and ask, "Hey, will you ordain me?" Even those jurisdictions that claim to have a strong formation program will often still ordain someone in the hopes that they will eventually form that person, but for now "we'll just go ahead and ordain them," because they seem like they'd be a great candidate. Then what you get is another priest added into the mix that hasn't been formed. Then within two or three years, that priest becomes a bishop, and the cycle continues. That's a problem.

I have been talking to lots of different people and it just seems to be a problem all over the place. It's not just one particular jurisdiction. Now, some jurisdictions are really working against this phenomenon. My statement shouldn't be seen as a universal condemnation of everyone, because I'm not condemning, I'm pointing out observations, but it's still there. It's a problem. I recently was contacted by a fellow who said, "I want to be a priest." He saw our website, www.youngriteusa.org, and wanted to be a priest. I advised him that the Young Rite in the United States operates as the Community of Saint George and asked him to read about the Community of Saint George and watch a video that I created on the Community. He eventually watched it and he responded and said, "I really just want to be a priest." I wrote to him and suggested that he go somewhere else.

We don't just ordain anyone anymore. It was frustrating that the Young Rite, has that reputation of "we'll just ordain anybody." That's something that must go away because if you haven't been properly formed, then how can you lead others? How can you create disciples? We will ordain you if you do the work!

MAYNARD: I think part of discipleship is discipline. They both have the same root, disciple - discipline. If we consider evangelization, the honeymoon phase where everything is rainbows and ponies and all that jazz and you're high on cloud nine, but eventually you come down from that cloud or you should come down from that cloud. There are people who don't ever come down from that cloud, and those tend to be the people who cause a lot of problems in communities because they're not grounded. I don't think you can be an authentic Christian disciple and not be grounded with both feet on the ground with your eyes forward and your arms outstretched, ready to do the work because that's what Jesus did.

Jesus was always present in very intentional ways to the people who were right in front of him. I think we have to make that transition. We have to come down from the cloud, we have to get into the dirt, and we have to say, "Okay, it's time to get moving and to be present." Anyone that's doing that will realize that there's a lot going on in the world, there's a lot of hurting people in the world. The earth itself is struggling and needs healing and needs God's touch. It takes discipline, a commitment to prayer every day throughout the day, a commitment to constantly renew your mind as Saint Paul says, but also a commitment to go out from your sanctuary and to have sanctuary by being in the streets. A discipline that whenever you are sitting with a homeless person who is high as a kite on something, and they ask you a question about God, did you brush them aside or do you entertain it and see what happens? Because even in that moment, God could have a move and, and make a way happen for that person. The next day that person could completely have their life changed.

Or if you were in a coffee shop, if somebody came up to you and you were wearing a clerical collar and they were absolutely enraged with the idea that you were a priest, because of everything that's going on right now with the clergy sex abuse scandals, how can you testify to them, to the love of God, to the extravagant grace of the Spirit and talk them down from that ledge? Gently touch that wound that they have seeping from their side, their spiritual side, and let them leave from your presence a little bit better.

Mother Teresa said, "If people leave your presence without smiling, you did not tell them about Jesus," which is the whole point is they need to be changed. There needs to be a noticeable difference. I've been in places with my collar on, and I've had people throw drinks at me because I represented something to them that they're angry about. There's a lot to be angry about when it comes to the clergy sex abuse scandals and how much of a testimony it is to be able to deal with that with grace and dignity. You can't do that if you're not constantly doing your internal work and learning to disarm your own demons, to do that internal work, to do that work of disarming yourself so that you can go into the world and be a presence for God in the world. I think that's how you embody discipleship.

KLING: One of the things that I think is important when it comes to forming people is being able to frame your faith in such a way that it is a part of your life, no matter what happens to you. In my work within hospice, there have been times when I have been with patients and their families, and family members will turn to me and say, "Why is God taking my mom?" I'm thinking to myself, "Your mom's 96 years old, what are you thinking? She's going to live to be a thousand years." That's the definition of absurdity thinking that my family members are not going to die, and it hits me every time, because my dad was 57 when he died, and I'll be 50 this year (2020). I'm thinking to myself, you had 40 some years extra than I had with my father.

Of course, I don't let that show because I'm a professional, but you should be able to pull on your faith, use your faith. Your faith should inform you, even in times of crisis and in times of joy, as well as times of sorrow. If you find yourself in a tough situation, whether you just found out that you were diagnosed with cancer, or you lost a child, or you lost a friend, your faith should still be there. I think that goes back to what you said about discipleship being linked to discipline. We shouldn't be preparing people to be fair weather Christians, but to be able to rely on that faith, to get them through those difficult times. Having that faith when times are good, and I think that's important too, because if things are going well and you're financially prosperous, you shouldn't put your faith on the back burner. If things are good and you only rely on faith when things are troublesome, that's just as bad.

There are people that will do that when they're doing well, they don't care about faith but when things are doing poorly, it's all about prayers for relief, then everyone becomes Job (from the Book of Job). You should have balance. Like all things in moderation, your faith should be constant, even in times of joy and in times of sorrow. I think that's the kind of discipleship that clergy in the movement who are educating others need to strive for.

MAYNARD: Thomas Aquinas says, "The first primary meaning of salvation is to preserve all things in the good," and I think that's what we're talking about. I like your phrase, "...not making fair weather Christians," to preserve all things in the good means that in every context, positive, negative, transformative, or whatever we remain grounded in reality of our goodness. God delights in us and having that discipline to keep that at the forefront of our soul, so that whenever something happens, like losing someone, you have the discipline of keeping that at the forefront of our mind, our inherent goodness reminds us to keep everything in perspective. It teaches us gratitude. If the only prayer you ever pray is thank you, that prayer is enough, because graciousness keeps everything in perspective.

KLING: That is one of the things that I pray every day, that I'm grateful for all the blessings that I have received.

MAYNARD: I think there's a lot of people right now who are immobilized, they're incapable of moving because they're stuck and confused about who they are. They're stuck because they've allowed a bishop or a pastor or church somewhere to repeatedly say to them that they are not worthy, that they are not valuable. They have internalized all these things that are contrary to the message of Jesus. Now they must be deprogrammed and returned to the truth of who they really are in Christ Jesus, as Aquinas said, "To preserve all things in the good." As a Movement of disciples, which is what we should be. Ultimately, a Movement of disciples that has to be the people who say, "Hey, let's work on that, let's unpack that, and then at the same time, teach how to develop a discipline of prayer, a discipline of reading, whatever you want to do that keeps you grounded in that constant state of understanding of who you really are."

"If you don't work on yourself, then much of your politics is merely projections. We have to walk our talk and do the inner

work that allows the outer work to be authentic and also effective." — Matthew Fox

"Concluding Thoughts"

Father Jerry mentioned a passage from the Gospel of Matthew. The fullness of that passage is Matthew 7:15 – 20:

> *"Beware of false prophets, who come to you in sheep's clothing, but inwardly they are ravenous wolves. You will know them by their fruits. Do men gather grapes from thornbushes or figs from thistles? Even so, every good tree bears good fruit, but a bad tree bears bad fruit. A good tree cannot bear bad fruit, nor can a bad tree bear good fruit. Every tree that does not bear good fruit is cut down and thrown into the fire. Therefore by their fruits you will know them."*

There is a lot packed in these verses. Vatican authorities would likely relegate all of us in the Independent Sacramental Movement as "false prophets," claiming that our fruit is bad. Prior to the Second Vatican Council the Roman Church would likely place every Christian leader who wasn't Roman Catholic, subject to the Bishop of Rome, into the category of "false prophet." This condemnation is due to the pre-Vatican II belief of *"Extra Ecclesiam nulla salus,"* or "outside the church there is no salvation." Prior to Vatican II this was taken literally, in that if you were not Roman Catholic you were outside of the Church.

The decrees of Vatican II, namely *Lumen Gentium*, extended the definition of "church" to include, in part, other branches of the Body of Christ, such as Protestants, as being in-part "the Church." Roman Catholic Traditionalists would claim that the pre-Vatican II position holds true with Rome being apostate and therefore included in the false prophet claim. Those of us on the moderate to progressive spectrum of the Independent Sacramental Movement would agree with *Lumen Gentium*, even if we reject the authority of Vatican II upon how we behave and belief as Christians.

Father Jerry's comments about humanity being, "…the beloved of God," is an echoing of Matthew Fox's *Original Blessing*, which is a post-modern reinterpretation of the classical belief of Original Sin. Likewise, the decrees of Vatican II are also a post-modern reworking of some of the classically held practices and beliefs of the Roman Catholic Church. The rise of ecumenism, and the Novus Ordo Missae are just two examples of the post-modernizing of the Roman Church. The rules of the game have changed and are continuing to change.

Are we still living in a post-modern world? Some scholars believe we have moved beyond post-modernism, which was a reaction to modernism and the industrial revolution. This new era that we find ourselves in now is referred to by some as "metamodernism." This is unchartered territory; we are living it now.

We live in a world where church attendance is down and growing is the "Spiritual but not Religious," along with other forms of DIY forms of spirituality such as Neo-Paganism, Wicca, etc. Where does the Independent Sacramental Movement find itself amid metamodernism? Is our existence a result of metamodernism? Our roots are in modernism, our rise and progression occurred during post-modernism. Will we mature and truly bear fruit in this metamodern period?

Pluralism has become normative; inclusion and acceptance has become commonplace. Exclusivism, radicalism, and fundamentalism have become anachronistic ideas rejected by most people. The Body of Christ is changing, and it is important that we wrestle with the culture that we inhabit. Reflecting on the fruit that we bear is an important part of being a Christian.

For Reflection, Contemplation, & Prayer:

- Are we living in a post-modern world? Or have we moved onto what some scholars refer to as metamodern?
- What is the fruit that the Independent Sacramental Movement produces? What are the good things being promoted?
- How do you see the Body of Christ? What is your vision of the Church?

"The Comic-Con of the Interfaith World"
A Conversation with Subdeacon Steve Avino

"For just as each of us has one body with many members, and these members do not all have the same function. So, in Christ, we though many, form one body, and each member belongs to all the others." — Romans 12:4-5

Steve Avino is a subdeacon within the Community of St. George, a jurisdiction within the Young Rite. He is a graduate of North Central College with a Bachelor of Arts in religious studies and received a master's in religious studies at Chicago Theological Seminary. He works as the acting chief operating officer of the Parliament of world religions and has dedicated his adult life to interfaith work, including helping to organize the 2015 parliament of world religions in Salt Lake City and the 2018 Parliament of the World's Religions in Toronto. Note: at the time of publication Steve is now a deacon within the Community of Saint George.

KLING: My first question, what is your elevator speech? How would you describe the Independent Sacramental Movement to someone who has no idea what it is?

AVINO: What I would say is that the Independent Sacramental Movement is within the Christian tradition and is in-line with Catholicism and Eastern Orthodoxy that believes in the validity of the sacraments as agents of God's grace and in apostolic succession. The reason why it's called Independent is because at some point in history it broke away from a larger group and maybe a Christian group that the person in the elevator might be more familiar with such as Roman Catholicism. That would be the baseline, but there's a lot more to it than that. Probably the most important things are validity of the sacraments, which the Independent Sacramental Movement comes from most, if not all the ISM groups that I know of believe in the importance of apostolic succession, that the apostles passed on, laid their hands on a bishop and the bishop consecrated another bishop and so forth for the last 2000 years. They have that lineage which is important. I don't know if all ISM groups feel that way, but that's my experience.

KLING: Thank you for sharing your perspective. I think all of them value apostolic succession. I know some individual priests and bishops who don't put a whole lot of weight into it, but still play lip service to it. I think generally it's something that is certainly valuable with us as a Movement because it's part of the seven sacraments that we promote. I appreciate your perspective, but my next line of questioning deals with your career choice, which is very exciting. Can you describe the Parliament of World Religions? What is it? What is it about and what has been your involvement?

AVINO: The Parliament is an organization that gave birth to the interfaith movement in the West in 1893 in Chicago, which is my hometown. The first Parliament of the World's Religions was held in conjunction with the Chicago World's Fair. They brought in thousands of people from all different religious traditions, including some early Independent Catholic bishops, and it was the first time that there was a mass meeting of religious leaders and people of different faiths in history.

The organization that I work for was founded in the eighties to commemorate the hundredth anniversary that was coming up from the 1893 Parliament. A group of religious leaders in Chicago got together and decided to do an anniversary event, and that led to the 1993 Parliament of the World's Religions, which was also held in Chicago. Since then, we've been having these international conferences every few years. For example, 1993 was Chicago, 1999 was in Cape Town, South Africa, and then in 2004 it was in Barcelona, Spain. In 2009 it was in Melbourne, Australia and in 2015 it was in Salt Lake City, Utah. In 2018 we held a Parliament in Toronto, Canada. I came on board in 2012, right out of college. I have since worked my way up and I'm now the acting COO (Chief Operating Officer) of the Parliament, and we're looking forward to the future.

KLING: What exactly do you do as Chief Operating Officer?

AVINO: I'm in charge of internal operations and the staff and the working between the staff and the board of trustees. It is a non-profit. So, we deal with all kinds of things that non-profit deal with such as everyday donations, fundraising, and then the programming aspect. Because of the situation with COVID-19 we are lucky to have a great online community where people can continue to have interfaith experiences online through our website and through our newsletter, through our forums on our website. We also have a membership program where you can join and get videos and content from all the past Parliaments. We also have an ongoing climate action program. There are six, what we call critical constituencies or critical issues that the Parliament deals with on an ongoing basis. There is dignity of women, climate action, indigenous peoples, countering war hate and violence, the next generation, and advancing justice.

We're working on that as our six issues. Some of it is, in progress, but our climate action program has regular webinars and lots of information. We just built a web hub for different faith communities to insert themselves on this map that shows what they're doing for climate action in their community. If you go to our website, you can find out all the different ways, different faith communities are helping in stopping climate change. You can go there to network and learn from what others have been doing.

I think that's, the thing that the Parliament is best at is we're conveners. We have historically done it and we continue to be the people that you go to, to meet other like-minded individuals who may not have the same religious beliefs as you. In fact, most of the time they do not, but you are all working to make the world a better place. Our mission is all about fostering interfaith understanding, but also bringing that understanding into action so that we can make a more peaceful, adjusted, and sustainable world.

KLING: It sounds like not only do you do these large events, but you're doing things in between the events to foster understanding.

AVINO: Yes, I think our bread and butter is the events, but we always have ongoing programs. The events, the great thing about the events is that they inspire people that come. The last event we had about 8,500 people, in Toronto, Canada. We had 10,000 people in Salt Lake City, Utah from all walks of life. The events inspire people to go back to their communities and start working on critical issues and working with people of different faiths, because if the religions don't buy into, for example, if the people of faith and the different religious traditions don't buy into stopping climate change, we can't really do much. Religion is so important in people's lives today, and that is so impactful that all the different communities need to be working together on these issues, or it won't happen. We won't stop climate change. We won't stop the violence against women. If the religions are not involved.

KLING: That's good that you bring people together and focus on certain issues that are important to our world and to our various communities. I certainly commend you on your work. Recently, you were ordained a subdeacon. Has your involvement in the Independent Sacramental Movement affected or influenced your work? Or is it just something that's in the background?

AVINO: I have been interested in ordination for years. I would say that working for the Parliament did affect my decision to become ordained. When I was younger, I had a more negative view of religion and what it does for the world. Although, I was a devout believer in God and a believer in the spiritual dimensions of reality, I thought that institutional religions were causing war, causing hatred, and was outdated. While working for the Parliament, although I did study religion in college, I realized that there's a lot of good that religion can do in the world. That there's a lot of religious people who are looking to do good and to bring about a better world. That inspired me to investigate becoming ordained. I was raised Roman Catholic, and I had a spiritual experience as a child.

I had epilepsy and was healed by a faith healer who was a Catholic priest. So, for me, that has always remained in the back of my mind since I was very little. That this faith has validity and when I learned about the different faiths around the world, I also saw validity and truth and sacredness in all the religions of the world. That has driven me my entire life. I wanted to be ordained so that I could bring, I know it sounds corny, but to make the world a better place and be an active agent in a spiritual way. Not just in my work.

KLING: I think that is essentially what it means to be called to ministry. You want to make a difference and doing something else doesn't make sense.

AVINO: Unfortunately, I would make a career out of it, but there's not really that ability to do so in today's world. The Parliament is a great way, where I can practice my ministry even without having a parish to go to and perform the sacraments. I feel like I can do good through my work and being ordained and having part-time church services and meeting with you guys once a year for Convocation, that kind of thing.

KLING: I think one of the advantages of the Independent Sacramental Movement is that it allows people to do ministry, but people are often bivocational and must secure another source of income. They're still able to live out their vocation; whereas I know plenty of folks from my seminary experience who are working full time as pastors in different churches and, many of them are miserable. They continue because that's how they make their income.

Fortunately, we don't have that problem. Now, the opposite is we don't make a living and several of us went to seminary and graduate school, like yourself, and received a good education in theological studies, but we are able to practice ministry in the fullness of who we are. For example, being in the Community of Saint George, if you are involved in your interfaith work and you're at a Hindu ceremony and you want to participate then you can, and we're not going to kick you out for being involved in that, in fact, we're going to applaud you for your participation. Whereas if you were in some other Christian denominations they may not approve.

AVINO: That is true. I feel like if I was part of a certain tradition, it would not be accepted for me to be involved in interfaith. One thing is the Roman Catholic Church in the mainstream, Roman Catholic Church, whatever you want to call it, has always been part of the Parliament and has been active supporters of the Parliament. Over the years, we had Joseph Cardinal Bernardin of Chicago at the 1993 parliament. We had the current Cardinal and Archbishop of Chicago in Toronto in 2018. The Roman Catholic Church has always been involved, in addition to the Independent Sacramental Movement.

The one thing that the Parliament does that I think few other interfaith organizations do or did is inclusivity. We have every type of religion and we do not discriminate against any religion. We have everything. In fact, we're famous for being the first interfaith organization to welcome Paganism into our meeting since the 1993 Parliament. I've heard people say that was the Pagans coming out to the world. We've always been inclusive of everyone. I don't know if I would get in trouble or be chastised for being part of the Parliament if I was in a "mainstream" denomination, but I would say that there's a lot of things that I personally cannot agree with. I'm more progressive on issues than the mainstream Catholic Church. So, I'm not really interested in joining that, you know?

The good thing about the ISM is that, like you said, you can be yourself, you can have your ministry, you can have your calling and live in the real world. You can have a job and have a life. I think it's important for all faith and all spirituality to intersect with the real world. I don't think it should be separate. That's a good thing about the Independent Sacramental Movement because it allows you to do that. I think you should bring your spirituality and your faith into all aspects of your life, and they should be intertwined. I feel like the Western faiths have left the modern world behind, and that has led to people leaving religion because they don't feel how it associates to their everyday life. That's one thing I wish that we could learn as a society in America, especially from other cultures that spirituality doesn't need to be divorced from the rest of your life.

KLING: Yeah. It should be integrated. It should be part of who you are.

AVINO: And religion should appeal to people's everyday lives and talk about real issues and not stay away from them.

KLING: Religion, spirituality, we shouldn't be afraid of tackling what we come up against and what we experience as humans. The Church used to do that, and I think you're right. In some ways it has disassociated from that, and in some ways, religion is an anachronism, and it shouldn't be.

AVINO: Yeah, and I understand why that happened because of the separation of church and state. You don't want to have that overlap too much, but there's a way of bringing spirituality into your life that doesn't impede on that wall between church and state. You know what I mean?

KLING: Religion should bring people together. It shouldn't drive people apart. It should build up communities and not cause division.

I remember when I was in college and I was involved in one of the feminist organizations called the Feminist Majority Leadership Alliance (FMLA). I discovered them at one of the student organization fairs. I was in my 30s. So, most of the other students were 18, 19, or 20. I was wandering around and I saw the booth for the FMLA, and I was interested in it. I said, "I'm real supportive of you guys." And they responded, "Well, you can join." I said, "Really?" So, I did, and we collaborated a lot with the Rainbow Alliance, the LGBT club on campus.

I remember giving a presentation at the Rainbow Alliance on religion and because a lot of the students had a very negative experience with religion because they were gay, and churches had rejected them. I talked about religion and talked about those religious traditions, whether they be Christian or Neopagan, or whatnot that are accepting of people for who they are. It was an eye-opening experience for some of the people in the organization because they had been so marginalized and so alienated by organized religion that they just assumed that religion was no longer accessible in their life.

It was neat to see some of them explore other options now that they knew that those options were available. I think integrating spirituality is important as clergy, and that's one of our theological tasks to do that and to help people.

AVINO: Yeah, definitely. I don't know if I've ever told you this, but I am a gay man myself. I've experienced that first-hand. I've seen plenty of people, when I say what I do, they run for the Hills. They don't see it as compatible. I know exactly what you're talking about.

KLING: Religion has done a lot to uplift society, but it's also done a lot of damage. I think we need to acknowledge that and do everything we can to fix it.

I think what you're doing with the Parliament of the World's Religions is certainly doing that. I want to ask you another question based upon your work with the Parliament, and it goes back to the 2015 and 2018 Parliaments. What are some of your takeaways from the 2015 and 2018 Parliament of the World's Religions? How are they similar and how were they different? Do you have any stories to tell?

AVINO: For me, they were similar. Salt Lake City was my first experience with the Parliament. I think people are biased from their first experience with anything, but I think Salt Lake was a very spiritual experience. I remember going home at night thinking, "Wow, there's 10,000 people here and they all just want to build a better world." You're not around that all the time, in your everyday life. There's a lot of negativity, and just to be there and see these different people of different traditions and the different clothing that they wear and the different cultures, ethnicities, genders, et cetera, all working together and being at peace! It really changes your outlook on the world.

I highly recommend to everyone to attend the next Parliament because it's a life changing experience. We've received that feedback many times, and even while I was working it was life changing. It changed my view of everything. Toronto was also a beautiful thing. I had to do the registration work, so I didn't get to see as many of the speeches and the programs, but it was a tremendous experience. I think the good thing about the Parliament is that you can go and experience so much. Some people say this is a negative, there's too much programming, but I think it's a good thing. You can go there and find a seminar on gaming and faith or something, any kind of interest that you have will come up. It's all encompassing, and it is a great to learn from each other and to come away from it with a positive outlook on humanity, and also with some ideas on how you can build on what you've learned and bring it back to your community.

KLING: Well, mentioned what to expect. Can you paint a picture of a typical day at one of the events and describe some of the things that people can do and experience while they're there?

AVINO: Usually there's two components, and they're at convention centres. Most of the event is at a convention centre and like any convention you'll have breakout sessions. So, you'll have hundreds of sessions that you can attend. There are hundreds of sessions to go to and there's different types of sessions. There are lectures and then there is group workshops. There are tracks of programming, for example, in 2018 we had our track set around the six critical issues that I already talked about. There was the dignity of women, for example, and you would have a Buddhist and a Christian women and panel discussion. There are secular topics too, it doesn't always have to do with religion. If it is a topic that intersects with religion, and you can go to so many different things. It's hard to say what happened, and maybe that is one of the issues, that it's all encompassing. It's like the Comic-Con of the interfaith world. You can see all kinds of things, and then there's also, usually in the morning and throughout the day, ritual sessions. You could attend mass in the morning and attend all kinds of sacred rituals throughout the day. People will be singing in the convention centre halls and dancing. In Toronto, I saw people who got engaged, which was a wonderful thing in the middle of the convention hall.

We have leaders from all over the world. Nelson Mandela spoke in 1999 and in 2015. I was lucky to see Jane Goodall speak. We have our major speakers at our plenary sessions. You have the breakout sessions and then you have major plenary sessions, which is usually built around a theme. For example, climate action had a plenary session. So, you'd have major speakers on a platform giving speeches about that issue. We also have a sacred music night and there will be a night of a concert of people, all kinds of religions showcasing the music from their faith and their tradition. That's always incredible. For example, in Salt Lake City, we had our music night it at the Mormon Temple where they have the Mormon Tabernacle Choir. The Church of Jesus Christ of Latter-Day Saints was nice enough to let us use that as the sacred music night, and we had Sikh, and Hindu, and Whirling Dervishes from the Islamic tradition. It's such a wonderful experience to see all this spirituality being enacted through music and dance. I can't say enough about how great it is to go. In fact, you can see a lot of this on our YouTube channel, but it's something that's a "once in a lifetime" experience. I think, there are interfaith events that are smaller, but there's nothing on this scale in the world outside of the Parliament. I'm proud of the work that we've done, and twice now I've helped to put on these events and I'm very proud of it.

KLING: Thank you for that illustration. I love the phrase you used, "the Comic-Con of religion." I love that, and that illustration helped me visualize it better.

AVINO: I should mention that for both Salt Lake City, Toronto, and in Barcelona, the Sikhs have a tradition called *langar*, where they give a meal to anybody who wants it. There's no restriction on religion or caste or anything, and it's part of their spiritual tradition that every week they prepare a meal and anybody who wants it can come and eat.

It's a spiritual practice for them. You must wear the turban and be respectful, but it's for everyone. They did that on a mass level in Salt Lake City and Toronto, where they fed thousands of people. In Barcelona, they fed thousands of people on a beach. It's incredible, and it's totally free.

KLING: Wow, that's neat! My next question is, what has been your greatest challenge within the Independent Sacramental Movement or within your interfaith work.

AVINO: With the ISM it has been finding a tradition or a lineage or church or community that is more interested in the actual tradition and history and spirituality. I guess the meat of things, instead of just like giving each person a glorified title or making things up as they go. I've always believed that it's important to not throw out the baby with the bath water. If you are being innovative in your spiritual tradition, it shouldn't come out of nowhere. It should be based on your history and what has worked in the past. I think a lot of people see things that are just a little bit out there, because the Community of Saint George is this perfect mixture of being innovative and respecting tradition. I think finding a community has been helpful for me, and there were a lot of places that I investigated within the Independent Sacramental Movement that were not that perfect mix.

They were more interested in either being super-conservative or they were so progressive that they threw out all the rules and they are just Pagan, or they are just making things up as they go. It's been great to work with the Community of Saint George because we are like the in-between place and I really enjoy that about us.

In the interfaith movement one of the issues that I see is there's a lot of emphasis on Abrahamic religions and one thing the Parliament does well is that they are inclusive of all traditions. You see smaller interfaith organizations where they just think of Christians, Jews, and Muslims, and just have that discussion or have that meet up. Whereas everyone is brought to the table with the Parliament, and that's why I'm proud to work for them because nobody gets shut out. Everyone is welcome to the table. I mean, I think that's a problem within the interfaith movement that there's to much of an emphasis on the Abrahamic traditions, even though I'm part of that tradition, I think it's important that we hear everyone's voices.

KLING: It sounds like a lot of the smaller faiths have been marginalized and you give them a voice and I think that's important.

AVINO: Definitely, we have a database of all the people, and their faith tradition, that have gone to the Parliament and it's extensive. Hundreds and hundreds of different traditions.

KLING: That's fascinating. My last question is, what has been your greatest blessing either within the Independent Sacramental Movement and within your interfaith work?

AVINO: I'm happy to have found the Community of Saint George. That is a blessing in and of itself, and I'm very blessed too, for all the experiences I had at Salt Lake City, and Toronto, and from all the people from around the world that I've met and have made friendships. It's incredible, and I'm grateful for the experiences that I've had working for the Parliament and will continue to have. Those are all blessings in my work with the ISM and the interfaith movement.

Obviously, there's a lot of things in my personal life for which I feel blessed. I think one of the problems with the modern world is that we don't spend enough time thinking about, this question because we don't spend enough time thinking about what blessings our lives have been. We often think of the negative things, especially people in my generation, but it's like, "I don't have what other people have," but you probably have a lot of good things in your life. If you sit back and think about it, you've been blessed.

KLING: Thank you for taking the time to talk to me today. Do you have any closing thoughts?

AVINO: I would just say that the Independent Sacramental Movement is a wonderful thing and there's a lot of people that don't even know that it exists. I mean, they are feeling like they're locked out from the "mainstream versions of Sacramental movement" and are turning to other places or turning to other traditions. There is a tradition that will embrace you and embrace your ideas. We are a little harder to find, but I really hope that we grow as a Movement. You hear about the emptying of churches in the US and in Europe. I think the ISM is one way to bring people back into religion and, I think my generation is yearning for spirituality and it keeps looking to the East for it. I think it's only because most people are unaware that there is a spiritual component in the Western religious traditions that doesn't come with all the baggage that the mainstream brings with it, and I hope that we can, I hate to say market it better, but in some sense, we have to make more people aware of this Movement because it's important. I think it will help people.

KLING: I agree. I've said it before, the Independent Sacramental Movement is the best kept secret within Christianity.

"There will be no peace among the nations without peace among the religions, and no peace among the religions without dialogue." — Hans Kung

"Concluding Thoughts"

It is no secret that as a world religion Christianity is on the decline. Islam is doing particularly well in terms of growth and even new religious movements like Wicca are drawing people. The message of Jesus has become less popular, and the Western world is no longer Christendom, and Christianity and religion have moved to the margins. Is this a tragic phenomenon? Is this something we should mourn? Some would say the decline of Christianity is a sign of the fall of our civilization as we know it; however, I see the marginalized state of Christianity and religion as an opportunity.

In my work with as a hospice chaplain I visit patients daily and get to know their spiritual and religious dispositions. Most of my patients and their families stopped attending church services a long time ago. Some consider themselves "spiritual but not religious" while others just embrace a cultural religious sentiment that includes a belief in God and a general understanding of Jesus. I do not think my patients are an exception, I think what I am witnessing is common throughout the country and much of the Western world. People are not attending churches.

While church attendance is dwindling, people still struggle with existential issues and they want answers, comfort, and a means to navigate through life. The Independent Sacramental Movement with all its scattered micro-denominations are in a unique position. We do not have a lot of disposable income that we can throw into evangelical endeavors; however, being in the margins of the margins we have a unique voice.

The Independent Sacramental Movement is a valuable part of the Mystical Body of Christ and those within this Movement have an opportunity to help heal the suffering of others, to help with those existential questions, and to be a presence in the world for the greater glory of God.

We have a message, but people will never hear it if we are silent. We need to speak up and preach the Gospel, and let the world know about the best kept secret within Christianity, the Independent Sacramental Movement.

For Reflection, Contemplation, & Prayer:

- What are the blessings within your life? What are some blessings that often get overlooked in your life? What instills within you a sense of gratitude?
- Have you had a conversation with another about their faith? Not to change them but to build mutual understanding. What was that experience like, and have you considered becoming involved in interfaith dialoge?
- What message should we be telling the world about the Independent Sacramental Movement? How can we share the message of the Independent Sacramental Movement?

"The Best of Both Worlds"
A Conversation with Jason Spadafore

"Therefore, keep watch because you do not know when the owner of the house will come back whether in the evening or at night or when the rooster crows or at dawn, if he comes suddenly do not let him find you sleeping. What I say to you, I say everyone watch." — Mark 13:35-37

Bishop Jason Spadafore has studied magic and Christian spirituality for nearly 30 years, with a focus on Catholic occultism. Known by his pen name, Agostino Taumaturgo, he lectures on these themes within the Christian paradigm. Our paths initially crossed in 2005.

KLING: Thank you so much for joining me again. I appreciate you taking the time to be with me this morning. You and I have both been involved in the Traditionalist Movement within Roman Catholicism and there are those within the Traditionalist Movement who are separate from Rome and some who have one foot touching the Vatican. One thing I wanted to talk about are the people who are concerned about validity. They're concerned about liceity and licit versus non-licit. The Roman Catholic Womenpriests Movement who are on the left of the spectrum, when juxtaposed against the Traditionalist Movement are also concerned with things like validity and liceity. I think this is an interesting phenomenon, that both ends of the spectrum, traditionalist and progressive, have similar characteristics. Can you speak on that to get us started?

SPADAFORE: I certainly can. On the one hand, I think this has a lot to do with being raised Catholic. When you're raised Catholic, or when you enter a movement that identifies as Catholic. I'm saying it that way, because I want to cover it in as much of a spectrum as I possibly can because there's a certain psychological thing where you either identify as Roman or you identify as a Catholic with Roman because Roman Catholicism is strict and says, all Catholicism is Roman. You cannot be Catholic if you're not Roman, this idea is opposing the branch theory within Anglicanism formulated around 1842 by a gentleman named William Palmer, which is what you find in Anglo-Catholicism, and that theory informs the Independent Sacramental Movement.

So, if you're raised Catholic there is a psychological thing that you must be Catholic. There is a psychological resistance against calling yourself, not Catholic. Somebody who was raised Catholic and now goes to a Protestant Mega-church is probably going to laugh, but for those who want to stay within sacramental Christianity, the idea of saying, "I am not Catholic," it's a difficult place to take yourself to. We can find this even as early as Martin Luther, he saw himself as the Catholic Church's faithful son and the Augsburg Confession toward the end it says that "what we teach is nothing different from the Catholic faith, even of the Roman Church, as known from its writers." That inclination to have a foot in the door of Catholicism is very strong. It can come from childhood. It can come from conversion. It can come from the culture, but there's a psychological need. The idea with validity and liceity, that goes along with it because to be Catholic, to have Catholic sacraments, you must have valid Catholic sacraments. That's how the thinking goes. To have valid Catholic sacraments, you must check a certain number of boxes such as form, matter, and intention.

To check those boxes, to satisfy that psychological need is strong. I can say this because in the Traditionalist Movement the need to identify as the "True Romans" is strong. It's so overpowering. You start making up excuses about liceity and validity you judge more or less accurately, but validity is not that hard to judge, but you start making up excuses about liceity. So, you make up excuses that we are Roman because we do X. They, over there, are not Roman because they don't do X, X, and X.

I did meet one of the Danube Seven at a function in 2003 (Note: Danube Seven refers to seven women who were ordained on a ship on the Danube river in Europe on June 29th, 2002). That's a story for another time, but I don't know exactly what their full level of justification is, but I know that in the Traditional Movement where my experience is, the justification is that we are Roman, because we believe, teach, and practice what Rome believed, taught, and practiced prior to about 1960 (Note: the time period of the Second Vatican Council).

Traditionalists will call modern (post-Vatican II) Roman Catholics "Novus Ordinarians" and those in the Independent Sacramental Movement will usually just call modern (post-Vatican II) Roman Catholics "Romans." You will hear me use those terms interchangeably. So, just be on the lookout for that. The average Novus Ordinarian defines

Rome as the physical city and the Vatican as the physical place with the physical chair, with the physical man sitting upon it. It's a very physical definition and the institution that flows from that physical location. The Traditionalist defines Rome as consistency with the teaching consistency, with the teaching of the Roman Catholic Church prior to roughly anywhere from 1958 to about 1962. That's where the cut-off date is, so that consistency of teaching, of ideological consistency. That's what defines Rome for Traditionalists.

I don't know how the far-left end of the spectrum define themself. I know that Roman Catholic Women Priests define themselves as Roman. My understanding of the Danube Seven is through similar ways, like for example, I know Traditionalists who have the same apostolic lineage through Bishop Carlos Duarte Costa, specifically through the Bishop Salomão Barbosa Ferraz lineage, since Ferraz was consecrated by Duarte Costa.

KLING: For those who are not aware, that's the Brazilian Church.

SPADAFORE: Thank you, yes. Carlos Duarte Costa was a Bishop of the Brazilian Catholic Apostolic Church. He was ex-communicated in 1945 because of his stance on social issues, and he started the Brazilian Catholic Apostolic Church. He consecrated Bishop Salomão Barbosa Ferraz and Ferraz reconciled with Rome and even sat in on some of the sessions of Vatican II. He was reconciled as a bishop.

There are several people in the Traditionalist Movement who derive their apostolic succession from the Costa lineage through Ferraz and there are a number of people in the Independent Sacramental Movements as well, such as the Roman Catholic Women Priests succession. The Danube Seven ordinations were on June 29th, 2002. They say that there was a Novus Ordo bishop who was present and participated in these ordinations, but this bishop's Identity has been kept secret to protect him. Since we don't know the identity of that bishop, I cannot say anything about that, because we don't know the identity. I cannot speak to any succession coming from him.

The bishop who was there, Rómulo Antonio Braschi, was of the Duarte Costa lineage through Ferraz, and was a recent Roman Catholic line. They could call themselves Roman Catholic and the Traditionalist Movement and therefore both are doing the same thing. I believe both sides are different, since they are in their ideology as different as they are in their theology and in their modality of ministry, and as different as they are irreconcilable. I do think that they both are operating from the same basic psychology that comes with being raised Catholic, that you must identify as Catholic, no matter what, especially if you were raised as pre-Vatican II Catholic. The amount of emotional force that it takes to break that conditioning, it is so strong as to be insurmountable in a lot of cases.

KLING: An interesting phenomenon that I've seen are people who were raised in a pre-Vatican II Roman Catholic Church, who long for a return to Roman Catholic tradition and who are fighting for the reestablishment of something that is important to them. However, I've also talked to people who are products of the post-Vatican II Church in the period where there was a lot of change in the church. Those post-Vatican II Catholics are seeing the Church make concessions to conservatism. It's certainly not a return to traditionalism, but a movement to try to make the Church more conservative, and they're longing for that time to return to Roman Catholicism of the 1970s and 1980s. The Church that they grew up in that was a church that was looking at reform, change, and hope. The paradox that I see is that certain segments of the population are longing for a Roman Catholic tradition that returns to a pre-Vatican II Catholicism and then there is another group of people that are looking for a post-Vatican II hope that they don't see any more. A hope that is lost and this creates a weird tension. Since we are talking about the Independent Sacramental Movement, which takes itself out of the Roman Catholic mould, within the ISM there is the creating of a Church that can have the best of both of those worlds and can be liturgically conservative, but still, have that hope that came out of the Second Vatican Council without having to be tethered to those Second Vatican Council documents.

SPADAFORE: I do think it's possible. I strongly think it's possible. For example, I don't really talk about the individual members where I was pastoring in Columbus, Chapel of Faith Ministries. The whole parish was about 80% disgruntled Catholics, and 20% Lutheran. That was an interesting mix and they all got along; we all knew each other outside of the church. There was overlap of various subcultures through knowing each other outside the church. It was a fun time. It was a time I remember fondly, and the thing is, we were liturgically conservative. The liturgy was in modern English because I put it up for a vote. Everyone voted for modern English, but it was a traditional liturgy.

The people themselves, they were not conservative, I wouldn't say that they were liberal either. They were kind of middle-of-the-road with a little bit of that "liking the reforms," and liking that hope. They weren't getting that in the other churches that they were visiting I wanted to jump ship because I think there's room for both, I think the two positions of tradition plus hope can be reconciled. I do think that was John XXIII's intention behind starting the Council if you read his opening address. What I think in the post-Vatican II period is that when the pro-Vatican II faction got control of the hierarchy, I think they took things too far.

I think what we're seeing now, what I call the conservative uprising of about 2005 onwards, is a reaction. The pendulum swung a bit too far, one way, we're going to have hope. We're going to have progress. We're going to have open dialogue. We're going to have freedom. They said that, but they also said, "We're going to take away your Latin mass. We're going to take away the things that you grew up with, and we're going to take away the things that you were told as a child that defined your Catholic identity." They went too far and that's what prompted the backlash.

KLING: I agree with your assessment. I have a question for you though. You're very connected with the Traditionalist Movement and I have a deep connection with it too. So, you will appreciate this question. Here's a hypothetical, let's paint a scenario. Let's say that you're in the role of Pope John the XXIII and you're convening the Second Vatican Council and since you're the Pope, you have control. We're going to assume that you don't pass away shortly after you convene the Council, that you're there to the conclusion of the Council.

So, you're the Bishop of Rome. You have full control to modernize the church as you see fit, through the decrees of the council and we're giving you a little bit more authority than what John XXIII had, but still, what changes would you make and what would you have retained?

SPADAFORE: If I was in his position, the first way I'd answer is by looking at what he said before the council. What he said before the council, the first would be his simplification of the rubrics of the Roman Missal. I love the fact he dropped the Easter Vigil readings from twelve down to four. I liked that because I don't like redundancy in liturgy.

Anyways. His encyclical, *"Veterum Sapientia,"* the Wisdom of the Ancients. This was a document that he promulgated, and it basically said all priests and all seminary professors either had to be fluent in Latin or lose their job. This is not a man who wanted to give up tradition. This is a man who loved tradition, also the case of Annibale Bugnini, for those who aren't familiar with that name of Annibale Bugnini he was the chief architect that created the Novus Ordo, the post-Vatican II liturgy.

What is interesting about Annibale Bugnini is that he was partially responsible for the 1955 missal under Pope Pius XII. He was calling the liturgical shots then too. John XXIII looked at Bugnini and said, "You're fired!" He fired Bugnini from his task of having anything to do with liturgy. It was Paul VI who brought Bugnini back. So, what we're seeing here on this level is we're seeing John XXIII who is a conservative man, at least where the traditions of the church are concerned. Now let's, turn and look at another part of his personality. John XXIII was also very open; he was open to new ideas. Look at his encyclical, *"Pacem in terries,"* which is an important document. The Cuban missile crisis, the threat of nuclear war, was the context of *"Pacem in terries."*

This was a man who was open to new ideas. He was open to dialogue with others. He was open to discussing the principles of others. He was very firmly rooted in his own principles. So, how would I modernize a church if I were in John XXIII's position? No one has ever asked me this question before. Truth be told, in the Traditionalist Movement I was willing to talk to people outside the Movement, and because of that I wasn't looked upon favourably. They still talk about me on the Trad Forums. About a year ago I found a forum post on one of the Trad Forums where I was the subject of an entire post and I left the movement back like 12 years prior, what the is wrong with these people? It shows how deeply obsessed some people can be.

So, if I were in John XXIII's position, and I would also add that after I left the Traditionalist Movement, I looked at the documents of Vatican II and I found they do have some good pastoral advice, which was his intention. First, I would follow his intention from his opening address of the Council, no new doctrine would be declared. Traditional doctrine stays. The other thing I would do, following his intentions, I would open dialogue with other religions. I would open dialogue with government. I would even open to dialogue with governments antithetical to

Catholicism. He did talk to the Soviet Union. He did not lift the prohibition against Socialism. He did not lift the prohibition against communism, which had been condemned by every Pope from 1849 up until about 2005 or 2011. He did not lift the restriction, but he did say it's okay to talk. It's okay to learn. It's okay to dialogue. It is okay to make changes in the way we approach the world and make changes to the way we engage with the world. It's okay to listen to other people's ideas.

If somebody else has a good idea, there's nothing wrong with acting on that idea so long as it does not compromise your own principle as a Catholic. That's pretty much where I would go with this if I were in John XXIII's position. I would open the windows. I would keep the prohibition on Modernism. The prohibition on modernism, insofar as modernism led to something other than Catholicism.

If it led to something that was not recognizably Catholic, then the prohibition would stay. If some of the tenants could produce a bolder, richer Catholicism, consistent with traditional Catholic principles, then I would see little harm in retaining it. I hope this makes sense. I guess what I'm saying is I would stay in the middle of the road, rather than going far on one extreme, like the SSPV [Society of Saint Pius V] or far to another extreme like Roman Catholic Womenpriests. Does it make sense in the middle of the road?

KLING: That makes sense. I thought that's where you would go. I would probably be a little bit more, radical. I certainly would retain the traditional liturgy. I wouldn't change the Tridentine Mass, the liturgy of St. Pius V. What I would do is I would allow married priests. That would be one of the first things that I would allow because forcing diocesan priests to live like monastics is criminal.

SPADAFORE: It's outdated. It served its purpose in the past.

KLING: It certainly is outdated, and it has no real theological basis. To claim that it does is disingenuous. I would allow married priests. I would start the process of investigating women priests. This would have been in the sixties. What I would have done is had women priests limited to women who are in religious orders that were cloistered and do that as a test run to see how it worked. Then I would open it up and expand upon it to mitigate controversy. There'd be people who would leave and whatnot, but by retaining that traditional liturgy and, by making some social concessions, for example, married priests, and then start to gradually open the priesthood to women. Those are the things that I would have done. I would have kept much of the tradition the same and try to maintain a strong *"Sensus Catholicus,"* which is the "sense of being Catholic." You walk into a Roman Catholic Church now and you may be confused. Is it Roman Catholic? Lutheran? Episcopalian?

SPADAFORE: It's kind of funny because in the Traditionalist Movement, they talk about the Novus Ordo having Anglican basis, but they don't know what they're talking about. I have a Lutheran altar missal from 1958. The service book and hymnal, this is eleven years before the Novus Ordo. If you look at it, the propers are the same as the Latin Mass. The propers, the lectionary is mostly the same, the actual order of the liturgy is based on the Latin Mass, but it also has a lot of features of the Novus Ordo, the prayer of the church, a Psalm between the first and second reading, actually three readings, it has so much. It is like it is based on a Latin Mass, but the Novus Ordo was based on it. Both were influenced by Taizé, but you can see the commonality, and like you said, if you walk into a modern Evangelical Lutheran Church, you're not going to see much difference between that, and your average Novus Ordo church built after Vatican II.

KLING: The jurisdiction that I'm with is the Community of Saint George, which is a Young Rite jurisdiction, which is part of the larger Liberal Catholic Church movement. We use a liturgy that's similar to the Liberal Catholic Church liturgy. The LCC was started in 1916 or 1917, and it's heavily based on the Tridentine Mass. So, other than the fact that it's in English and some of the prayers are changed to take away the more doom and gloom aspects of the Catholic tradition; instead, focusing on the resurrection as opposed to being stuck on Good Friday. However, if you look at the liturgy it's going to look very similar to the Tridentine liturgy, at least in part.

SPADAFORE: Back to the thought experiment. Married priests, I've got a twofold thing on that because on the one hand, it's out of date. When it was imposed in 1139, it was imposed for good reason. At least the way I was taught it was that the priests we're using the parish property which was supposed to belong to the people. The priests were using something in the feudal system so they could pass the parish property onto their sons. So, to keep the parish property in the hands of the people, the Pope said, "You're not allowed to marry anymore." That way they didn't have legitimate sons and they couldn't pass the property on. If what I was taught is correct, then in that context, it was a good law to pass for a good reason. The problem is we live in a time where that rule has outlived its usefulness. It's no longer a necessary rule, it's no longer there for property protections. Obviously, it could be dispensed with and a law that outlives its purpose is no longer a good law.

KLING: Right and for a thousand years, there were married priests and then they did away with them. Then they rewrote the narrative to make it sound like it had always been that way, and that's something that the Roman Catholic Church is famous for doing, for example, Ultramontanism and the rise of Papal Infallibility after the First Vatican Council, they really painted a picture that it had always been that way, but it wasn't. Just like clerical Celibacy was never always a part of the priesthood.

SPADAFORE: Clerical celibacy is a lot less important than Ultramontanism in the big scheme of things. One is doctrinal and the other is disciplinary. The appeal there, with Ultramontanism would be like the Easter Controversy, the Acacian schism, and matters of that sort. I can't say that Ultramontanism is revisionist so much as it is, cherry picking and it would not exist in the pre-Tridentine Church, because that level of centralization did not exist prior to the Council of Trent. With the issue of married priests, you said they try to say it was always that way? You missed an important point, because what was said is not that it's always been that way. What was said, and you hear this in a Traditionalist Movement, it was a matter of positive divine law. That's what's being said. That takes clerical celibacy from being a disciplinary question to being a doctrinal one. Whereas it is not doctrinal. The Church has admitted celibacy was a preferred state of life, referring to things Paul said in Corinthians saying, "I am not married I would rather, you not be married, but it's better to be married than to burn if you can't control your desire."

It's easy to take that, Paul was just giving a confession about marriage. Paul doesn't say "He must be," but whoever would be a bishop or an overseer to translate the word more collectively, "Let him be the husband of one wife." Let him have his family in order, because if you can't keep your house in order how can you run the larger house of God? Paul is not saying he must be married. He's saying, let him be married, and he's using the marriage as a tool for vetting this potential bishop's suitability as a bishop. So, the whole thing is yes, it was optional. The discipline with the Orthodox is only to draw the bishops from amongst the celibate, often monastic clergy. So as a theological matter, it's a theologically a moot point one way or the other, it's a disciplinary matter. The question is, does this discipline suit the best interests of the church, currently? They recognize that when disciplines do not suit the best interests of the church, they can and must be changed.

The question I would have regarding married clergy as a pastoral matter and strictly, as a pastoral matter, is a question of money. If we are waiting on the professional clergy model, where you have a man who is living in a house on church property who receives a regular pay, basically his entire support, housing, food, utility bills, all that his entire support is being given by the church institution off the backs of the donations from parishioners. It is cheaper to support a single man than it is to support a man, his wife, and his family. I'm saying wife, because we're talking about the Roman Catholic Church and the Roman Catholic Church does not permit gay marriage. Obviously, it would only be a man married to a woman in the rectory. It would cost the parishioners more to support a man, his wife, and his family. We could assume that they're going to have children. It's a financial concern, it must be considered when making this decision. I don't hear a lot of people on either side of the debate talking about that.

KLING: I think that's somewhat of a myth, and it's problematic. Let me explain, here in my local area, I live in Massillon, Ohio, and the town next to us is Canton which is the home for the Romanian Byzantine Rite Catholics, their cathedral is in Canton. The diocese spans the entire United States, and all their priests used to be married except for their bishop, I assume that is still the case. I think the reason why John Michael Botean is the bishop is because he was the only priest who was celibate. All the other priests are or were married. All the other priests serve parishes, and let's look at those parishes. Those parishes are not nearly as large as most Roman Catholic parishes, yet they can still afford to pay the priest who's married and has children.

I think, maybe the Roman Church should stop exploiting its diocesan clergy by giving them room and board and a vehicle but paying them $10,000 a year. Instead, they could pay them a good wage and give their priests a housing allowance and let them go buy their own food and take care of themselves and be adults and not have somebody taking care of everything.

SPADAFORE: I think you're giving a good place to start here. We can talk about the financial model for the Romanian Byzantine Rite Catholic Church. Let's look at their stewardship model. Let's compare what expenses they have with that of the Roman diocese and vice versa, what things could be paired down? What expenses does a Roman diocese have and would a Roman parish have expenses that it doesn't need to have? So, what you're telling me is that there is a model that works. It's just a question of either influencing that model or adapting that model to do something that will work. That's great, and there are Protestant churches that had full-time married clergy.

KLING: I work as a hospice chaplain. I get paid. I have a lot of student loan debt, but I own a house. I have two cars, and I'm able to support my wife who's a stay-at-home mother. We have a two-and-a-half-year-old. There are Episcopalian clergy who make six figures. I don't think clergy needs to make six figures, but you can certainly make a living wage, be able to support a family modestly and get by, and if you're wanting to become a Roman Catholic priest, who's married and make a lot of money and be able to send your kids to Harvard and Yale and drive a BMW. Well, maybe that's not going to happen. Maybe you should be content driving around in a Hyundai Accent.

If you're willing to live frugally and humbly, you can still etch out a good life and allow your partner to stay at home and raise the family. It's not impossible, but a lot of these priests, they're celibate, the church is not paying for their family, and they're living well. They have no debt and no real expenses.

SPADAFORE: So, what this goes to, this goes to what you're telling me. It can work. It goes back to modelling. It can work. There are models that make it work, and I'm not talking about making six figures or going to Harvard or any of that stuff. No one who goes to the priesthood for the right reasons goes into it to get rich. I think we can agree on that as an absolute, if you want to get rich, there are plenty of other ways to do that. That involves a lot less stress and a lot less headache than the priesthood, but it goes back to the model, a model that is possible. It's just, a question of finding the right model. There's also the question of the whole stereotypical preacher's kids' behaviour, how to reign that in. The Orthodox Churches seem to do a very good job of that. So, learn what they do.

The idea of married clergy, I've never had a problem with it, but I've never had a problem with it in theory. I think we've taught this one to death, but the model is workable. The model exists. The rule itself is out of date. It has served its purpose therefore it has expired. It is expired therefore it can no longer be considered a good law unless there is another equally strong valid reason for the law to remain on the books.

"If God created shadows, it was to better emphasize the light." — Pope John XXIII

"Concluding Thoughts"

In my conversation with Bishop Jason Spadafore the topic of apostolic succession came up several times. Apostolic succession is contained within the sacrament of holy orders and the succession is the spiritual lineage that goes back to Jesus Christ who instituted the sacrament of holy orders and therefore passed on the succession. It was first passed onto the apostles and then unto their successors and so on. The ideal is that every deacon, every priest, and especially every bishop can trace an unbroken lineage back to Jesus Christ. Ordination within apostolic succession is essential, and mandatory, for the efficacy and validity for most of the other sacraments. Any person can baptize another person, and within the sacrament of marriage the couple are the true ministers of the sacrament; however, the five remaining sacraments need either a bishop or priest to officiate those sacraments. Therefore, apostolic succession is necessary for the administration of the sacraments. Apostolic succession requires a bishop laying hands upon the person being ordained and that laying on of hands is an energy transfer from the bishop to the person being ordained. That transfer produces an indelible mark, an ontological transformation, upon the soul of the person being ordained. They are changed forever. This sacramental alteration is like the sacraments of baptism and confirmation in that they also produce an ontological change in the form of an indelible mark upon the soul; a person changed forever.

A person cannot "take back" their baptism, their confirmation, or their ordination. These sacraments will influence you for life, and you cannot turn them off. Therefore, before accepting ordination to the priesthood or episcopate you should ask yourself, "Do I accept this ordination or consecration for the rest of my life?" You might find yourself, in the future, in a position where you may no longer possess a desire for priestly or apostolic ministry; however, the status of your soul is not changed by your willingness to "leave" a sacramentally ordained or consecrated life. It will still be there even if your spiritual disposition changes. This is something important to consider, and to evaluate in your life.

Something else to consider is the person who is ordaining or consecrating you. The originator of the priesthood/episcopacy is Jesus Christ; however, when an ordination or consecration is conducted those individuals within the succession are also passing something of themselves on to the new ordinand, and this is an important consideration. Things to consider:

- Is the person who is about to ordain/consecrate me a person with whom I would normally be "in communion" with?
- How do I view the person ordaining/consecrating me? Do I respect him or her?
- Would I ordain/consecrate the person who is ordaining/consecrating me if the situation where reversed?

These are important questions to ask yourself because an ordination/consecration is an immensely powerful energy exchange and the energy passed onto the new deacon, priest or bishop will affect each of us in different ways. What is the personality of the person ordaining or consecrating you? I suspect their strengths and weaknesses could potentially pass on via the energy exchange; therefore, you might be cautious with whom you allow to ordain or consecrate you. For example, my ordaining bishop was the late Archbishop John Gilbert, and he was a quirky individual, but I was fine with that because I too am quirky. My consecration included three bishops, as is customary, and included Archbishop John Gilbert as well as Archbishops Albert Stubblebine and Rima Laibow, MD. The late Albert Stubblebine was a retired US Army major general who was involved in the US Army's Stargate Project (remote viewing and psychic spying), and Rima is a medical doctor specializing in psychiatry. I am excited about my apostolic lineage and gladly accept the quirks, strengths and challenges that may have been passed onto me during my ordination and consecration.

Again, something else to consider is how you plan on coping with the changes that will take place after an ordination or consecration. Instead of looking at this energy exchange as, "I'm a new priest" or "I'm a new bishop," think of it as you have now become a priestly initiate or episcopal initiate into the sacred mysteries of the priesthood and episcopate. The essence of the priesthood and episcopate is mystical in nature and less about administrative or jurisdictional characteristics -- these are constructs resulting from church polity and not intrinsically linked to the mystery of the sacrament. The mystery of the sacrament is about the sacraments themselves and not about any newfound power you might think you possess over others. The effect of the sacrament of holy orders is upon the state of being of the person ordained or consecrated. All too often I have seen bishops within the Independent Sacramental Movement focus their attention on the administrative side of the episcopacy. This is not what the sacramental initiation of consecration is about -- it is about the fullness of priestly initiation and the fullness of the sacrament of holy orders.

Things to consider before ordination and consecration:

- What was my life like now, before ordination or consecration?

- Am I equipped to deal with a major change in my life?

- Am I ready to deal with the added responsibility that this change will bring upon me?

Things to consider after ordination and consecration:

- How has my life changed since ordination and consecration?
- Do I find myself depressed? What will I do about this depression?

- What is my support network, do they understand ordination and consecration? Do they support my decision? What sort of support do I have from other priests and/or bishops?

Having a support network is important for a new deacon, priest or bishop. It is important because the sacrament of holy orders effects each person differently, based upon the context of their life. Whatever you are going through at and during the time of your ordination and consecration is exacerbated by the ontological transformation of the sacrament of holy orders. Be mindful of your mental and spiritual state before your ordination or consecration and plan accordingly. Be prepared.

For Reflection, Contemplation, & Prayer:

- What are your thoughts on clergy getting paid to preach, administer the sacraments, and perform other ministry skills?
- What are your thoughts on the clerical state, or how clergy including priests and bishops should live? How is the clerical state distinct from a monastic state? How are the two similar?
- If you were in the position of Pope John XXIII, how would you have shaped the Second Vatican Council?

"Passionate About Sacraments"
A Conversation with Kevin Daugherty

"Yet you, Lord, are our father. We are the clay. You are the potter. We are all the work of your hand." — Isaiah 64:8

Father Kevin Daugherty of Lincoln, Pennsylvania, is the co founder, and priest of Kindling fires: A New Monastic order within the Convergent Christian Communion (formerly known as the Anthem Network). Kevin was ordained to Christian ministry in April 2013, became an ordained elder within the Convergent Christian Communion in October 2017, and was commissioned an abbot in June 2018.

KLING: What are some of the things that you'd like to talk about today? Why don't you go ahead and get us started?

DAUGHERTY: Well, basically, when we were discussing coming back, we had a couple different topic ideas. Interestingly enough, the Holy Spirit worked a little bit into this because my partner and I, we were visiting a Lutheran Church yesterday, and this Lutheran church was very unique. They're a smaller group. They're located in a former Byzantine Catholic Church, and most of the members are former Roman Catholics. Instead of identifying with the Lutheran church they identify as an evangelical Catholic Church in that their services are a blend, of course they have the typical ELCA Lutheran books of worship. They have various Lutheran worship services, but then they blend those services in with material taken from the Anglican churches as well as the Roman Catholic Church. For example, when they say the "peace of the Lord be with you," instead of saying "and also with you," they say, "and with thy spirit," which is something that you see in the Book of Common Prayer and Catholic services. That really begs the question as to what exactly the word Catholic means. Last time we spoke we talked a lot about the word evangelical and what it means. Here in this Lutheran congregation, we have evangelical Catholics. What does evangelical mean for them? What does Catholic mean for them? It's worth talking about.

KLING: I'm fascinated that it's a Lutheran Church, I would have thought that the switch from Catholic to something else that the

Episcopal Church would have been more in line with their sense of identity. I'm fascinated that that they went Lutheran.

DAUGHERTY: It wasn't that the church switched. What happened was there was a Lutheran congregation, and then over time, they had lots of converts from Catholicism. The church eventually became predominantly ex-Catholic, even though the church started out as Lutheran.

KLING: Where is this church located?

DAUGHERTY: The church is in Pennsylvania, just outside of Pittsburgh.

KLING: When thinking about the word Catholic we should start with the textbook definition, we can start there and then move outwards. Of course, Catholic means universal. When you recite the creed, One Holy Catholic and Apostolic church, you're always going to have somebody in a Protestant church who says, "I'm not Catholic." Catholic means universal, as in the universal Church. If we were to replace the word Catholic with the word universal in the creed, then it could be confused with Universalism, which is a theological belief that everybody receives salvation, everyone is saved, everybody goes to heaven. I'm not sure that's useful because not everyone in the Independent Sacramental Movement believes in Universal salvation. Using the English translation of Catholic to Universal may be problematic. What are your thoughts?

DAUGHERTY: Thinking about the issue of Universal versus Catholic, I can see the word Universal being even more obscure. The reason why is because, like you said, there are theological traditions that use the word universal for their theological beliefs. The other thing that is a problem is when we say Catholic there are other implications with it. When we say Catholic, it includes a liturgical form of worship. Catholic refers to a type of sacramental theology and refers to a particular historical legacy. When we just say universal it can be confusing, because in addition to talking about the historical Catholic and Orthodox churches we are now also taking the word and expanding it to refer to modern contemporary Protestant churches or new religious movements like Mormonism or New Thought, that the word becomes more obscure and hard to use.

KLING: I agree. Coming out of the Liberal Catholic Church tradition, we don't have a problem with universal salvation. The confusion with translating Catholic to Universal and the confusion with that being associated with universalism is not a problem for me; however, it would become a problem if it is associated with the universalism side of Unitarian Universalism, because that is a very different approach to Christianity, then the Liberal Catholic Church tradition. Then it gets confusing.

DAUGHERTY: There's a lot of confusion with that word. When the Universalist Church in America switched and joined the Unitarian Church, it became something different than what they were historically. Historical Universalism was raised in historical Catholic theology. There are plenty of church fathers who were Universalist in their beliefs. Roman Catholicism is open to the doctrine of universalism. The Orthodox Church is open to it and the many Lutheran churches are too. I remember seeing an article from the ELCA, and their Presiding Bishop Elizabeth Eaton was saying that she believes that hell was probably empty. Universalism as an historical orthodox belief is distinct from what the Unitarian Universalist Association has now. There's a branding problem where two very different schools of thought have now happened into using the same word, the same language.

KLING: Going back to the word Catholic without the association with the English translation of universal, but just going back to the word Catholic. The word Catholic evokes a certain feeling. You either like Rome or you don't but there are grays areas. I will acknowledge that, but there's something behind the word Catholic, that's important to unpack. Do you have any initial thoughts?

DAUGHERTY: Would you say there are certain assumptions that we bring in with the word Catholic? When we talk about it, we have to have an explanation, a type of deconstruction of what our assumptions are, that sounds right.

KLING: Let's say you're fine with the word Catholic. You like the word Catholic; it evokes a positive, emotional response for you. What does that mean? When I was at the monastery, Christ the King Monastery in Cullman, Alabama, the superior Father Leonard used to talk about what he called the "*Sensus Catholicus*" or the sense of being of Catholic. The underlying culture of Catholicism. There's Catholic culture and it was more evident in pre-Vatican II Catholicism. I would think because you can go into a Catholic church today, you can go into an Anglican Church, you can go to a Lutheran Church and unless you pay attention, you may not know the difference. You and I would probably know the difference, but the average layperson may not. The *"Sensus Catholicus"* isn't as "in your face" as it would have been 60 years ago, 70 years ago, but there was something about being Catholic and about Catholicism, something that was special, and it evoked an emotional response. In the Independent Sacramental Movement, a lot of people don't want to divorce themselves from the term Catholic because they're afraid that they might lose this "something special." Does that make sense?

DAUGHERTY: I think so. The word Catholic has a nostalgia. The word Catholic has a firm history. There's an identity to it. This is why so many Independent Sacramental Movement churches and jurisdictions tend to act like tiny Roman Catholic churches, with a similar structure, similar liturgy, similar language. Such as with the ultra-traditionalist Roman Roman Catholic splinter groups. They even see themselves as the true Roman Catholic Church. My counterpoint to that though is I'm not sure that there ever was truly a firm Western Catholic identity. That's something that we imposed on the word Catholic. The reality is that the Orthodox Church is a Catholic Church, the Assyrian Apostolic Church of the East is a Catholic church. The St. Thomas Churches, the Christians of India, which come from the Syrian church, are Catholic churches. I would argue that most Anglicans are Catholic, and even the Lutherans comfortably fit into the Catholic world. This is part of the balancing act. The word Catholic does mean universal, and it applies to all these different streams of Christian thinking that have different types of services, different rites, different cultural backgrounds, linguistic backgrounds. It's tough to pinpoint really what the word Catholic means sometimes, because all these different churches come from the same historical base. You're from the primitive church, from the Apostolic Church, from the church that originally called itself Catholic and Apostolic and the ecumenical creeds. All these different groups diverged from and evolved from that original source. They have a lot of common aspects, a similar liturgy, similar sacraments, similar theology, but I'm not sure there's a cohesive identity.

KLING: I certainly agree with you when you say that the Orthodox are Catholic, that the Oriental Orthodox are Catholic. I'm not so sure if you're using a lowercase "c" or a capital "C," but I don't know if it really matters.

DAUGHERTY: I don't really think it matters that much, whether capitalized or not. When it comes to the term Catholic, we like to capitalize it and we associate the word Catholic with the Roman Catholic Church specifically, but we're wrong to do that. If you go back to church history, there have always been self governing Catholic churches. We saw that with the Celtic Church for a long time. We we saw that with the Orthodox churches in places like Ethiopia and in Persia. They've always been Catholic and with a larger C, but they were never part of Rome. They were never part of the The Roman Catholic Church.

KLING: Thinking back to my own experience within Roman Catholic traditionalism, I have an affinity for that worship style. That is, for pre-Vatican II liturgy, pre-Vatican II liturgical customs, and divine office, etc, etc. I never really connected with this modern *Novus Ordo* style church. When I saw the liturgy books for The Young Rite and the Liberal Catholic Church tradition, I noticed a similarity in worship style to the pre-Vatican II Tridentine liturgy but in English. There's something there, there's a lot of things changed, but it has, at least for me, that "*Sensus Catholicus,*" that sense of Catholicism. It was easy for me to embrace the Liberal Catholic Church tradition, because with it we have one part traditional one part esoteric or open to "newness." In The Young Rite we are socially progressive, and it was the best of all worlds for me because it still had that sense of being Catholic without some of the bad trappings that I have seen promulgated and promoted by Rome.

DAUGHERTY: Do you feel that the liturgical reforms that the Roman Catholic Church made in 1960s diverged too much from what you consider to be a historical Catholic tradition?

KLING: Yes, absolutely. 100% There are some things that they did that the Byzantine Rite church has always done such as concelebration, or multiple priests at the altar, and concelebration is fine. Some of the other practices of Vatican II are unnecessary. They turned Roman Catholicism into just another option. If you look at an Episcopal or high church Anglican, they look more Catholic than some current Roman Catholic churches and if you go into some older churches that used to have an elaborate high altar the altars are either taken down or they're covered up and then what looks like a table is just put in front and that's sad to me.

DAUGHERTY: I understand your disappointment. There's a trend towards secularization, of the beauty and majesty. A question for you, do you consider the Book of Common Prayer, the Eucharistic Rites in there to be firmly Catholic or not? And the reason why I asked is because many of these services from the prayer book, especially the older forms, such as the 1662 version, or 1928 version, those are in many cases just directly taken from the Sarum Rite we saw in England within the Catholic Church.

KLING: I've used the Book of Common Prayer many times. I've used it for communion, I've used it for anointing, and I've used it for funerals and commendations. I'm okay with the Book of Common Prayer. For me it does have the *"Sensus Catholicus"* that I talked about, but it's the Anglican tradition. A similar but different tradition from the Roman Catholic tradition. They have common origins, the Anglican Church has retained a certain feel that remains Catholic. I can respect that but I recognize that it's different. I prefer to use a Book of Common Prayer rather than the modern Roman liturgy, the *Novus Ordo*. That's just a weird bias, from being a former traditionalist. If you've ever been involved in the Traditionalist movement, even though you may now be a million miles away from it in your current context, there's always something there. You can't get rid of it completely. For example, I do not like "Eucharistic ministers." I have no use for them at all, zero use! Have and use more deacons, or sub deacons maybe, but have more deacons. I do not like Eucharistic ministers. I've had people say to me, "I'm a Eucharistic minister," as if it's a level of clerical hierarchy within the church. A Holy Order within the church. It was designed for large communities where it would take over 20 minutes to distribute communion. I can guarantee you that there are very few, if any churches, here in the United States, where it's going to take more than 20 minutes to distribute communion. Sadly, many churches use Eucharistic ministers. That's not what they were intended for, but they've evolved into something where people can become "Eucharistic ministers" and go distribute communion in nursing homes and elsewhere. That's lazy. That's what the priests should do. If the priests can't do it, then they should have deacons distribute communion.

DAUGHERTY: I'm wondering which came first? Many Episcopal and Lutheran churches also have some form of lay Eucharistic minister. What they will do is have a monthly cycle where one month the pastor or priest will visit nursing homes, and the next month, there will be a break. You'll see a lay Eucharistic minister distributing communion. I'm wondering which one came first? Perhaps it was a Protestant innovation that the Roman Catholic Church incorporated?

KLING: It was a Protestant innovation. I have no use for it at all. If you need people to distribute communion, you make them a deacon. I'm okay with women's ordination. So, if the only people in a congregation are elderly women who can go distribute communion, then make them deacons. Of course, the Roman Catholic Church won't ordain women. Here in my local area, I live just south of Akron, Ohio and I work in hospice as a chaplain. I interact with Catholic clergy frequently, because I have Roman Catholic patients and they need to be anointed. There are some who have asked me to do the anointing, and I'm perfectly happy to do that, but many of them want their priests to do it, and I'm fine with that too. Out of three Roman Catholic priests in my local area the youngest is middle aged. You're dealing with a priest shortage in the Roman Catholic Church, but they will not ordain ordain women; however, they will make them "Eucharistic ministers" to go distribute communion. That does not compute to me. I had a patient once who had Alzheimer's, they took her to the dining room at the nursing home because that's where the Catholic Eucharistic minister was distributing communion. They didn't have an actual mass, of course, not in the the dining room of the nursing home. This Eucharistic minister was distributing communion to all the Catholic residents and my patient had a mild mental breakdown because she said, "I'm Catholic. I'm Catholic." She thought she was at a Protestant service. She didn't realize the Eucharistic minister was duly commissioned by the church to distribute communion. She thought it was all part of Protestantism. If if you're 90 years old, and you're suffering from Alzheimer's and when you think of the Roman Catholic Church, you think of the Church of your youth. The church she remembered was not the church she experienced in the dining room of the nursing home.

DAUGHERTY: I stumbled into some similar circumstances while visiting nursing homes. Whenever I'm in a place like that I usually identify as Independent or Independent Sacramental. Occasionally, I'll make use of the word Anglican because Anglican is a broader word than say Episcopalian. The reason why I'll do that is that it helps to distinguish what I do from the Roman Catholic Church. People will see the collar I wear and see a Roman collar, even though it was invented by Presbyterians, and popularized by Anglicans. There are stereotypes that people will attach to the priestly office, and I often avoid the word Catholic when it comes to talking to people. Because of that people have memories, such as senior citizens in nursing homes of a Roman Catholic Church back in the 1940s and 1950s. I don't look like that or act like that, but because of the collar, because of the the ministry I'm doing, it confuses them. It appears like I'm a Catholic, a Roman Catholic priest. I'm not and they don't really know what to make of it which is why I avoid the word Catholic. The Roman Catholic Church has its own unique practices and tendencies and it can be confusing to people because they lump the words "Roman Catholic" and the word "Catholic" and when they think about it, especially older people, they often think Roman Catholic as in the church before Vatican II. It's a complicated thing.

KLING: It is very complicated! As you may have noticed, I get passionate when I talk about certain things and I didn't realize this topic would bring out some things within me that I hadn't really thought about in a long time. For me, the word Catholic evokes an emotional response. When I joined the Roman Catholic Church I was baptized by a priest who's now deceased. His name was Father Joseph Terry Marks and he was originally ordained in the Archdiocese of Louisville, Kentucky. He left the diocese and affiliated with the Society St. Pius X[th] because after communion one Sunday, one of the Eucharistic ministers was pouring the Blood of Christ down the drain. Father Marks about lost it. He said, "No, we don't do that." He ended up going to the archbishop to talk to him about this and the archbishop responded that he was overreacting. That it wasn't that big of a deal. It was at that point that he realized he was done with the archdiocese, and he became a traditionalist and eventually became the priest and pastor of Our Lady of Fatima Chapel in Richmond, Virginia. He was the priest who baptized me, and I remember that story because that was so important to him. The belief in transubstantiation, the idea that the bread and the wine become the Body and Blood of Christ and the action of pouring the Precious Blood down the drain was horrific to him. That is important. That is part of the *"Sensus Catholicus"* of Catholicism. When I went to a United Methodist seminary you could see the grape juice stains on the on the floor near the table, because the grape juice would spill on the floor from time to time. When I was at the monastery, if for any reason some of the Eucharist fell on the floor, you'd have every monk on their hands and knees addressing it, because we would not allow that to happen, or to be ignored. That might seem strange to some people, but it's important. If it's just a symbol, then why do we have priests? Anyone could officiate at the altar! But it wouldn't be an altar, it would be a table. We wouldn't be offering the sacrifice of the mass; instead, just a meal.

DAUGHERTY: I find your narrowness to be something of an interesting contradiction since you are coming from a Liberal Catholic perspective. The Liberal Catholic Church, at least from from my study of that tradition, seems to be theologically broad. It borrows heavily from Theosophy and different schools of thought like Theosophy.

KLING: That goes to show you that can be diverse, you can be a pluralist, but you can still subscribe to solid sacramental theology that is Catholic. For example, my emphasis on transubstantiation and the real presence in the Eucharist and in the transubstantiated wine becoming the Blood of Christ. You can believe in the importance of this and believe that it's okay to ordain gays and lesbians, you can still subscribe to transubstantiation and believe that it's just and valid to ordain women. You can subscribe to transubstantiation and still believe in that it's okay to go into a Hindu temple and honor Brahman as an aspect of the Holy Trinity. For me that is what is Catholicism, that is the Universal Church. It's not about conservative or liberal. The term Liberal Catholic Church doesn't necessarily mean "liberal" as in how we see "liberal and conservative" today. Just because I'm in the Liberal Catholic Church tradition, just because I'm in The Young Rite doesn't mean I abandon sacramental theology. On the contrary, if a priest comes to me as their Bishop and says, "I designed my own Eucharistic liturgy," I would say, "Great, let me see it." If it doesn't adhere to strict sacramental theology, then I will tell that priest, "You cannot use this and represent us." Just because we are progressive and open, and open to experimentation, does not mean we play with the sacraments and doesn't mean that someone can deviate from the proper matter, form, and intention of the sacraments.

DAUGHERTY: It sounds like from your perspective that the word catholic and the word sacramental are directly tied. The two words are almost the right hand and the left hand of the whole. If I understand you correctly, it sounds like sacramental theology is what defines what is Catholic for you?

KLING: I would agree with that, because without the sacraments, there is no Catholic.

DAUGHERTY: My opinion comes closer to what you see in the Anglican Church with the Lambeth Quadrilateral. they have the ecumenical creeds, especially the Apostle's Creed and the Nicene Creed. The historical Episcopate locally adapted, and scripture and the sacraments. They they emphasize a few different things. For me, I would use a little bit broader definition. It wouldn't just be about sacraments. For me, it would also be about such things as I see in creed. The reason why I mentioned the Nicene Creed specifically is because it's the one statement of faith that all the major historical Christian churches have come to agree upon. There are some variations. There are some different versions of the Nicene Creed, there's a couple different clauses that changed different communions. When the Greek Church Fathers came together, the two councils of Nicea, rather the council of Nicea and the council of Constantinople, they produced the Nicene Creed. Churches everywhere came together and adopted the Nicene Creed as their statement of faith. I consider beliefs and doctrines into that as well, not just sacraments.

KLING: I don't disagree with that; I don't disagree with that at all. That's fine, but the church is more than just the creeds. There's the expression "Lex Orandi, Lex Credendi," the law of prayer (worship) is the law of belief (faith). You worship the way you believe; you pray the way you believe. Your worship should be an expression of your beliefs and your values, your doctrines and whatnot? That's important. Having gone to a Protestant seminary, I can tell you, the one thing that was missing was sacramental theology. We studied a lot of the Creed's. We studied the doctrine of the Trinity. We studied the Incarnation. I took a worship and music class. We studied baptism, we studied the Eucharist, sort of but not really. Sacraments were discussed, but not in the sense of a valid sacrament or an invalid sacrament. We didn't talk about matter and form or intention. None of that was part of the curriculum.

Once, when I was in seminary the president of the school officiated a communion service and he decided not to use the words of institution, he just assumed them. It was a United Church of Christ communion service, even though was a United Methodist elder. He assumed the words of institution but didn't use the words of institution. I walked out, and paradoxically I was serving a Unitarian Universalist parish at the time.

DAUGHERTY: I can relate from where you're coming from. My denominational background is in Baptist and Anabaptist churches and most of my training when starting out in ministry was in the Mennonite Church. I knew I was having a shift in my thinking and that I would I end up somewhere else, because when I start getting more and more involved with the Mennonite Church, I realized that I missed liturgy and the sacraments. Most of my friends and colleagues are also charismatic and I'm also charismatic. It was weird to me how we firmly believe the spirit being present and all the different things within the church. For example, prophecy, or laying on of hands, and baptism. But when it came to the Eucharist, Oh that's a symbol. The Holy Spirit is literally present in all these different things but when it comes to the most important part of the service, which is the Eucharist, then that's all symbolic. I can relate to your frustration with Protestant seminaries and churches where it seems like they've given God a demoted status, where God isn't present in physical life anymore. From my experience, a lot of these churches have swapped out the Eucharist as being the center of service to the sermon, with the pastor as preacher, as being the center of the service. That has always bothered me.

KLING: Right, me too. I like good preaching, don't get me wrong, but that's not what we are there for, in worship. I come from a type of Catholicism, from Traditional Catholicism, where when I would hear the priest say, *"Hoc est corpus meum,"* I get tears in my eyes, it's emotional. When you go from that to some of the things that I've seen in Protestant worship and in some modern Roman Catholic services I respond with, "No." The *"Sensus Catholicus,"* is the sacredness that's inherent in the liturgy, in what I consider good liturgy. That's extremely important to me.

DAUGHERTY: So, here's a follow up question, because you talked about the Protestant seminary, where does the line between Protestant and Catholic end? The reason why I ask this is because we have traditions like Lutheranism that were founded originally to reform Catholicism. The intention was to take the historical Catholic Church and merely reform it to make it less corrupt, or the Anglican Church, which was originally found as a national Catholic Church. The King of England had a clean break with the Roman Catholic Church and the Church of England was originally just a Catholic Church in England, but then the second generation embraces a Reformed theology. Of course, fast forward a few hundred years to the Oxford Movement, in the 19th and 20th centuries, which pushes Anglicanism back towards the Catholic side again. Where's the line? Where would you draw the line between Protestant and Catholic? Is it possible that many historic Protestant churches are also Catholic churches?

KLING: That's a difficult question for me because I have focused most of my attention on the Independent Sacramental Movement. I don't really think too much anymore about the various Protestant expressions of Christianity. I'm not sure that I could, at this point, draw a line between Protestant and Catholic. If there isn't Apostolic Succession, then, for me, it's a moot point and it doesn't matter.

DAUGHERTY: I see. The thing with that is there are Anglicans in the Independent Sacramental Movement, plenty of us. Same with Lutherans. For example, the Independent Lutheran Diocese, they may not have Apostolic Succession yet, but I would include them.

KLING: I would include Anglicans; I would include Anglicans who are in the Independent Sacramental Movement into the Catholic umbrella that we have been talking about. I would include them because there is a lot of fluidity within the Independent Sacramental Movement and because of that fluidity there are people in Anglican jurisdictions that have been influenced by Old Catholic theology. There's a lot of cross fertilization and I can respect that exchange of ideas.

DAUGHERTY: The lines get very blurry; especially because the official Old Catholic Church, the Union of Utrecht, recognizes the Episcopal Church USA as an Old Catholic Church. So, the lines do get very blurry. Also, the Lutherans, there are some Lutheran Churches that you could argue have some form of Apostolic Succession.

KLING: Sure, I would agree. You and I have talked before and you are aware of my disdain for Martin Luther. I do not like Martin Luther because of his essay, "On the Jews and their lies." However, I did have an opportunity, when I was at my Doctor of Ministry intensive a few weeks ago, to meet two Lutheran pastors, and they're great guys. I enjoyed spending time with them. I spent a week in the intensive with them, and we lived on campus that week. I got to see them after hours and we hung out a lot, and I really got to appreciate them and their perspective. The Evangelical Lutheran Church in America (ELCA) has redeemed itself somewhat in my mind. I wish they wouldn't use the term Lutheran but there's a lot of good people there, I still have no use for Luther. Anyhow, we were talking about how Apostolic Succession is creeping into the Lutheran Church. There are some branches of Lutheranism that are opposed to it, opposed to having bishops, but there are other Lutherans who welcome getting closer to the Episcopalians and therefore are getting exposed to Apostolic Succession through the Episcopal Church. This goes back to our previous look the word Catholic. I've been talking about the *"Sensus Catholicus,"* and Pope Leo 13th declared Anglican Holy Orders invalid. While I believe Pope Leo was wrong, it does raise some questions for me that I really haven't thought too much about. I haven't invested a whole lot of time in this subject and I certainly don't believe in being the Apostolic Succession police in getting caught up in Apostolic lineages. What's your lineage? I don't do that. If someone says, "I'm in Apostolic Succession, and I'm in the Independent Sacramental Movement." I tend to give them the benefit of the doubt and welcome them as a brother or a sister, but there's still a bit of apprehension based on Leo 13th and his papal bull, *Apostolicae curae.* Does that make sense?

DAUGHERTY: It does. In listening to your comments, it sounds like you have some extra bags left over from your Traditionalist days.

KLING: I have a lot of baggage, and I know it!

DAUGHERTY: Which is why it's unusual for me when I hear that you're so LGBT affirming and supportive of the ordination of women. When it comes to your sacramental theology and Apostolic Succession you are extremely traditionalist.

KLING: I would agree but would add that just because we're in the Independent Sacramental Movement doesn't mean we should play roughshod with the sacraments. I do not believe that at all. We should have solid and well-defined sacramental theology. All our theology should be sound, and I don't care how progressive or liberal you are, you should be able to tell me about the doctrine of the Trinity. You should be able to tell me the doctrine of the Incarnation, and we should be able to discuss it. I had a guy once contact me wanting to be ordained. I was in seminary at the time, and he contacted me and wanted me to ordain him. I asked him to tell me about the doctrine of the Trinity. He said to me, "I don't really believe in that." He couldn't discuss the doctrine of the Trinity; he had no clue. I told him to go find somebody else. I've said that story before. Whether or not you embrace a certain doctrine that the historical Church has embraced, you should be able to articulate it and discuss it. You can say, "I don't know if I believe it, but this is what the Church teaches." If you can't do that, then to me, that's a problem. There are a lot of clergy in the Independent Sacramental Movement that I suspect if I asked them to describe the doctrine of the Trinity they could not. I'm okay with them saying that they reject it, but they should be able to articulate a doctrine that the historical Church has embraced before they say they don't believe it. That's a big hot button for me.

When it comes to sacramental theology, there are three things that are important. Matter, form and intention. For example, if you were going to baptize somebody, you use water. You don't use Coca Cola or whiskey, you use water. If it's under extreme circumstances, and the only water that you have is, a puddle out in the road. If the water in that puddle is mostly water, then you can use it to baptize, but if that water is mostly mud, then I would question whether you could use that to baptize because water is the proper matter for baptism. If you go to baptize somebody, and you pour water on them, and say, "In the name of Jesus, you're baptized," that's not the right form. The right form is Trinitarian such as, "I baptize you in the name of the Father and the Son and the Holy Spirit." You can say Holy Ghost, it doesn't matter, but you get the point about proper form. If you baptize somebody "In the name of the goddess and the Sun and the whatever," and you start quoting from Gnostic texts, then that's not baptism either.

It's important that if we are part of the Independent Sacramental Movement that we emphasize good, solid sacramental theology. That's my perspective. It's important because we identify as a sacramental movement, so sacraments must be important to us and bringing the sacraments to others. If we don't believe in the sacraments, then why are we a part of this Movement? Does that make sense?

DAUGHERTY: It makes a lot of sense. The Anthem Network (Note: now known as the Convergent Christian Communion) was originally not part of the Independent Sacramental Movement, we've only recently changed our governing structure and started making the connections to bring us into the Movement. When I first listened to my Bishop, my bishop now, talking about the ISM I was apprehensive. I've seen far too many small Independent Catholic groups have a very high view of themselves. They often see themselves as the one true church or they'll have insane titles, such as the "Archbishop-Cardinal-Metropolitan of all of Russia," with a house church in the middle of Milwaukee. I was very apprehensive, but over time a couple things happened. First, I grew to trust my now bishops, even though they wanted to go in this direction, I was apprehensive, I went with them in the direction. The other thing is how I believed that the broader charismatic movement believes in the Spirit of God literally being in all aspects of our life, but for some reason, when it came to the sacraments, they were just symbolic. It was inconsistent to me and I would watch as I was doing ministry, I would watch as I'll gave people communion, I would anoint people, I would bless people. I could see this visibly improve their spirits, clearly lift them up because of the sacraments. For me, I've come to really emphasize the sacraments. When I look at the sacraments and I look at sacramental ministry, God really works through that. I can see why most of the Christian church is sacramental. When you consider the Roman Catholic Church with over a billion members, the Orthodox churches with a few hundred million in communion, if you include Lutherans who are sacramental, for Protestants. When you consider this, you're talking about most of the Christian church embracing a sacramental theology. Even if for some of them, it's only a couple sacraments. For others, it's seven plus. For me, I agree with you. It's very important that we have a strong and robust sacramental approach, and a sacramental theology, and of sacramental liturgy.

KLING: I agree. I must emphasize, based on some of the things you've said, that just because a particular jurisdiction or priest or bishop is a pluralist or progressive does not mean they have weak sacramental theology. Let me be the case in point. My sacramental theology. I was trained by Roman Catholic traditionalist. I embrace those teachings and I haven't deviated from them. When it comes to liturgy, we can experiment with prayers, we can experiment with combining Western and Eastern practices and I love all of that! I love looking at Ethiopian Orthodox liturgy and Coptic Orthodox and Syrian and Tridentine styles and the Liberal Catholic Rite and all sorts of liturgies. I love liturgy, but just because you can embrace a multitude of diverse liturgical approaches doesn't mean you have weak sacramental theology.

DAUGHERTY: It sounds like we're touching on something else that is also important, which is you can have unity without uniformity. You could have a oneness approach to the faith. You can have a unified or Catholic or universal Christian faith without having uniformity across the board where everyone must do the exact same thing the exact same way. One final question for this conversation. Considering the broadness of the word Catholic, which that's the one thing we've been able to agree upon here is that all these different historical sacramental churches are in some way Catholic, whether they use a small "c" catholic, or large "C" Catholic. The question is, do we hold fast to the word Catholic and strongly insist that we're Catholic, or do we surrender the word to the Roman Catholic Church? Because in this country, the USA, the word Catholic is typically synonymous with Roman Catholic and even the Eastern Orthodox Churches has decided to just say that they're the Orthodox Church because it confuses people to say Orthodox Catholic. Typically, when you say Catholic there is an immediate association with Roman Catholic. What's the solution there? Do we hold fast to the word Catholic and have that conversation explaining the word or do we use something else such as Independent Sacramental Christian?

KLING: I think it's time to abandon the word Catholic because when we use the word Catholic, we almost always use the word Independent in front of it. That's problematic. If we abandon the word Catholic, then what we have left is Independent Sacramental Movement, but that too is problematic. Then what? If not Catholic and not Independent Sacramental Movement, then what? Any last words Father Kevin?

DAUGHERTY: It's always important to remember that we have as Paul says, "We have one faith, one Lord, one baptism." We need to emphasize our Catholic with a small "c," our catholic faith but at the same time, we need to be loving about it. We need to be broadening our horizons a little bit with our use of the word Catholic.

"The spiritual virtue of a sacrament is like light; although it passes among the impure, it is not polluted." — St. Augustine

"Concluding Thoughts"

Recently I was at St. Raphael's Bookstore in Canton, Ohio. It is Catholic bookstore and I visit there from time to time to stock up on Trappist beer and ale. The local Catholic bookstore is the only local business that carries the beer produced within Trappist monasteries. One day, while I was visiting St. Raphael's Bookstore I got into a conversation with a graduate student in theology from the local Roman Catholic college, Walsh University. I do not know how the conversation got started, but I started talking about the Independent Sacramental Movement. He had no idea the ISM existed and was interested in learning more. As we talked, I mentioned that I had been a monk at Christ the King Monastery in Alabama.

When I mentioned Cullman, Alabama the woman who was working at the bookstore mentioned Father Leonard Giardina. I perked up and responded, "Of course I know Father Leonard, he was the prior at Christ the King Monastery where I was a novice." She told me the story of her uncle being a priest and how he would take her down to Alabama to visit with his friend, Father Giardina who was pastor at Sacred Heart Parish in Cullman, Alabama. Before Father Leonard founded Christ the King Monastery, he had been the parish priest at Sacred Heart Parish. She and I talked about her experiences down in Alabama when she was a young child and would play at Sacred Heart Parish. It was nostalgic for both of us. For her she remembered her joyful youth and for me I recalled my time as a Benedictine.

When I left the monastery, I eventually found myself living amongst the Romanian Byzantine Rite Catholics. Once I had the pleasure of serving at the divine liturgy at The Basilica and National Shrine of Our Lady of Lebanon. The priest was Father George Gage and I served at the liturgy with his, at the time, 10-year-old son. Several years later, I'm working as a hospice chaplain and Father Gage comes up in a conversation I was having with a colleague, a Roman Catholic lay-woman hospice chaplain. I mentioned that I knew of Father Gage and that I had served at one of his liturgies during my sojourn with the Romanian Greek Catholics.

The point of both stories is the interconnectedness of humanity. The impact you have upon someone can take years to bear fruit. The relationships we have and cultivate influence who we are as people. Each conversation I have, and each encounter I have with another has an opportunity to help transform and change who I am. I am a different person today because I got to know Father Leonard Giardina, O.S.B. He was not perfect, he had several faults; however, his influence over me and my life is still felt and the last time I spoke with him was over thirty years ago. He was one of the important mentors in my life.

Mentorship is important within the Independent Sacramental Movement especially because a lot of the clergy within the Movement have had insufficient formation and training. Mentorship is about relationship and having a good mentor can help one grow and mature as a deacon, priest, bishop or Christian. Be mindful of who considers you a mentor and recognize the responsibility you have entrusted to you in forming and shaping another person.

For Reflection, Contemplation, & Prayer:

- Who have been the mentors in your life? What has their influence been upon your life? Are you a mentor for others? How are you influencing the lives of others?
- What are your thoughts on the term "Catholic?" Do you think the Independent Sacramental Movement should continue using "Catholic," such as "Independent Catholic" as a source of identity and as a descriptor?
- What is your ideal form of liturgy? Are there liturgical practices that are important to you?

"Trouble with Train Wrecks"
A Conversation with Bishop Gregory Godsey

"Beware of false prophets, who come to you in sheep's clothing, but inwardly are ravening wolves." —Matthew 7:15

Bishop Gregory Godsey has served as Presiding Bishop of the Old Catholic Churches International since 2015. Born into a Roman Catholic family, he had a disastrous first encounter with the Independent Sacramental Movement. In 2002, Bishop Godsey founded the Ancient Apostolic Communion, which merged into the Old Catholic Apostolic Church. In 2012, he was named Bishop Ordinary of the Diocese of St. Maximilian Kolbe, which covered Alabama, Florida, Georgia South Carolina. Bishop Godsey is the editor of Convergent Streams: The premier magazine of the Independent Sacramental Movement.

KLING: One of the things that I want to discuss is something that I'm not sure how to name, but I think the working title is "the train wrecks within the Independent Sacramental Movement" and there are plenty of them out there. I thought we would just take some time and talk about those train wrecks that we have experienced. I'm also looking at the last issue of *Convergent Streams: The Premier ISM Magazine*, and there's an essay by one of your Bishops, Bishop James St. George, who wrote an essay titled "Empty hats, the silent and ever-pervasive scourge of old Catholic/ISM movement," and that's a very appropriate title. I like that, "the ever-pervasive scourge," that's a little bit more dramatic than train wreck, but it certainly gets the point across. I thought I would read a couple of sections from this essay to kind of give us a springboard in which to frame our conversation.

The first one is, and this is the words of Bishop James St. George. He writes,

"It saddens me to see so many of our clergy dress in fancy attire or liturgically, inappropriate clerical garb, or willfully misusing their officer status to harm another, or to pretend they are better than others. These empty hats live to do one thing, create more empty hats. And then those hats create more and soon we are made of entire churches and orders filled with empty hats and hearts that could care less about real mission or ministry. Then he goes on to say, say

what you might about all the things wrong with the Roman Catholic church, but despite their imperfections, they train good priests and ensure that the rules are the rules like them or not. Then he goes on again to say, what happens when we allow for such things to happen within the Old Catholic church, independent sacramental movement. What happens when we allow empty hats to collect regalia, post fancy images that self-aggrandized, but not follow the normative rules of formation and ordination. What happens when we amass greater libraries and more clothing and liturgical vessels and try to engage in bigger and better organizations while never fixing the plague that is within."

I thought those were good words, and I thought we would use them to start off this conversation. Any initial thoughts?

GODSEY: Well, I completely support what he wrote, he is not only a Bishop in our church but a regular contributor to Convergent Streams. I think it's important to remember, as he wrote, that there seems to be a great amount of resistance to the idea of education and a little education can go a long way to resolve a lot of the issues in our movement. For example, if you go to the hospital and you have appendicitis and they come to you and say, "Well, we got Dr. So-and-so here, he was trained in medical school. Top of his class and performed hundreds of these appendectomies and has been a surgeon for 20 years, and he's willing to do your surgery, or you can have John the janitor who's never gone to medical school, has no idea what that appendix looks like, but he watched a YouTube video about appendectomies, and he really wants to give it a try. Which would you rather have? I want the surgeon any day because John may, kill me on the table. We, as clergy are no different, we are spiritual healers. We are spiritual physicians, and we can do real temporal harm to a person here on earth. We can do everlasting damage to them, and I think the exact thing I said was, "Well, John as an ill prepared clergy person can risk damaging your soul and cause your separation from a loving god for all of eternity, and that's a greater burden."

KLING: I had a professor in seminary, her name is Dr. Linda Mercadante, and she used to say quite frequently that, "bad theology kills." I agree with that. I saw that very prominently when I did my chaplain residency in Clinical Pastoral Education. As a resident, I would often encounter pastors that would be there visiting their parishioners, and I could see bad theology at work. For example, you have a cancer patient, the doctor says you have two weeks to live, and the local pastor is in there saying we can pray for a miracle. Jesus answers our prayers, and if we have faith, they'll be answered. When that person dies, the family is like, "We didn't have enough faith, our faith wasn't strong enough." Bad theology kills, and with a lot of people that I've seen in the Independent Sacramental Movement, they have no theology. They don't even have bad theology. I mean, they have bad theology by default, but they can't articulate theology. You can't teach what you don't know, and there's just a lot of that out there.

GODSEY: I like to call it bumper-sticker theology.

KLING: I want to make sure I speak from my own truth and I want to put out the disclaimer that I have made mistakes. I've been a Bishop since 2004, and I was ordained a deacon, priest, and a Bishop all at the same time. I don't recommend anybody do that. That's a mistake, and that's a mistake that I allowed to happen to me, and I won't make that same mistake on somebody else. I don't want to say I've been part of the problem because after I was made a Bishop, I didn't, go off and create my own jurisdiction and do tons of photo ops. It took me 10 years before I bought my first miter, but my point is a lot of people have and they made some of the mistakes that I made, and they just run with it and create havoc and that's a problem.

GODSEY: I would also echo some of what you said. I made mistakes early on too, and that's why I'm so stringent about the fact that we must educate our clergy. I know how ill-prepared I was in the beginning. I have spent all that time since, everyday work and I'm currently on track to be in a CPE residency program here in Augusta, South Carolina starting in September. I'm furthering my education by going back to college, to get a degree, to back up all the learning I've done in those intervening years. I've been a Bishop since 1999. I would encourage anyone who is looking for a fast track to slow down. You need time in formation, because it's so important to understand all the nuances that are involved in being a clergy person.

KLING: When I was ordained and consecrated, I had a high school diploma. I had some experience in the church. I had been a novice at a Benedictine monastery. I understood some aspects of church life and what that meant; therefore, I'll give myself a little bit of a pass. It wasn't just, "Here, you're a Bishop and there's no reason for it, just by the fact that you're a nice guy." There was some background there; however, after I finished, after I was consecrated, I eventually went to college, went to seminary, did four units of CPE, et cetera. When I was in college, I worked at a Unitarian Universalist Fellowship as an Education Director, and when I was in seminary, I was served at another Unitarian Universalist Fellowship as their consulting minister. I had that experience which helped me become a better Bishop, but I wanted to make sure I mention that not to "toot my own horn," but to say that I know what it's like to get put in a situation where you are a potential train wreck. I get it, but if you're driving a train, that's out of control, you can slow that train down and do things right.

GODSEY: You can put the brakes on.

KLING: You can make it right! If you find yourself a deacon, a priest, or even a Bishop, when you probably shouldn't have been, you can put those brakes on and get the formation that you need. Then wear that miter with dignity and respect. There's a couple of situations, I don't want to mention any names, not try to make a lot of enemies, but there are individuals that I know that come to mind. The first individual was somebody that I had encountered before I became a Bishop in the Independent Sacramental Movement, but he came back on my radar around 2007, and at the time he had created a website and was pawning himself off as a Unitarian Universalist minister and running his own congregation outside of his home.

He was claiming to be a Unitarian Universalist minister, and at the time I was working at a Unitarian Universalist Fellowship, and I contacted Boston, the Ministerial Fellowship Department within the Unitarian Universalist Association, in Boston, and asked them, "…is this person a minister in good standing within the Unitarian Universalist Association," to which they responded, "…absolutely not." Two weeks later, his website was down. I assume their attorneys got in contact with him. My point was this same guy, just a few years later was now referring to himself as a patriarch of an Independent Sacramental Jurisdiction, claiming to have doctorates from some university in Jerusalem. I saw that and I just rolled my eyes. There is nothing wrong with someone going from one thing to another, a lot of us have, but it's another thing to one minute, you're a Unitarian minister or you are claiming to be, and the next minute you're a patriarch claiming to have advanced doctoral degrees. That's insulting to those of us who are working on our education. You have people who claim to have degrees that they didn't earn. Just because you're a Bishop does not make you entitled to claim you have a Doctor of Divinity. That's one example of some of the nightmares that I've seen.

GODSEY: I have also encountered people like that, and an example is a bishop who set up a jurisdiction back about 15 years ago. It grew to be a large jurisdiction, he was an archbishop in their jurisdiction and began setting up a unity group in the Independent movement, which gained a lot of popularity, only to find out that not only had he never been to seminary, he never had any education behind him, but he also had never actually been ordained or consecrated. That's a serious issue that we have because there is so little oversight. We have the potential for these problems to occur. One of the things that I had toyed with for the Independent Sacramental Movement database have been a verification service that provides you kind of a seal on your listing that says that we verify you as being ordained, having an education et cetera. We've never really hashed out the entirety of it, but something like a certification.

KLING: That's a really good idea.

GODSEY: The problem with it is the time. It's going to take a lot of time to do it because verifying that information is going to be difficult. It's going to be time consuming. The Independent movement is not very good at keeping records. Bishops sometimes don't always get certificates to clergy and then of course, some of the time records are lost and people die. There's a lot of issues, but it's certainly something that I consider doing. Speaking as a fellow chaplain, you know that chaplains have certifying agencies. The ACPE, APC, the BCCI process, the board-certified chaplain process and CPE training and everything that you must go through. Why would we not have the same type of process within the ISM. Some way to show this person has legitimately gone through some sort of process, and a description of that process. This would have to be fluid to a certain degree because we do have so many ways of teaching our clergy. I think the important thing is that they at least be respectful of that, but also stopping those that would just ordain anyone without any training, without any background review of that person.

KLING: I've ordained people that I shouldn't have ordained. I've ordained people without putting them through proper formation, and I recognized that it's a problem. It's problematic and the same patterns keep showing up with people that are quickly ordained. Everyone that I have ordained quickly, and it's not been that many, but those that I have ordained quickly could be better priests. If I would have taken my time, formed them properly, I believe they would be better priests. I know one that I ordained too quickly, he promised to do formation later, but because I was in the area halfway across the country, he convinced me to ordain him. I did not give him any faculties, but it didn't matter he was still ordained. Two weeks later, he went somewhere else, and I think in about a year and a half time, he's been in six or seven jurisdictions. That is crazy, but I must take some responsibility for those mistakes.

GODSEY: We see that a lot actually, jurisdiction shopping it's a big issue in the ISM.

KLING: I see people changing jurisdictions for reasons such as, "I don't like the jurisdiction's name. I wish you had a different name. So, I'm going to look somewhere else." I just roll my eyes.

GODSEY: I'll readily admit that in my past I've ordained people too quickly. At least three or four that I can think of off the top of my head that I ordained too quickly. Then there are those that even though you try to put them through formation, they just absolutely refuse, one excuse or another, as to why they can't do it. Yet, they still expect you to ordain them. It creates a problem in the ISM. And I've experienced that this morning with an individual who took exception to my desire for clergy to be educated, they don't understand Catholic piety or polity in a very basic level as a lay person, much less as someone who is wanting to be ordained. They're setting their own ordination date and preparing to be ordained, but if they don't understand Catholicism then how can they possibly become good priests?

KLING: One thing that come to mind is when dealing with people who are train wrecks within the Independent Sacramental Movement, is if someone says they're ready to be ordained and they want to be ordained right now, and they have no patience, and it must happen now, is to ask them some simple questions. I ask them some basic theological questions, such as, can you explain to me the doctrine of the Trinity, can you explain to me the hypostatic union, can you tell me about your

Christology, and if they cannot respond appropriately then they don't need to be a priest until they go through a solid formation program. They need to be able to articulate basic theological concepts without having to think about it.

GODSEY: One of the questions on our application is a modern theological question. Most people should be well versed in it, I would think. It's not like they have 2000 years of division between when it was discussed and now, and that question is on the Immaculate Conception. I throw that in the application to see how the applicant responds. I can't tell you the number of wrong answers that I get from people who pass themselves off as highly educated and ready for ordination. Even priests and bishops seeking incardination, they often answer with, "when Jesus was conceived in Mary's womb." It makes me wonder about the level of formation that we have in the ISM that these people can become clergy and not understand some of the most basic theological questions.

KLING: Yes! The Immaculate Conception is a curve ball because a lot of people get that wrong.

GODSEY: I would expect clergy to at least to be able to get it right, because how can you educate the lay people if you don't know yourself?

KLING: If I was to do a face-to-face initial interview with somebody who is convinced, they are ready to be a priest right now, I think one of the things that I would do is sit down with them before we even discuss theology or incardination or ecclesiology. I would sit down with them, take out a rosary and say, "Okay, you lead it. You pick the mysteries that you want to do, and you lead it. Let's say a rosary together. Let's pray together." I guarantee you, half or more, of those seeking ordination "right now" cannot pray a rosary.

GODSEY: I think that is probably accurate.

KLING: But they probably have $600 worth of vestments already.

GODSEY: That's the other side of this, a huge travesty is the train wreck bishop. I used to call it "dolly dress up," and people who have no formation, no idea of what they're doing, can't even properly say mass. I'm not saying this to be snobbish of anyone. If you're using whatever literature you're using and you can't follow the rubrics, you can't say mass properly. They can't say mass, and yet they have thousands of dollars invested in vestments, and they look beautiful in the pictures, but there's nothing there. I call it smoking mirrors, or dolly dress up, but that's essentially what it is. There is nothing there.

KLING: Right? Here's another situation for you. There was a guy that contacted me sometime last year, he was local. We met at an International House of Pancakes (IHOP) for breakfast to talk. I didn't want him to meet me at my house, because I didn't want him to know my address. We met at an IHOP and we're sitting there talking and I find out that he was consecrated a Bishop through the internet on a Zoom meeting and I told him that his "consecration" is not legitimate and that it is not valid. He said to me, "I thought so that's why I wanted to meet with you." He wanted me to consecrate him a Bishop. I'm sorry, but anybody who's going to get consecrated through the internet and thinks that it is legitimate shouldn't be a Bishop unless they go through a lot of training and formation. I told him, "You are more than welcome to apply to join The Community of Saint George, we have a process. You go through the minor orders. You'll be a sub-deacon for a while. You'll be a deacon for a while. Eventually, you'll be made a priest if you do the work, but you probably not become a bishop. If you are, it will not be while you're in your early to mid-twenties." He said, "Great." He ended up ghosting me and I found out that he found somebody who consecrated him a Bishop. I just shake my head.

This is the kind of mess that we see far too often. Yes, you and I have made mistakes. We learned from them those mistakes quickly, and we made efforts to correct those mistakes. Some of these people, I think they really think what they're doing is good. The IHOP guy I was telling you about, he found a jurisdiction in the United Kingdom that would incarnate him, and now he is responsible for educating and training all their clergy in the United States. You can't teach what you don't know.

GODSEY: That's right. And that's perpetuating that cycle, an empty hat cycle. That is the whole notion that "he's a good guy he's got a great heart," so," we're going to ordain him and consecrate him just because." I'm not going to debate the fact that the person may have a great heart, but you're right. You cannot teach what you don't know, and for a lot of the ISM jurisdictions they are setting themselves up for failure by continuing to perpetuate this. I don't want to make any enemies, but I have 22 years, you have 19 years. There are others of our brothers and sisters who have as many or more years in the Movement. We're the pillars of this movement now. Look around you. Peter Paul Brennan, Francis Facione, these people are gone. We are the pillars of the movement now and it behooves us to speak up and say, "We have to stop." We must do that because the ISM could be the Emergent Church of tomorrow. We could be the church that captures all those young people who are falling away from their faith because they're tired of churches that refuse to bend, refuse to grow, and refuse to expand. We could be that outlet, but only if we're willing to confront our own demons and fix our problems.

KLING: That's right. If somebody is listening to this and they think, "...are they talking about me?" Well, maybe we are, but if you are a train wreck and you are listening to this, there are plenty of people out there that are willing to help you. They're willing to offer you an olive branch and say, "Hey, let's put the past behind us and let us work to help you learn the things that you need to learn, fill in the gaps that you're missing." Unfortunately, it takes a certain degree of humility, a virtue that is lacking within many folks.

GODSEY: And it takes a commitment, and a lot of people don't have that kind of commitment.

KLING: If you're about ready to start a CPE residency program, your whole life is going to be turned upside down. The process will change you, and it will make you a better person. If you let the process work. It changed my life, having gone through a CPE residency program. But you must be able to be vulnerable, to be humble, to be willing to do the work; otherwise, you're not going to make it, and there are so many out there that are not willing to do the work. It's so sad because I agree with you, our movement has so much potential. It's not going to reach that potential If we don't police ourselves, if we don't take charge of this movement and say enough is enough, we need to raise the bar.

GODSEY: That's one of the things that we're looking at in our jurisdiction, a change of course. We've spent the last year focusing on a simple message of deepening our commitment and this first year is a five-year process. The first year of deepening our commitment to church and faith with each year having a different commitment focus. One of the things that we've been looking at is our own training program and one of the things that we have decided is all our candidates are going to be trained as chaplains because chaplains are called to do so much more than a parish priest is called to do.

If you can be a chaplain, you can learn to incorporate a lot of that education into yourself and you can also be a good parish priest. Part of that training is going to be a CPE-like program where they're going to have to go through a program, built by people in our jurisdiction, who have units of CPE. They're going to help us develop a program that's very much like CPE, so that our candidates must do introspective work. They will have to look at their biases and their blind spots and begin working to resolve those issues within themselves through that process.

KLING: That's wonderful. I think every jurisdiction needs to implement a similar program. I know I currently adjunct teach at a local college. I teach mainly medical ethics; however, I'm currently designing a course in spiritual care for nurses and social workers. It is a course designed to give healthcare workers, who are not chaplains, the basics of pastoral care so they can navigate around those emotional grief-stricken environments, that are the mainstay for chaplains, and be able to function properly and effectively in those environments. I thought about taking the syllabus and the curriculum that I'm designing for that course, rework it a little bit, and use it within our jurisdiction.

We have a couple of modules on spiritual care, but I thought about using the spiritual care course to replace those modules and have a super module. The way our formation program works is we have an LMS system, a learning management system, online. We have all the modules there and all the proscribed readings, that students will need to purchase. You submit your work directly to the LMS system. It will notify the mentor that you've submitted a paper. Then they'll set up a time where the student and mentor can talk about it. The program is designed for reading, reflection, writing a paper, and then talking to your mentor about it.

I'm under no pretense that anybody coming to our jurisdiction needs to get the same level of education that I did. There's no reason why anybody needs to straddle themselves with so much student loan debt. It's almost criminal to demand that of another person, but that doesn't mean that they can't take advantage of what I know, and what other mentors in our program know. I would have loved to have had the opportunity to learn from somebody without having to go to seminary, because seminary was a long-drawn-out experience. I loved it, but a lot of student debt. It would have been nice to have been in a jurisdiction where I could have received the same level of education. It may not be accredited, but the same level of education, and then I could have gone for an MBA and made a better living.

I think all of us, all of us that are serious, we do it [chaplaincy] because we like to do ministry. As a full-time hospice chaplain, I love what I do. I was visiting a patient just last week. He's in his 70s and he's dying of cancer. I meet with him and his wife, twice a week. I was holding his hand after I said a prayer and when I said, "Amen," he started crying. That's why I do the work that I do, to try and make a difference in the lives of others. Good pastoral care is an art, and I practice my art whenever I have the opportunity.

GODSEY: I agree with you, and I find that families in the hospital setting are so appreciative of the work that we do. It's particularly difficult during the pandemic, as you're aware. Finding ways to connect families with their loved ones when they can't be in the hospital with them. Our chaplains have been using phones and iPads, using FaceTime, so they can at least help people see their loved ones, even just to say goodbye. It's heartbreaking, but it's also a blessing for me too. To be able to be there, to be able to provide that level of spiritual care for people and to give them some amount of closure. There has been a lot of funerals, especially with COVID, families are not being allowed to see the body after death. There is a level of closure missing. We give them an opportunity for that process to start, that feeling of ending to begin. I can tell you from experience that most of the clergy in the ISM don't have any kind of educational background at all and are not willing to learn. They're not going to be able to do that kind of ministry. Hospitals and hospices are not going to let them come in and minister to people as a chaplain unless it's their own parishioners because they're just not going to put themselves in that kind of risk. Unleash that kind of…

KLING: Liability.

GODSEY: It's a liability, a huge liability and that's another thing, probably for another discussion someday, but there's a huge amount of liabilities that we accept as ISM clergy, and as bishops for the clergy under our care. I know jurisdictions that say, "Well, they're contracted employees, we assume no liability." The courts don't typically accept that as good enough. Doesn't meet the smell test, and if you have direct authority or supervision over them, technically they're not a contracted employee. You're liable for any mistakes they make and for any damage they do. That's why it's important for us to tighten this up and do better.

KLING: That's a good way to put it, do better. I want to make one more disclaimer. I know, when talking about education and when talking about formation, one of the things that gets brought up almost every single time is, "what about those people that have learning disabilities?" I don't know if I've mentioned it before, but I have dyslexia and for most of my elementary school experience I was in what they called LD or Learning Disability class, back then in the 1970s we called it "happy class" and I got to ride the little bus to school. When I make jokes about the little bus it's coming from my own experience, because I had to ride a little bus. I remember getting beat up a lot by the neighbor kids because I was different. I didn't go to the same school that they did because the little bus picked me up and took me to a school on the other side of town. I struggled with dyslexia throughout my school experience. In high school, I knew I was labeled and marked. Nobody ever said to me, "You should go to college." I was well into my mid-twenties before I ever went to college because I thought I was too dumb and I could never go to college, but I overcame these feelings. I overcame it and I'm working on my fifth degree now. I'm in a Doctor of Ministry program. My point is, I worked through it. I overcame it, and so can others. If somebody really has serious issues, I will certainly work with them, but I wouldn't use dyslexia or other learning disabilities as a crutch to get out of doing the work.

GODSEY: Very true. I think that a lot of people think that you're discounting people with learning disabilities. I think that they also consider the idea that we expect clergy to be the perfect person. There was a time, not too long ago, that if you were Roman Catholic and wanted to be a priest and you were blind or had eyesight issues that you were denied. If you were missing fingers or a hand, you were denied. If you had any kind of major physical disability, you were denied. That speaks of perfectionism. One of our clergy is on the Autism Spectrum and highly functioning but is Autistic. We worked with him very rigorously through training and he's a priest now. A very good priest who pays attention to detail, always learning, always growing, and always expanding. He was willing to commit to the process and that's what is important. He was willing to commit to the process, and I would echo, that anyone who has a learning disability that I am willing and able to help you go through that process to get the same education we give all our clerics. It may take a little longer, it may require a little more personal attention to make it happen, but that shouldn't exclude you, if you're willing to try if you're willing to learn.

KLING: That's right. Before we end our discussion, I don't want to say this was negative, it was necessary, but I know some people might think, "Wow, this was a very negative discussion and I'm sorry you feel that way." I've been wanting to talk about this topic for a while because it's been building up. When you've been in this movement for so long, you see things and sometimes it just eats at you. The Independent Sacramental Movement has so much potential, and I hate to see it be squandered by people who are wearing these empty hats who are playing games and who aren't taking it seriously. Being sympathetic to those who may think this is negative, can you wrap us up with some closing thoughts that are totally different? That are positive and could cheer people up as we end our discussion.

GODSEY: Absolutely. You know, I've had people who say to me, "Well, if you hate the movement so much, why are you still in it?" To be honest with you, they're amazed that I ask myself that same question. I don't hate the movement. I really don't. I think we have such great potential. We have the potential to be the 21st-century churches of spirituality. People are looking for what I like to call Emergent Catholic. I have toyed with putting that out there as a term to use, Emergent Catholic, because we can be that light and path of hope for people who've lost faith and lost hope in the mainstream churches, but we can't shy away from looking at the dark corners, the areas where we can improve.

I don't think this is a negative discussion, as much as it is looking at those dark corners and saying, "These are the areas we can improve." We can learn to be better, and we can become that church for the 21st century. The movement to bring people back to spirituality, not just, religion. It's going to require everyone to put effort in things like Convergent Streams. The whole purpose of Convergent Streams is to highlight the best of our movement and to put forth the fact that we're not all like those empty hats. Put effort into the ISM Database or any of the other things that I do to support the ISM. I do believe there is hope and I do believe it is worthwhile. So that's why I think it's important that we all pull together, and we work together to shed light into those dark corners so that we can be the best that we can be. So, we can be a better version of ourselves.

> *"Merciful and loving God, sometimes we, your children are lost, and need found. Sometimes we wander and need guided. Sometimes we suffer and need comfort. Sometimes we conflict and need peace. This day, as it comes to a close, we ask that you find us, guide us, and give us the comfort and peace that only you can provide. Amen."* — An Evening Prayer (by David Oliver Kling)

"Concluding Thoughts"

When I was in seminary there was a fellow student who ended up leaving seminary because he could not cope with being a graduate theology student. He would skip classes so he could play World of Warcraft which was starting to consume his life. While I do not know for sure I suspect he was on the Autism spectrum and was unable to adapt to seminary life. He struggled with several things such as what denomination he would settle into and how he could find his way in this world.

Recently, my daughter Vivianne Leona was diagnosed with Autism. She is an adorable toddler, but she struggles with communication, activities of daily living, and has epic meltdowns. I have been advised by people close to me that I too may be on the Autism spectrum, although I have never had a formal diagnosis. My exposure to Autism and issues surrounding autism spectrum disorder has me thinking about neurodiversity and the Independent Sacramental Movement.

I know there are clergy within the ISM who have struggled with feelings of acceptence and have felt it impossible to navigate through the ordination procedures within mainstream "big box" denominations. That feeling of, "I don't feel like I belong," and seeking to find a spiritual home that is fully accepting and welcoming. I wonder if the Independent Sacramental Movement has become a safe space for the neurodiverse.

For Reflection, Contemplation, & Prayer:

- If you are a part of the Independent Sacramental Movement, what keeps you here? What pulled you in, what has kept you here, and what sustains you?
- Have you struggled with feelings of acceptance? Has finding a community that you feel welcoming and encouraging been a challenge for you? If so, what steps did you take to end up where you are now?
- What do you feel should be the priorities within any formation program in the ISM? What should formation programs focus on during the training and development of clergy?

"The Greatest Danger"
A Conversation with Rev. James Ishmael Ford

"As Jesus was walking beside the Sea of Galilee, he saw two brothers, Simon called Peter and his brother Andrew. They were casting a net into the lake, for they were fishermen. "Come, follow me," Jesus said, "and I will send you out to fish for people." At once they left their nets and followed him. Going on from there, he saw two other brothers, James son of Zebedee and his brother John. They were in a boat with their father Zebedee, preparing their nets. Jesus called them, and immediately they left the boat and their father and followed him. — Matthew 4:18 – 22

The Reverend James Ishmael Ford has walked the spiritual path for more than fifty years. He's danced with Sufis, studied with Gnostics, lived in a Buddhist monastery, and was ordained a Zen priest. Later he was also ordained as a Unitarian Universalist minister and preached from the high pulpits in old New England churches. He was a co-founder of the Boundless Way Zen network and was its first abbot. Today he is guiding teacher of the Empty Moon Zen Sangha and leads the Anaheim Zen sangha hosted by the UU Church in Anaheim. James served as a UU parish minister for twenty-five years. He is minister-emeritus of the First Unitarian Church of Providence. Today he serves as a consulting minister with the Unitarian Universalist Church in Anaheim and is an adjunct professor at the University of the West. In addition to his role as a Zen priest and Unitarian Universalist Minister James also holds ordinations within the Independent Sacramental Movement as well as several initiations within Inayat Khan Universalist Sufism. He has blogged as Monkey Mind for more than a decade and is the featured speaker at the Empty Moon Zen YouTube channel.

KLING: I know it has been a long time since you were involved in the Independent Sacramental Movement, but I am curious how you would describe the Movement to someone with no idea what it is. What is your elevator speech on the Independent Sacramental Movement and how would you succinctly define it to somebody inquiring who has no idea what it is?

FORD: I have not actually given this a great deal of thought. In fact, honestly, I haven't given it any thought, so I'm not sure how succinct I can be. It was Mark Twain who said, "If I had more time, I would have been briefer," but let's see... Independent Sacramental Movement. It's rooted in Christianity and it is driven by a deep affection for, and sometimes and idolatry of, a particular form of ministry through apostolic succession. Which is the belief that Jesus commissioned the apostles who commissioned the bishops and that there is a line that continues down through history. It's a wonderful venue for people who are square pegs, surrounded by round holes. It is a trap for people who are perhaps a little too interested in the abstruse parts of Christian ecclesiology and occasionally, you run into a Saint.

KLING: I like when you said, "square pegs." In some ways those involved in the Independent Sacramental Movement are in their own little Island of misfit toys. For those of us who are in it, you have to love it because there are a lot of square pegs.

FORD: Yeah, and then the odd saints. That part is important to hold up, it's easily dismissed. It not only can look like, but it can actually be, people playing church.

KLING: And that's a problem.

FORD: And it's a significant problem, too many jurisdictions, not enough parishes.

KLING: Yeah. That's very true. Well, you were only briefly a part of the Independent Sacramental Movement. Can you talk a little bit about your experience and why you moved on to other endeavors?

FORD: Sure, it was a hot 15 minutes. I was living in a Buddhist monastery and then left. It was a cultish organization, and I was glad to be done with it. I thought I was even done with Zen particularly at the time, and I was still trying to reconcile my childhood Christianity. I was living in the Bay area and discovered the Liberal Catholic Church, in Oakland. It's a congregation that I believe may even still exist, but it's floated around several physical locations for decades. I attended for a couple of months and then I moved to Southern California. There, I was working in a bookstore, which was one of those little spiritual crossroads. I met a lot of people involved in a lot of different things, and one of them was Dean Bekken who was a Liberal Catholic priest in one of the great schisms. He was the pastor of the little church, which was, I think the only legal, Liberal Catholic Church in the United States. There's a larger body, but it had to call itself the Liberal Catholic Church Province of the United States. I forget all the nuances. Anyway, I found him interesting. He was a lawyer and pastored a little church, and then I met another Independent Catholic, Bishop Julian Gillman. We became friends and I was wildly casting about looking for what to do and attended his services, and of course, in most of these Liberal Catholic congregations, we're talking two, three, four people showing up. I think he was one of the larger groups, he had five, six, seven people showing up.

I was trying to find something, and he offered to ordain me and that seemed right. So, he ordained me and then another Independent Catholic priest who had started a small congregation, said he was moving and asked if I would like to be the pastor. I ended up becoming pastor of a little group, half a dozen people. We ended up renting space very nominally from Bishop Bekken. I don't know, the whole thing lasted a year. It became apparent to me that I was in way over my head, and I had things I needed to do before I was able to tell people what to do. I resigned, left, and then moved up to the Bay area. Back in the Bay area I started studying Sufism.

And again, I met another Independent Catholic Bishop Mikhail Itkin. He ended up consecrating me a Bishop just as I was leaving the Sufi community and resuming Zen practice. There was a moment where I was trying to start a community that had Zen meditation that was influenced by Universalist Sufism but included a sacramental element. I thought it was a good idea that not many other people did. I left that, trying to remember the precise timing, but when I left, I felt the Sufi path was not really mine at all. The sacramental tradition kind of went with it, and I threw myself into what would become a 25-year intensive training in the Zen tradition. Then for what I felt it lacked, I became involved with Unitarian Universalism. So that's kind of a very large nutshell.

Oh, and I think the other thing is that when I began seminary, at the Pacific School of Religion, I recall that I could get an academic Master of Arts if I just added in another year of worth of coursework and wrote a thesis. The original intent for the MA was to be a study of Zen in North America. I did all the coursework and all the preparation for the degree, and then just as I was ready to move into the dissertation, as I was graduating with a Master of Divinity the lead professor said he was going to retire. There wasn't time for me to write on Zen, but I had written a paper that involved original research, and I should turn that into my thesis. And so, my Master of Arts thesis was on, an exploration of Christian Episcopacy specifically through the lens of the life of an Independent Catholic Bishop Mikhail Itkin. He was an interesting figure, in fact, he embodied most of the bad things about the Independent Sacramental Movement and several noble things. He's an early leader of the spiritually influenced Gay Liberation Movement, and he was there for several things in the early days of that whole phenomenon. I knew just about everybody, and I sat down and did formal interviews with Itkin.

KLING: It sounds like when you were ordained in the Independent Sacramental Movement, and then when you were later consecrated within the movement, that you didn't have much formation or any formation. I'm interested in juxtaposing that experience with very little to no formation with the experience that you had within Unitarian Universalism. A seminary education and probably an internship. I'm interested, do you think if you had better formation that you may have stayed, and can we talk a little bit about formation and looking at the two different types or lack thereof and just reflect on it?

FORD: That's a very rich question. I think part of what was at practice for me about the Independent Catholic Movement was I had no clue what I needed. I'm not positive how much I would have been able to bend into actual formation. There are two different types of formation, there's ecclesiastical formation, the things that make you a successful minister. And then there is spiritual practice, which is a major driver for me. In my life, I felt that my formation as a parish minister as a minister that was a conventional Western style of formal academic training, internship, some testing, and guidance along the way, were enormously important. How I made a living and I think I did good. I think it was helpful to people. It made me a living. But spiritual insight? I didn't think Unitarianism, or any Christian formation is worth, on the spiritual side, is worth anything, or worth very much anyway. This is one of my little soapboxes.

KLING: Yeah, go ahead. I want to hear it.

FORD: For instance, it looks to me at some point in the 1960s some Episcopalians thought, "Well, geez, we're lacking spiritual formation. I think I'll start a school," and so creates the Shalem Institute. Then there's just all these copycats that go around and they're like community colleges for spirituality. You get a little taste of this practice and a little taste of that practice, and you're introduced to some of the mistakes and there's nothing wrong with it. Except at the end of the course, you're given a certificate where everybody pretends that you're now a spiritual director, and that is a significant problem.

Within the Christian churches, there's a gigantic lacuna around the interior life. The Orthodox have some things, but they hide it away in the monasteries and the list ends there. There are a few things where people have tried to restore things and you see some real attempts at spiritual practice such as the Centering Prayer Movement, with Thomas Keating and, you start seeing some of these interesting thinkers that are popping up now who seem to be trying to engage authentic spiritual lives.

KLING: It sounds like your spiritual life came from your Zen practice and your professional life, that paid the bills, came from your Unitarian Universalist ministry.

FORD: Yeah. That's a harsh way to phrase it and significantly true. For the last 20 years of my life, it has been an attempt at ever greater integration of my interior life, my spiritual life, and my public ministry. How I serve the world, useful or not.

KLING: Did you sense this back when you were trying to do this Independent Catholic and Sufi hybrid?

FORD: It was like the germ of an idea, is what I thought, but I wasn't ready. I didn't have the chops to do it. I did not have the insight. I was not ready to be the leader of such a thing, or a director. I needed another 20 years of spiritual practice.

KLING: I'm not saying I completely disagree with you, that there seems to be a lack of spirituality within Christianity. What kind of advice can you give to change that? I'm speaking primarily on behalf of folks within the Independent Sacramental Movement. What advice can you give to them based upon your experience of having been in the movement, having left, but being well trenched in a highly spiritual path, which is your Zen practice, but also involved in professional ministry?

What advice can you give to heighten the spiritual life of those who are trying to make Independent Sacramental practice work?

FORD: Well, I think the greatest danger of the Sacramental Movement, as I see it is spiritual arrogance and with that a confusion of titles. What I would encourage people to do is, embrace humility and find a real spiritual director. I think a real spiritual director can be a formal practice like Zen or insight meditation, or any of these things that are now open to people. You don't have to be Buddhist to do them, or it could be as simple as identifying some truly wise person you know and apprentice yourself to them. Ask them and say, "Can I visit with you? Can I talk to you? Can I ask you questions?" And then listen. The practice of listening, the practice of presence, the practice of constantly returning to the moment that we encounter and between those two things then you can do the other stuff at the same time. You can pursue whatever it is that's calling in your heart to be doing, usually it's some form of ministry if you're involved in the Independent Sacramental Movement. Allow yourself to realize that maybe your motives were not clean and to work on looking at them, seeing what is healthy? What is not healthy?

KLING: That's a good point. Talking about motive, everyone enters the Independent Sacramental Movement for different reasons. For myself I didn't stumble upon it. I was involved with the Traditionalist Catholic Movement. Those are the folks that reject Vatican II and…

FORD: Yeah, like Pius…

KLING: …the Xth. Yeah, the St. Pius the Xth movement (after St. Pius X) and the St. Pius the Vth movement (after St. Pius V), both are part of the Traditionalist movement. I was involved with that in the early nineties, but in the Liberal Catholic tradition that you were in, and that I'm in now, I got involved with that through accident. It's a stark contrast with those individuals out there within the ISM who go out searching for somebody to make them a Bishop. Often those folks don't have a single grain of humility. I know I'm making a judgment call, but I think…

FORD: I've met them.

KLING: You've met them, so you understand. There's a difference when somebody stumbles upon the movement and when someone goes around begging for consecration. I know in organizations, for example, like the Unitarian Universalist Association that this does not happen. It's a daunting process to become ordained there, but…

FORD: And that's true of any of the mainstream churches. That's true of the Episcopal Church. That's true of the Catholic Church. Normally, there are a lot of barriers between an aspiration and ordination. I don't know how the Independent Sacramental Movement can get around the fact that someone can feel there's something right, and want to do it, and then the first time they run into a no, all they have to do is send an email to someone else and 15 minutes later, they're ordained or consecrated or whatever.

KLING: And that's a problem.

FORD: It's a significant problem. There's a proliferation of jurisdictions there are very few parishes. I don't think that's the only marker for ministry, I think chaplaincy is very authentic. I think teaching is very authentic, but in the Western tradition, the congregation is the syncronon. The church and is found in the two or three, and in formation, preparation, testing, and acclamation are all part of a long process. Does it have to be quite as long? I don't think so, but there needs to be something.

KLING: This is something that my own jurisdiction has tried to address. We've tried to create a formation program that mirrors a seminary program. Students are going to learn basic skills, like how to preach, how to do pastoral care, how to offer the sacraments, but they're also going to get a spiritual formation. Learn about Christian mysticism and Christian esotericism. They will learn about the history of the Movement and about basic Christian history and get all the touchstones that you would with a seminary education. Not a "here you go, you're a priest, now you're a Bishop." We stopped doing that because it is so problematic, and it's frustrating because you ordain someone and then they go somewhere else. They bounce around among three or four different jurisdictions within a year or two. That's not uncommon. That's not healthy. It's not healthy for them. It's not healthy for the Movement. It makes us look a silly. I've been pushing for the idea of focusing on formation. Let's focus on building community based on stability and not on collecting titles.

FORD: Right and therein lies the possibility for the Independent Sacramental Movement, but it is going against the tide or at least it appears to be from the outside.

KLING: If you look at the Movement from an outsider's point of view it seems dysfunctional, and that's a problem. It's a problem that only those who are in the Movement can fix. In the Unitarian Universalist Association, in the United Church of Christ, and the Episcopal Church USA, they all have a long and daunting process to ordination, and it can take you years. I have an Episcopal friend who was recently ordained as a deacon, and it took him seven years before the bishop finally ordained him. How is the process in the Zen community?

FORD: Well, that's a fascinating conversation. Well, to me, it's fascinating. I'm not sure how it is for many other people. There are a number of different expectations for different schools of Zen. There is the Zen in Japan, and in Korea, China, and Vietnam. All having their own indigenous expectations. Then there is the riot of lineages that have started taking root here in the West. In the West, I'm a chronicler of this. I wrote a history on Zen in North America a few years ago, and I'm interested in that side of it. When Zen started becoming something established in North America, in the late 1950s and 1960 there would be people who would start undergoing the actual training practices and I'll circle back around to that. There were people who had for whatever internal reasons needed titles and a phenomenon occurred where people would simply make it up. They would just say they had Dharma transmission, and there's this whole kind of rap that you say, "Who gave you authorization?" And the response from fakes is, "In real Zen you wouldn't ask a question like that, asking shows you don't know anything." There is a little tiny cottage industry of people who did that, who had some training or no training at all, but needed the title. As Zen continued to develop these kinds of people started to disappear. Now, if you want to be a Zen priest it's maybe twice as hard as it is to an Independent Catholic priest. Meaning not very difficult.

There is a kind of bleeding out where this kind of phenomenon is occurring, and I don't know what to say about it. I worry about it. The actual formation to become a Zen teacher or a priest, two different terms in Japanese Zen which is the areas in which I practice, are in the West the normative practice, usually takes about 10 to 15 years of serious practice with a teacher. Then to show aptitude in leading retreats, many of them. It's practice-based so, the real question is, do you do the Zazen? Usually in most cases, there's a group called the Americans Zen Teachers Association, where there's so many ways one can get credentialed. They're just trying to be a support group for people, and you need to have had a formal meditation practice of retreat practice of being on the pillow almost all day. 10 hours a day for about a year, and not in a one-year stretch, but over time, usually 10,15, or 20 years.

That's the one way of formation that is very common and the other is koan introspection. This is kind of like a curricular spiritual practice, semi-objective. I've heard of people doing it in five years, but normally the forms that are available in the West, it usually takes a serious practitioner when they get what they're doing 10, 15, 20 years. In Japan, where the spiritual practice is somewhat different since you're trying to prepare ministers for temples. The average formation period is about three years to get a credential. That's assuming you have an undergraduate or university degree.

KLING: About the same as a Master of Divinity?

FORD: It's like a Master of Divinity except that the formation is not academic. Its monastic. You live in a monastery, a very strict monastic situation for that period of time.

KLING: That's fascinating.

FORD: Yeah. And I could go on, that's the short version.

KLING: I want to give you the opportunity to share any closing words or thoughts that you would like to share to people who are in the Independent Sacramental Movement.

FORD: I have this hope for the Independent Sacramental Movement. I live a life between. I often say, I have a physiology of faith. I stole the idea from Erasmus, "He is having lunch on a Friday, and eating a sausage. Some friends come up and say, 'Erasmus you're a Catholic priest.' And he says, "Yeah my heart's Catholic, but my stomach's Lutheran.'" In my physiology of faith I say, "I have a Buddhist brain. I really believe that the core analysis of the Mahayana traditions is as close to accurate as anything human beings have ever come up with, but I have a Christian heart. I learned how to read, out of an oversize King James Bible on my grandmother's lap."

I dream of Jesus and Mary, and that gang, but I have a rationalist stomach in Unitarian Universalist circles, I'd go into a congregation and you would understand a little bit of this, but I could tell people I'm more rationalist than you are, and that was probably true. I believe we're in this great time of turmoil and experimentation. I think there's a place for Sacramental spirituality and Buddhist practice, and I really would encourage people to look at Insight Meditation, Zen meditation, look at whether there's a spiritual practice for you in that and a discipline for your own personal life. Then I'd be curious in a decade or two, what would emerge. An Independent Sacramental Movement that also conveys an authentic spiritual discipline that is profound and insightful and can open hearts. What a community could arise out of that? I would encourage people to think about it. Maybe even, look online about what Buddhist practices are available in your neighborhood.

> *"A humble man is never rash, hasty or perturbed, never has any hot and volatile thoughts, but at all times remains calm. Even if heaven were to fall and cleave to the earth, the humble man would not be dismayed. Not every quiet man is humble, but every humble man is quiet. There is no humble man who is not self-constrained; but you will find many who are self-constrained without being humble. This is also what the meek humble Lord meant when He said, 'Learn of Me, for I am meek and humble of heart, and ye shall find rest unto your souls.' [Matt 11:29] For the humble man is always at rest, because there is nothing which can agitate or shake his mind. Just as no one can frighten a mountain, so the mind of a humble man cannot be frightened."* — St. Isaac the Syrian

"Concluding Thoughts"

I think about ISM clergy such as Bishop Mikhail Itkin and Bishop Dean Bekken and their legacies and contributions to the Movement. One challenge within the Independent Sacramental Movement is keeping records and keeping history. There is not a lot of literature available on the ISM and when priests and bishops die, their stories are often lost. This is one of the hopes with the "Sacramental Whine" project, to record, maintain, and preserve the stories, thoughts, hopes, and expectations of our greater ISM community.

There are some giants within the ISM, such as Herman Adrian Spruit, the Archbishop and founder of the Catholic Apostolic Church of Antioch. I remember when I was a teenager, stationed in Washington, D.C. I stumbled upon a metaphysical bookstore and was looking around and discovered a magazine called, *"Gnosis."* This was in the late 1980s. In the back of *Gnosis Magazine* there were advertisements, classified ads, and box ads within the classified ad section. Every issue, that I can remember, always had an ad for Sophia Divinity School, the seminary of the Church of Antioch. I discovered other 'zines and publications at the metaphysical bookstore and one had photos of the ordinations within the Church of Antioch, and I remember seeing photos of Patriarch Herman and his wife, Matriarch Meri Louise Spruit, performing ordinations.

Everyone has a story, and our collective stories tell the full picture of the Independent Sacramental Movement. The ISM community is not a homogenous group that speaks with one voice; instead, we are a divided community with some branches cringing at the existence of other branches. There are the moderate Independent Catholics who look at those on the Gnostic or esoteric side and wish they didn't exist. There are the Traditionalist Catholics and Old Calendar Orthodox who insist they are not part of the ISM. The ISM is a very diverse group with many different stories to tell. I am surprised more academics have not looked to the ISM for research opportunities. There are a lot of interesting stories out there and my hope is that in the decades to come people will look back and read the words here and find some connection.

For Reflection, Contemplation, & Prayer:

- What do you think is the greatest danger within the Independent Sacramental Movement? Is it spiritual arrogance and a confusion of titles, or something else?
- What are your thoughts on syncretism and hybrid religious and spiritual practices such as an Independent Catholic and Sufi hybrid?
- What are some authentic spiritual disciplines that could be incorporated into an ISM community that would open hearts and bring about a connection to God?

"In the Same Chapter"
A Conversation with Father Jerry Maynard

"Sitting down, Jesus called the Twelve and said, 'Anyone who wants to be first must be the very last, and the servant of all.'" — Mark 9:34

In this chapter, I am joined by the Rev. Jerry Maynard as we address a question proposed by Bryan Bombardier on the Sacramental Whine Facebook group. Father Jerry and I discuss Bryan's post with additional commentary by Subdeacon Tim Olivieri, Father Stephen Gallagher, and Swami Prakashananda Saraswati.

KLING: The first thing I want to go over was a post that was made on the Sacramental Whine Facebook group by Brian Bombardier. He wrote the following,

"A thought from the cheap seats on the past few podcast episodes:

I have listened to the podcast for a while now and really appreciate the hard work. The past few episodes have created cognitive dissonance for me though.

A major message that I heard was "the ISM is not doing a good job forming priests." Point taken. The answers presented to this problem lately have a major theme. They seem to wish to model the ISM after the Roman church. Seminary education, standardized educational competency, uniform preparation, homogeny of thought, etc. Of course, I understand this isn't the only intent but it is the overwhelming impression that I received.

For a group that strives to create Vatican-free Catholicism, this seems like a very Vatican-like method. I was just thinking that forming priests as they did for the first 1500 years of the church isn't a bad idea either. Maybe focusing on bishops and their indiscretion with regard to handing out ordinations is more important than the standardization of the process. At the same time, this idea was definitely covered. It's probably a "both-and" kind of situation.

Any thoughts? Again, easy to say from the peanut gallery..."

Do you have any initial thoughts, on this post? I certainly do, but I was going to let you talk first.

MAYNARD: I think it's interesting because it does bring up an ongoing insecurity in the newsprint. I do think that we go on and on about how we're independent and free from Rome and free from the Vatican. Yet there are some of our communities in our movement who very much are not Independent. They're adjacent to Rome or the Vatican. And really their only distinguish mark between them like if you go to their, their liturgies, the only way you can identify that they're not Roman Catholic is the fact that they may have a woman on the altar who is functioning as the priest. And that's not a dig at them, that's just their way of doing things, and that's not just an ISM thing. The association of Roman Catholic Women Priests and the Roman Catholic Women Priest Movement at large is very much like that.

I think there's an interrelated insecurity in both movements, and that insecurity is the fact that the people who gravitate towards both of our movements tend to gravitate towards us because they have a shared sensitivity to the overall theme or mission of our movements and want to participate in some way. Oftentimes, I think people in ecclesiastical movements tend to think that the best way to participate is to be ordained, which is a question or an issue that has to be addressed as well. I think the overarching thing is in the Roman Catholic Women Priests Movement, a lot of the women who go to that movement are older. They're older, they're retired, they've lived lives and they've just never been able to live this way in life because it's not allowed in the Roman church. They go to this group and the majority of people who are ordained in their movement are older retirees, and that's because they have the money to afford to do the Education. If they lose their jobs, they don't have to worry about it because they're not working anyway. They've already lived a life socially to the point where they don't have to worry about being ostracized, or having to constantly defend themselves, although that is certainly present in some contexts. Whereas in our movement, I think a lot of people come to us because they have the capacity to be educated. They may want to be educated and they may even want a traditional seminary education with degrees, even if they can't get accredited degrees, because it comes out of a place of feeling like I'm not authentic. It's an imposter syndrome manifestation. I think part of the reason why some jurisdictions overly focus on trying to mimic Rome or to mimic Utrecht, the Old Catholic Union of Utrecht, is that it comes from a place of insecurity, of feeling subconsciously, like we're frauds. If we get called out as a fraud we can say, "Oh no, we did everything the same way that you do. Just not with your permission."

KLING: So, it's like a compensating for imposter syndrome?

MAYNARD: Yeah. I think that's really the overarching thing that's happening and part of how we remedy that, and we kind of massage it out of tension, is we need to learn, to give ourselves some grace and know that God doesn't despise us. God delights when we do the work of justice, including practicing justice in our life. When it comes to living out the vocation that we know we're called to, even though institutions might disagree. I think also, it's a maturity thing. It's one of those things that doesn't really go away until you keep persisting in it until you've been in the movement for a long time. I know we've talked about how this comes up occasionally, for you and for me. It's one of those things that just the older you get and the more wisdom you gain in life, the less it becomes a monkey on your back. I don't really think it's a solution that can be solved or it's a problem that can be remedied with an infrastructural change. I think it's a problem that is remedied by spiritual growth and development and companionship.

KLING: I think you raise a good point. We talk about spiritual growth. One of the things that the author of this post Brian mentioned was why mirror the current state of Rome, mandating a seminary education, standardized educational competencies, et cetera. Why not use an older model? One of the first thoughts that came to mind was my time at the Benedictine monastery in which I was a novice. The community was part of the Traditionalist Movement and as such had a huge disdain or suspicion for secular education. The thought was, "you leave here, you go to college, you'll lose your faith." Ironically, it was in college that I left the Roman Catholic Church, but the thing is they did not do education just because they looked down upon a college education. They still had formation. We met every week in a classroom setting we called it *tyrocinium.* It was the school to learn how to be a monk and we would talk and reflect upon just what it was to be a monk. Oftentimes, it was Father Leonard lecturing us on how bad we were and how our minds wandered, how we talked too much. I'll give you an example. We were able to watch a movie maybe once a week if that. Usually more like once a month and it really had to be a mild sort of movie. I allowed the movie "The Princess Bride" into the monastery and the Father Leonard had a chance to view some of it and said, "Stop! This is banned. Never again, will you watch this. The only movie you can watch is 'The Sound of Music,'" and from that point on the only movie we could watch was "The Sound of Music."

My point is that part of our training was how to be a monk. The other part of the training was in theology, and mostly sacramental theology. We had to write papers and we wrote them by hand with paper and pencil. We didn't have computers or typewriters. We wrote papers and we presented those papers. Then we had to go into a bubble, so to speak, and be critiqued by our peers. Then we could defend what we wrote after everyone had their say. That was how we learned, and it was phenomenal. My education in sacramental theology comes right out of traditional Benedictine monasticism and traditional Catholicism. That was probably more along the model that Brian is advocating for when he says, what about the first 1500 years?

The problem with that is for example, in The Community of St George, where I'm with, we have people in our formation program, in Chicago, in New York and Texas and we're not living together in community. We're scattered around the United States. We talk on the phone, usually at least once a month, sometimes more, but we meet face to face once a year. We don't have that day-to-day community in which to form or educate our would-be clergy. We can't work in that first 1500-year model that the church enjoyed. We just can't. We're operating in a very different paradigm, but we must be able to educate our clergy. Am I advocating for a seminary education? The word seminary comes from the Latin word, semen, which means seed. We're working from a type of education that plants the seed of one's vocation and builds upon that. In one sense, yes, I am advocating for a seminary education. In the sense of, "You need to have a bachelor's degree before you can get this graduate degree." No, I don't advocate for that.

I don't advocate for anybody having to go to college and then seminary and get so much student loan debt they'll be crippled for life. I don't advocate for that at all. What I do advocate for is for jurisdictions to have a sufficient program, to educate clergy and I've said it before, I'll say it again, "You can't teach what you don't know." Just because you're a Bishop doesn't mean you know anything. It just means someone laid hands on you but doesn't mean you're qualified to lead a formation program. I know plenty of bishops who aren't qualified to say mass, let alone, lead anybody in formation.

Standardized educational competency? I would say I do advocate for that. I also advocate for individuality and people finding themselves in figuring out what they feel called to do. Some people are called to be parish priests, some people are called to be chaplains, some people are called to be educators. Standardized educational competency means you're not necessarily an expert at pastoral care. It just means if you go into a room with somebody actively dying and family is present that you're not going to embarrass yourself, you're not going to embarrass the jurisdiction that you're with, and that you're going to provide sufficient pastoral care to these people that is going to help them.

MAYNARD: Yeah, and I think people forget that religion is about 90%, maybe even 95%, culture. It's how we behave with each other. Formation, especially in a religious community, is more about forming you and having the consciousness, or the mindset, or the hermeneutics, of the community that you're with, because there's a way of being in that group, there's a way of being a Zen Buddhist monk. There's a way of being a Benedictine monk. There's a consciousness to it. There's a way of being a Dominican, and when somebody asks you why you chose the Dominicans versus the Benedictines you should be able to vocalize and show through your life, the difference between the two groups and why you felt called to one or the other.

Formation must not just talk about the head, the left brain, and the right brain, it must also focus on integrating your awareness, and your lifestyle. Part of the reason [religious] orders developed particular ministries is because those ministries developed out of their mission. For instance, when the Dominicans were first started, they were itinerary preachers. When Dominic founded the order, he made it a very clear point that he wanted his brothers to be well informed about scripture, theology, and philosophy, because at the time, there were so many heresies. Dominic lived at a time when many priests were so ill-informed and so unknowledgeable, they were not allowed to preach. Most people don't know that for a long time the only person that could preach in the context of the Eucharist was the Bishop, and the Bishop wasn't always present at every parish to preach.

Therefore, the liturgy of the word, for a long time in the Western Church, was often just reading a scripture and there was never any humble edifying exchange done, except if the Bishop was present. Priests were not properly trained to do that. When Dominic founded the order, he made a point to be sure that his brothers were trained to be preachers. That's why they're called the Order of Preachers, to combat heresies and false ideas. Ultimately, out of that mission and out of the importance of planting that seed, they, the Dominicans could on as their real, most solid vocation, which they still do to this day, is being educators, primarily university educators. The first universities in Europe were almost exclusively run by Dominicans. Sadly, some of the Dominicans did other terrible things, such as the inquisition, but that's another story.

My point being is that formation must include the cultural element. You must understand why we pray this way, why we dressed this way, why we eat in silence while somebody is reading scripture to us or reading from the rule of the order. Know why as Franciscans we sleep on the floor, while Benedictines don't. There's a reason to all of this, and all of it testifies to the overarching reality that we are trying to live the Incarnation, which is about helping people to realize that Christ, the anointed one, came down into time and space and simplified our experience. Everything that we do should reflect that anointing. I don't necessarily think, as I would assume you would agree, that getting a degree, no matter how good it is, no matter if it's accredited or not, indicates to me that you have done that or that you're doing that. It just indicates that you went that route, and you spent a lot of time in an area, and you've got something to show for that time. It's more a marker than an indicator of how much, you know.

KLING: One of the things that Brian also mentioned was, "uniform preparation, homogeny of thought, et cetera." I want to comment on that. I don't agree with the uniform preparation. I'll give you an example, I'm a presiding Bishop in the community of St. George, a jurisdiction of the Young Rite, which is a part of the Liberal Catholic Church tradition. I'm also an associate Bishop in the Convergent Christian Communion, which is a jurisdiction very different from the community of St. George. The Convergent Christian Communion has an Evangelical side, a Charismatic side, and a Sacramental side, and of course, it's the Sacramental side that's my primary connection with them. They also have an evangelical and charismatic element. There are some folks that are a part of the Convergent Christian Communion that have approached me to help them with their formation. I'm not going to put them through the same program that I would put somebody in the community of St George, different ministry context. Each context requires a different formation plan.

Even though it's the same person doing the mentorship, I'm going to do the mentorship in a differently for each context. There are some elements that I would want them to know that are different than I would want people to know in the community of St. George. There isn't necessarily uniformity of thought. Each jurisdiction has their own peculiarities. If let's say a jurisdiction has an identity of being Celtic, and there are several out there, then Celtic spirituality should be a part of their formation. Because that is a big part of who they are as a church. Just as a jurisdiction that talks about being charismatic should teach about the origins of Pentecostalism, for example, as opposed to teaching the history of the Liberal Catholic Church movement.

Uniform preparation when it comes to areas like homiletics, pastoral care, those sorts of things, then uniformity is not necessarily a bad thing. Sacramental theology should be uniform. If you don't have proper matter, you don't have proper form or proper intention, then that could cause a problem, because if somebody says, "Oh, I'm part of the Independent Sacramental Movement, but I had my ordination through Zoom or Skype." I would respond, "Yeah, I'm not going to count you as being a part of this movement." Some uniformity is good, but there is also plenty of opportunity for individualization per jurisdiction, like what you were talking about with the Dominicans.

Another thing I want to address is homogeneity of thought. Within the Community of Saint George, we have a formation program and, in that program, you're going to read certain books. You can disagree with the books and the authors that you read, and that you write about. It's not like, "read Bishop Leadbeater and accept his writings as gospel." No, you can disagree with him and that's fine if you disagree, say why and peel back the layers. If I had somebody that said, "I don't believe in the doctrine of the Trinity," that's not necessarily a deal breaker for me per se, but you got to at least study the doctrine, be able to explain it, and if you can explain it, but then tell me why you disagree, then I'll listen. Homogeneity of thought in some areas, yes. When it comes to sacraments, that's important to me, but in other areas, somebody can have a high Christology, somebody can have a low Christology and still, potentially find a home in my jurisdiction.

MAYNARD: I think there's also this whole issue of semantics. I think we oftentimes are talking over each other or talking through each other and we don't realize it because we're so committed to our narratives that we cannot read between the lines and "do it midrash" as Jewish folks like to say, and really understand deeply. Thích Nhất Hạnh talks about if you truly want to live, you must look deeply within. It doesn't just mean with your life, but with everything. I think we must have enough self-awareness to know that maybe we're saying the same thing or similar. I like to say, and I say it all the time, "We don't need to be on the same page, but we should at least be somewhere in the same chapter."

You might be a faster reader than I am, or you may be slower than I am, but if we're in the same book and then in the same chapter, I think we can be okay. There are just different life experiences that we have in this movement and that informs our understanding of the Divine. That's something that shouldn't be educated out of us. We must be, and I know this bothers some ISM people, but I'm a believer that we must accept the reality; otherwise, our theology is not only immature, but I also think it's disingenuous. We must be mature enough to say that things are happening, and things are being said that are coming from God and we need to listen. As the UCC likes to say, "God is still speaking." I think we must be mature enough to address that and include that in our formation.

Also, if somebody comes to you and they're 40, 50, 60 years old, and you're arguing with them back and forth about something that you have to just be like, "they're not going to get it and that's okay," because they've already lived life and they're not gonna want to change that much. There must be some of that too. Yeah. I don't know. I think it's a personality thing, probably more than an education thing. I've seen many programs in different ISM jurisdictions, and one of the common realities I think among them is they all have tidbits in each one of their formation programs that's geared to what they believe in the world. The Ascension Alliance covers a wide range of topics in their formation program because they're open to a wide range of topics and practices and that's okay. That's a part of who they are, and they need to have a formation program like that because that's their consciousness. That's the way that they want to show up in the world, and that's fine.

If you're a part of a jurisdiction or want to start a jurisdiction that is more traditional then great, have a traditional Roman formation program. Fine, I personally would question whether that's useful to the body of Christ, but that's a whole different topic that I think needs to be addressed at some point. If that's a part of your mission, great, because not everybody that goes into your program is going to know the same thing. Not everybody that gets through the program is going to agree on the same things. One of the things that I always point out is that we don't need to know the same things. We don't need to agree on the same things, but there should be assumptions that we take into scenarios or situations that we should be able to agree upon in some way, shape or form. For instance, when we talk about the sacraments, I can tell when somebody does not come from a sacramental background, like I do. When they make assumptions about the Eucharist that a born and raised Roman Catholic or Orthodox person would never think about doing, that's not because they have a bad formation or whatever they just weren't brought up in that understanding that you would never assume to celebrate mass, I don't know, in the ocean.

KLING: I think it is a matter of formation. I really do and let me give you an example. When I incardinated with the Young Rite, this was before the community of St. George was formed in the United States. When I came on as a Bishop in the Young Rite there were several priests who were already present. They had been ordained by Bishop Marcus van Alphen and some of them went, elsewhere. The ones that stayed, including one that I ordained according to the Young Rite's laissez faire approach to formation, eventually said to me, "I no longer wanted to be classified as a celebrant because I don't feel like I know what I am doing." Imposter syndrome essentially engulfed them and took over, and it's not about going with a model, a Vatican-free model, or moving away from a Vatican like approach it's about giving people the proper tools to be able to function effectively as a priest, in an environment where they may be encountering clergy of other denominations and feel like they are just as good as everybody else. It's like, being in a surgical room and you have two surgeons, one was trained at Harvard and the other one was trained in the lowest possible tiered medical school. Both feeling like they can do this surgery and not feel any doubts about it. You don't want your surgeon to be like, "I'm not sure I can do this, but I'm going to really try." A lot of ISM clergy are like that. If they are put into a situation that requires them to do ministry, many of them are like, "Ah, I'm not sure." They don't know how to function, and we need to be able to prepare them to function. Otherwise, we do a disservice to them when we lay hands on them.

MAYNARD: Yeah, and I think that's also a question of confidence and it goes back to my original thought about spiritual growth. That's why I'm a believer that part of formation should be spiritual direction or spiritual companionship. I think anybody that's ordained should at least for one year have a "big brother or big sister" that has been in ministry for a good amount of time.

KLING: I still go to a spiritual director and meet her every month. Spiritual direction is important if you're doing ministry.

MAYNARD: Yeah, absolutely, and preferably somebody that's not in your jurisdiction or maybe not even within your… Maybe somebody who's older than you. If you're a man, maybe a woman or vice versa, or if you're transgender another trans person, that way there's not a reflection.

KLING: Mine is a few years older. She's a woman. She was a United Methodist elder, but she's retired, even though she's in her 50s. She's retired from ministry and now she is a family therapist. I think everybody in ministry should have a spiritual director because the benefits are just wonderful. Just having someone to talk to about your spiritual life is helpful, and it goes back to ongoing formation, something I wanted to discuss. I want to address one of the concerns that Brian had. I have talked about "train-wrecks," and we discussed a lot about formation. I want to be clear as to what I was referring to as a train wreck.

A disclaimer, I think it's fine that people have a history, or a spiritual journey, that is all over the place, my journey has certainly been a long and winding path; however, my point is that you can't really go from, let's say one day and literally on June 1st, you consider yourself a Wiccan High Priest, and then by, let's say June 10th, you're an ISM Bishop with no formation or training, and suddenly you think you have all the answers to Sacramental Christianity, that you should have all the teaching authority of a well-trained and formed bishop. Especially, when you've only read a few articles on Wikipedia.

MAYNARD: Yeah.

KLING: That's what I'm talking about. That is a train wreck.

MAYNARD: Absolutely.

KLING: That is a problem. I know plenty. I know people who are very spiritually fluid that practice, for example, Zen Buddhism, and they're also a Christian or they practice various forms of Paganism and they're also a Christian. I know people who are culturally Jewish and still observe some of the High Holy days but are also Pagan. That's fine. I'm not saying that's wrong. What I am saying is you can't add an ordination or consecration in the Independent Sacramental Movement like you would if you were a Freemason and you decide to join the Elks or Odd Fellows or decide to join another order and add it to your collection of fraternal order memberships. Just because you're a Bishop doesn't mean you automatically have authority. You have the sacramental authority by the right of your consecration, but there's something else to consider. People respect action, people respect wisdom, and people respect knowledge. Just because you're a Bishop, you have a title, and you wear a cassock that's purple doesn't entitle you to my respect. It just doesn't.

MAYNARD: I agree with you, and I think that that's a train wreck and I certainly do not by any stretch of the imagination discount spiritual fluidity. I do practice inter-spirituality in my prayer life. I practice Zen Buddhism. I also have a deep relationship with Starhawk and the Reclaiming Movement. If I try to throw a stone at that glass house, that would be hypocritical.

KLING: It would be very disingenuous.

MAYNARD: Yeah. Yeah, exactly.

KLING: And the same is true for me, but it would be like me saying, "I'm a Bishop in the Community of St. George. I'm now going to start practicing Zen and start calling myself a Zen priest." If you want to also be a Zen priest, you need to go through Zen priest training.

MAYNARD: Then people would really come down hard on you because to become a Zen priest is extremely intense. I mean, becoming a Catholic priest is nothing compared to their formation program, but that's part of the reason why they don't have many Zen priests. It's hard to go through the program.

KLING: It should be hard to become a Bishop in the Independent Sacramental Movement. It should be, but it's not and that is frustrating.

MAYNARD: Well, and we get crazy characters. I'm not going to name anybody, but we get lots of the characters out there. Ultimately, I think it goes back to what fosters the most genuine manifestation of the vocation that God has planted within all of us, and is it bearing fruit in the world around us that is deeply in need of the grace and healing power of God? If it is not, if all it's doing is increasing the number of vestments that you have in your closet and how many fancy pieces of paper that you'll hang on your wall, I think it's not only disingenuous but it's immoral and I think it is deeply harmful to the body of Christ. I do think that Brian brings up some good points though I think maybe he should get a little bit more out of the peanut gallery and get more involved and bring some of those questions into the circle because I think they're good questions to have. It also brings up what people see when they see us, and I think that's important to remember, especially as we build our movement.

KLING: Exactly. He says, "...maybe focusing on bishops in their indiscretion with regard to handing out ordinations is more important than the standardization of the process..." That sentence seems problematic to me because bishops seem to be too eager to ordain. That's a problem, and I've been guilty of that. I can confess that and beg for forgiveness. That certainly is a problem, but is that more important than the standardization of the process? I'm not sure I understand what he means by standardization of the process, but I'm going to go back to you must have a good solid formation. You must be able to provide some basic ministry skills. You don't have to go overboard. For example, if I walked into a church today and someone said, "The pastor isn't able to preach for whatever reason. Can you preach in his or her place?" I should be able to respond with, "Yes, I can do that," and with no notice. "Just give me a Bible, give me 5 minutes and I can get up there for 10, 15 minutes, 20 minutes, maybe more and preach." It's not going to sound horrible. It may not win any awards, but I'm not going to embarrass you either, nor am and I going to embarrass myself. I can do that because I've taken a few homiletics courses, and in seminary I served a Unitarian Universalist fellowship, and I did a lot of preaching.

Being able to do those basic ministry skills, that's important to being a priest or deacon. There have been priests in my own jurisdiction that I inherited when I incardinated as a Bishop that when we got together face to face, I assumed that they would be saying mass and they didn't, because they didn't know how. That's a problem with the Bishop who ordained them, but that was a problem that I inherited. The challenge is when a Bishop has priests under his or her charge who don't know how to say mass and they live two States away, that should never be an issue, but it is an issue, and it is challenging.

MAYNARD: I think that when it comes down to it, I think the responsibility falls with the bishops. I think it's important for us to remember that when you identify yourself as a priest in the United States, there is a lot of baggage that comes with that term. There are also a lot of expectations that come with that term. You must be able to have the spiritual maturity and the confidence and the ego to be able to step up and address those expectations and that baggage and be willing to carry it as much as possible. When you tell somebody you're a priest, almost instantly, they may come to you and start telling you everything that happened to them that day. Or they might say, "Oh, my mother is dying of cancer. Can you pray for her?" That will happen almost instantly, and you must have the backbone to be able to keep your feet flat on the ground and minister almost at an instant, because that's what happens when you designate yourself as a priest or as a minister of any kind. Part of that is having confidence and knowing that you know what you know but also knowing that there are places that you don't know, but that you're willing to learn. Often that last part is what I have found most people in the ISM do not have, which is they are not willing to learn.

> *"Many poets are not poets for the same reason that many religious men are not saints: they never succeed in being themselves. They never get around to being the particular poet or the particular monk they are intended to be by God. They never become the man or the artist who is called for by all the circumstances of their individual lives.*
>
> *They waste their years in vain efforts to be some other poet, some other saint. For many absurd reasons, they are convinced that they are obliged to become somebody else who died two hundred years ago and who lived in circumstances utterly alien to their own."* — Thomas Merton, *New Seeds of Contemplation*

"Concluding Thoughts"

I appreciate Father Jerry's commitment to "Sacramental Whine." On the Sacramental Whine: An Independent Sacramental Movement Group, our Facebook group, there were two responses to Bryan that I thought were worth sharing, the first is by Subdeacon Tim Olivieri:

"So, let me jump on in here since when I was a guest on the podcast some months ago, we talked about formation AND I was in formation in the Roman Catholic Church.

The RC Church requires 2 years of pre-theology (philosophy) training with prescribed coursework. Off the top of my head, the coursework required was intro to phil, ethics, logic, philosophy of religion, cosmology, epistemology, ancient, modern, medieval, two semesters of Latin and one semester of Greek.

That was so you could get into a theology program which, in the U.S. typically results in an M.Div.

I was educated as a seminarian by Jesuits. The priests who oversaw my education were educated by Fathers of the Congregation of the Holy Cross when they were in seminary (my order did not have its own university, so we outsourced). Those in my order who completed their theology years in Rome did pre-theology and theology under the Dominicans.

There is a lot I take issue within the Roman Church. But there is also a lot that they do well and that other denominations also do similarly. A few of those things are standardized educational competency which is a hallmark of a seminary education.

There is nothing wrong with educational standards. Even in the RC Church, there can be deviations from the norm. Far too often, however, in the ISM we conflate the words "formation" and "education." Education can absolutely be a component in formation. The two things are separate, however. There are denominations that rely on education solely. Earn an M.Div. and get ordained. There are some apostolic traditions where the formation is almost entirely on the job training. My grandfather studied to be a Greek Orthodox deacon locally with his priest, completed no formal coursework and received training largely in liturgy with very little theological prep.

The point is that priests need to be formed. That formation can be adjusted and adapted. Within the ISM, however, it is not at all uncommon to find priests who received ZERO preparation. They cannot celebrate Mass. They don't understand sacramental theology. These basic elements are ignored by some jurisdictions.

Far too often we treat it as an either or. Either we subscribe to a highly regimented, expensive educational program or we do absolutely nothing to prepare a person to receive Holy Orders. There is plenty in the middle."

Father Stephen Gallagher responded to Subdeacon Tim and wrote,

"I concur with your conclusions. I also received a Roman seminary education in the diocesan system. I wasn't ordained in the Roman church and so I didn't complete the M.DIV but I completed 3 years total including 2 years of theology and I completed the philosophy coursework prior to theology. Standardized forms of education are important for those who want to get into accredited ministries. I'm talking about chaplaincy programs in the VA, hospital or Federal prison. If one just wants to do it yourself like an unofficial chaplaincy where someone shows up at a nursing home or does a house church which are common things in the ISM don't require accreditation. Education is only one piece in formation. Pastoral formation involves actually working with people in a pastoral setting. What I see happening is an ordination or consecration pic shows up, but we have no idea of the person's background. We see that a person has collected vestments but that's all we can tell from a pic. That's why a caption or short Bio is good."

Addressing the comments of Father Stephen, I think you can do fine ministry without an accredited education. I'm not advocating that clergy within the ISM go out and get massive amounts of student loan debt to get a formal education. If you want to be a professional chaplain, yes, you will need it. But if you want to do a volunteer prison ministry or visit residents in a nursing home then a solid formation system within your jurisdiction is enough. Just because someone is in a nursing home does not mean they shouldn't have someone sufficiently trained and formed providing them ministry. They, the residents, are important too.

Another member of the group, Swami Prakashananda Saraswati, posted the following:

"Well, a few observations. The comments on training are very revealing. Whilst a basic education in theology etc. is undeniably important, the emphasis on a college education is not necessary. That is a western and recent development. It is easy enough to get

caught up in the glamour of intellectual achievement. But that is not what the priesthood is about. Education and pastoral formation have traditionally been covered in the past as part of "reading for orders," which should necessarily include the formation of personal spirituality.

I'm so surprised that this has not been mentioned. I would not consider anyone as a candidate for Holy Orders unless they already had a sustained and deep personal spiritual practice and were able to hold and sustain the fire of the Holy Spirit and the additional intensity of Apostolic Succession. We do our candidates no service by ordaining them into something they neither understand nor can handle.

This, alas, is the root of some of the sexual issues and mental disturbances arising amongst clergy. And that's not just the ISM but also mainstream denominations who seem to have dismissed their lack of direct knowledge by explain ignorance with "oh, it's a Divine Mystery." Offering spiritual development and practice as part of formation is not an option, it's a responsibility.

Candidates for Holy Orders should likewise be looking closely at their prospective Bishop's own depth of understanding and practice."

The "reading for orders" model is essentially a mentorship model which is exactly what we, in the Community of Saint George, offer to people interested in our formation program which to go back to Bryan's initial post really harkens back to earlier formation models instead of a formal seminary program; however, "reading for orders" should not mean, "read these books," and poof you are good to go. Swami Prakashananda seems to favor an Eastern pattern of learning. My understanding is that the Western model is more intellectual and the Eastern model (that is, Eastern Orthodox) is more mystical. Eastern in the sense of Asian or Hindu and Buddhist models seem to favor praxis or actively doing something such as meditation or yoga instead of or in addition to academic study. I advocate for all three in a good formation plan. Some intellectual study (such as discussions on sacramental theology), some mysticism (such as discursive meditation, recitation of the Jesus prayer and Rosary), and practice (such as the liturgical or divine office).

Formation is something that I talk about often. It is an important issue within the ISM because it is often neglected. When I was in seminary there are two professors that stick out on this topic. The first was the late Dr. Kendall McCabe who said, "Seminary is the place where you wrestle. If you're not wrestling here, you don't belong here. It is the place where you know if you have a calling or not." Such a great quote. Formation is where you work on your "stuff." It is where you struggle with the things that will get in the way of doing good ministry. Clinical Pastoral Education, for example, changed my life. For the better. This is the point of formation. When I was a philosophy major in college, we used to joke that education, specifically as philosophy majors, brought about an ontological transformation. But it is true, education and formation, if done right, brings about a change in who you are and how you function. It, if done right, will change you forever and give you the tools to be a successful minister of the Gospel, a sacrificing priest at the altar, and a compassionate listener.

The second professor that I thought about when looking at this topic of formation is Dr. Linda Mercadante, and she used to tell us in class that "bad theology kills." And I have seen the effect of bad theology. When I was in my chaplain residency at St. Mary's Medical Center in Huntington, West Virginia I was visiting a patient who I had seen several times over a series of months. When I finally met his wife, it was after the doctor had told them the patient had two weeks left to live. I asked the question, "What are you going to do with these two weeks?" The wife immediately responded, "We are going to pray for a miracle." The patient's face suddenly changed, a defeated look. As I was leaving the visit, I was washing my hands and overheard their local pastor, who I discovered had never went to seminary, respond when he was told the patient had two weeks to live with, "Have faith, we will pray for a miracle and cure this cancer." Bad theology kills. A miracle never happened. The patient died and his last couple of weeks was filled with prayers for a miracle that never happened and a wife who was dismayed because she must not have had enough faith.

We don't exist in a vacuum. We encounter other people, who we must serve. Clergy within any faith tradition have an obligation to be sufficiently formed and prepared for ministry. Being a bishop means more than just putting on a miter. Being a priest means more than standing at an altar trying to figure out rubrics. We must take our formation and education serious, as a community and say NO to those who relegation formation to the realm of optional. It is not optional; it is necessary and beneficial to the community.

For Reflection, Contemplation, & Prayer:

- What are your thoughts on spiritual fluidity? The idea of people being a Christian and something else? Such as being a Christian who also practices Zen meditation or engages in Wiccan ritual.
- Why do you think some people within the ISM are unwilling to learn? Why are some unwilling to "do the work" of formation programs and prefer to "shop around" until they find a jurisdiction that will ordain them without much actual work?
- If the phrase, "bad theology kills," is true, what do you think are some examples of "bad theology?"

"Seeking Integration"
A Conversation with Dr. J. Richard Paszkiewicz

"People were also bringing babies to Jesus for him to place his hands on them. When the disciples saw this, they rebuked them. But Jesus called the children to him and said, "Let the little children come to me, and do not hinder them, for the kingdom of God belongs to such as these. Truly I tell you, anyone who will not receive the kingdom of God like a little child will never enter it.'" — Luke 18:15-17

Dr. J. Richard Paszkiewicz (in ecclesia The Most Venerable Sunyananda Dharmacarya) is a priest, psychotherapist, martial artist, healer, chef, writer, and academic. In addition to being ordained in the Independent Sacramental Movement, Dr. Paszkiewicz is a fully authorized Buddhist teacher, who has been given teaching authority in the Japanese, Korean, and Vietnamese Zen schools. He has studied and taught Buddhism throughout the world, lectured at numerous colleges and universities, and has appeared in and written for various media outlets, in addition to serving as an official delegate to numerous notable Buddhist events, including the first White House Buddhist Leader's Conference, and the United Nation's World Day of Vesak. Dr. Paszkiewicz is a registered yoga teacher with the Yoga Alliance and has trained in the Bhakti Yoga tradition in West Bengal, India where he lived as a Brahmacari and personal assistant to a preeminent guru. Academically, Dr. Paszkiewicz has earned a host of degrees, and completed a clinical residency in pastoral counseling at the University of Kansas Hospital, and has subsequently earned dual board certification both as a Pastoral Counselor and as a Clinical Chaplain. Currently, in private practice as a counselor, consultant, and coach, Dr. Paszkiewicz has served as a chaplain in a variety of settings, from health care facilities to law enforcement agencies. He is the founding Convener of the Kaw River Valley Chapter of the College of Pastoral Supervision and Psychotherapy, where he also serves on the national Certification and Ethics committees.

KLING: My first question is what is your elevator speech? How would you describe the Independent Sacramental Movement to someone who has no idea what it is?

PASZKIEWICZ: I love that question. In retrospect, I think I've had a few answers to that over the years, at one point I was a little bit more interested in the mainline identity. I would say, "Well, we're like Episcopalians but different," and that usually would sum it up for people but these days I would probably say something like, "We're a collection of diverse individuals that value, as a mystery, the celebration of the sacraments that are traditionally Catholic."

KLING: I like that you mentioned the Episcopalians because when I'm with colleagues, I work in hospice as a chaplain when I'm around chaplain colleagues, and if they ask me, I will respond that I'm like the Episcopalians, just a little bit different and that's usually good enough.

I'm intrigued by your spiritual journey. Your spirituality seems very fluid, combining several spiritual elements. Can you describe how you weave together, Buddhism, Christianity and all the elements of your spiritual path? I'm especially interested in your story within the Independent Sacramental Movement.

PASZKIEWICZ: I sometimes say that I'm something of a one man walking interfaith show and not necessarily by choice. I was born into a Roman Catholic family and baptized in Germany, where my parents were stationed in the military. Coming back to the States, we had a very Catholic family. My dad went up 10 and my grandmother had rosaries on every bedpost and a crucifix in every corner. My parent's marriage didn't last forever, and after they got divorced, neither one of them thought to reconcile with the Roman Church. So, we floated around as Christmas and Easter Catholics with my father, but we'd always sit in the back. We wouldn't participate in communion and that was sort of that for a couple of years. At some point, my great-grandmother who was the matriarch of the maternal side of my family passed away, and my mother grieved that deeply. She responded affirmatively to a knock on the door from the Jehovah's witnesses one day.

So, from the time it was in fourth grade until I graduated high school, I was raised in the Watchtower Bible and Tract Society. Attending five hours a week of meetings and three or four conventions a year with the Jehovah's Witnesses, and my father responded to that interestingly. He was, for all I knew up to that point, Agnostic, but I remember him distinctly saying, "That cannot be the only exposure you have to Christianity." His answer to that was to join a very socially progressive United Church of Christ congregation. Every other weekend I grew up going there and I remember being a 12-year-old with big questions being in dialogue with these two traditions every week. I started making meetings with our UCC pastor as a 12-year-old.

KLING: Wow.

PASZKIEWICZ: Those pastoral meetings were an important thing for me. I learned some great things from the Jehovah's Witnesses and their theocratic ministry training that all literate young men must go through. I learned some good pastoral ministry skills and good expository preaching skills. I still reference some of that today. It was solid formation in a way, but I wasn't exposed to mainline thinking until I started having these meetings with the UCC minister. I remember her referring to me, 12-year-old me, to John Shelby Spong's "Why Christianity Must Change or Die: A Bishop Speaks to Believers In Exile." That was huge. That spoke to so many of the questions that I was having. My father, at that point, had come out of the closet as a gay man and we struggled with that conversation between traditions and congregations, and I had big questions around issues like that too.

Long story short, by the time I was 18, I was kind of fed up with Christianity. I had gotten tired of this conversation that was always competing. These alternative views of how one should live their lives and the eschatology of it all. I just stepped away. I'd been involved with martial arts since I was about five years old and, the appendant Asian philosophy intrinsic to all that and I decided that I was going to go explore East Asian religion and wound-up kind of couch surfing if you will, between Buddhist monasteries across North America. I eventually found myself living in West Bengal, India, studying Bhakti Yoga at the feet of a guru as a *brahmachari*, as a novice monk.

Eventually, I just realized that I needed more and more integration, but I started finding as I was traveling Asia that I was homesick. Not just linguistically or culturally, but the container of food and the comforts of daily American living. I started having this interesting longing for the symbols of the sacred of my youth, those earliest experiences of the smells and bells of the Catholic liturgical tradition. As luck would have it, I came back to the States. I settled back into my normal routine, but still stewarding this longing. One of the meditation groups I was leading was at a Unity Church that also hosted several other religious groups including an Independent Sacramental congregation.

I saw the board change one day and then what is this Independent Catholic thing happening downstairs on Sunday morning? I stumbled in with my Buddhist vestments on my daily habit of a Buddhist monk and attended mass and was welcomed with open arms. That was my introduction, my accidental introduction to the Independent Sacramental Movement, and that welcome really inspired to me a vision of, "hey, maybe I can pursue this, this Christian spiritual longing in an integrative way." I can be exactly who I am with these people. I don't even need to change my dress and I can explore this location that popped up out of nowhere. So that's how I organically ended up with these different influences.

And I'm not going to pretend to say that it's all neat, but I can hear voices like Paul Tillich, speaking towards matters of ultimate concern, voices like Mircea Eliade speaking of the importance and the centrality of the sacred and the pursuit of religion. Those are the themes that I've pursued in my ongoing cultivation of integration in my spiritual path. Ways to explore the sacred that transcend time, space, culture, language, and symbol. I find myself deeply informed by my early experiences, by my culture as a Western person but also deeply informed by the mysticism of Eastern religion that I find deeply lacking in mainline Christianity. That's the big integration point for me. That was a lot.

KLING: That's fascinating.

PASZKIEWICZ: I think you asked about the Independent Sacramental formation specifically, is that where you were going?

KLING: Yeah. I hear how you stumbled upon the Independent Sacramental Movement and I know you're a priest. How did that manifest?

PASZKIEWICZ: Sure, so that initial engagement, which lasted, around four years before I was ordained was very interesting. Like I said, being able to just be who I am, this Buddhist monk showing up and attending mass and being offered the sacraments was fascinating to me. I started researching more, the bishops that led the congregation that I was attending had come from the Catholic Apostolic Church of Antioch. They pointed me to some of the writings of the Spruits and other folks in that movement. I eventually started reading some of the other literature like John Plumber's book and reading everything on the web and realized that there were other groups. There's one called the White Robed

Monks of Saint Benedict, a jurisdiction that practices Buddhist meditation, and there are others.

I didn't quite know how to fit it all together, but my bishop locally had a formation program that they began putting me through. That lasted about four years and it just kind of continually asked these questions about why are you doing this? Where do you find value in this? The big vocational questions wrapped up in small assignments and I eventually participated more and more in the daily life of the church. Eventually, the point came where it was offered that I could be ordained a priest and that made a lot of sense for me. I was trying to find a point of expression in my vocation that would allow me to live in a culturally recognizable way. I'd been confused for a Muslim on the street with the habit of my Buddhist tradition and that wasn't always helpful at social justice events. It wasn't a problem being recognized as a Muslim, but that wasn't my identity.

How could I find a public expression of my vocation that made sense within my own cultural and linguistic container? That was the big impetus. I explored that and finally submitted to it and said, "Yeah, this is something that I'm called to. I don't know exactly how it'll work, but I'll go through it." I had gained contact with another Independent Bishop in New York who was supportive on this path and came to Kansas City and his jurisdiction supported my ordination. One of the funniest parts of it that I joke about that embodies the quirkiness of the Independent Sacramental Movement, or the quirkier side of it, is that they thought that maybe just being a priest was not good enough for someone of my background. So why not just consecrate me as a Bishop the day after my priesthood? I politely declined. I'm very happy being a priest and just doing that work. Only in the ISM, can we say, "just being a priest."

All three of the bishops participated in my ordination, which was supported by many of my local colleagues who attended, and we had it in a beautiful little chapel. I went from there and co-pastor the community that had formed me for another three years.

KLING: They offered to consecrate you and you politely declined. What thoughts do you have on the proliferation of bishops within the Independent Sacramental Movement?

PASZKIEWICZ: I think I have two frames of mind about it. If you'll forgive the horrible turn of phrase, "too many chiefs and not enough

Indians" has been thrown around in the ISM for some time and I think that's legitimate. I think that is part of the problem that we have with jurisdiction forming and blowing apart so quickly because we have individuals that don't have a good psychodynamic formation process, we have a lot of power seeking and a lot of ego stroking that goes on. There's a place for that to be lived out healthily within a religious vocation that people can be seen and recognized for who they are and offer services to people and they can fulfill their need to be needed as caretakers, all those things, can be done healthily. When people are offered these big titles and big hats and shiny vestments in such a relatively short period of time, they don't get the full effect of the formation process that minimizes the ego's unrequited need for recognition over time. That becomes a problem, especially when we look at the traditional lens that a bishop is lording over a diocese with a lot of priests. I don't know that that's necessary either, especially in our post-modern religious setting of the 21st century. I think that there's a way to approach ordination as initiation as an initiatic wisdom where we can look at the minor orders and the major orders as being points of intentional formation that leads toward intentional eldership that doesn't demand huge congregations or a huge diocese to be legitimate, but I think formation is ever important. It's not a problem for me having a proliferation of bishops, if there's a reason for them to be a Bishop. That doesn't have to be having many priests, although I think that's part of it, but I think it means having a verifiable formative process that has given them some wisdom that would constitute intentional eldership. That they can be pastors of the community that forms around them organically in a meaningful way that's not just haphazardly offering Eucharistic deliberation.

KLING: I like that. Two thoughts that came to mind as you were talking, the first one goes back to my own experience within Benedictine monasticism, and you can probably relate to this from your exposure to monasticism within the Buddhist tradition. There's a difference between ordination and the profession of vows, at least in the Christian monastic sense. It is easy to go from layman or lay person to Bishop in the Independent Sacramental Movement but in my experience as a Benedictine monastic nobody joined as a postulant and said, "I think I should be in solemn vows tomorrow; I think I'm ready for solemn vows." No, you go from postulancy to the novitiate to simple vows and then eventually solemn vows. I've heard very few people jump from the aspirant or postulant phase all the way to solemn vows within the religious order context. When it comes to ordination, let's just jump to the end, whether you're ready or not. That's one observation in the Independent Sacramental Movement.

Another observation, which goes back to my involvement with Freemasonry. I don't know if you're familiar with the fraternity, but I've been a Freemason since 1997 and I started out with male Craft Freemasonry within the Grand Lodge of Ohio and now I'm with the International Order of Freemasonry for Men and Women, Le Droit Humain, which is a Co-Masonic organization and has both men and women. Within male Craft Freemasonry, they often have what they call one-day classes where you can go from not being a Mason to being a Master Mason receiving all three degrees in one afternoon. Then the lodge crosses their fingers and hopes that the new Master Mason comes back and becomes involved. It's a guessing game. Whereas in Le Droit Humain, you must write several papers before you can progress to the next degree. There's a time frame that you must endure between degrees. You can't just go from one to the other quickly. You take your time and fully participate in the lodge and their education program. By the time a person is a Master Mason within that system of Freemasonry, the odds are strong that they're going to remain because they've invested so much time and effort into it. I've seen so many go through one-day classes that if you initiate a hundred, you may have 10 that become active. Those are some observations that I see paralleling the Independent Sacramental Movement.

PASZKIEWICZ: I would say if our numbers are that good, that maybe 10 stay out of a 100 in the ISM, then that'd be great, but I think we probably have fewer numbers than that, we have folks that are consecrated a bishop in an afternoon and practice that until they realize they're not getting those unmet psychological needs fulfilled and then they go on to the next thing. Maybe Freemasonry or something else? There's value in formation and there's value in waiting and marinating. I think that one of the beautiful points of the ISM is that we do have the flexibility to look at somebody's life holistically and if they have a legitimate calling we can, fast-forward things sometimes if it's appropriate to a certain level of service and initiation if you will, but too often, it's just done to falsify numbers with hopes of building up a large jurisdiction and when you're building it up that way, it might as well be pillow stuffing, it's just stuff that pops out easily. I think we have a lot to learn and not just trying to mirror traditional formative processes and big denominations but providing meaningful formation that gives our folks stick-to-itiveness and a presence that has contiguity in our communities.

KLING: One blessing, that I refer to as our sacred advantage, is that we are small. We're a collection of micro-denominations and as such we can develop strong relationships with one another. For example, if you were to go into the United Methodist system for ministry, it is very byzantine with so many committees, so many boards, a lot of impersonal conversations; however, we have the advantage of building solid relationships and having good one-on-one mentorship, but you can't teach what you don't know. One-on-one mentorship works well when you're being mentored by somebody who knows what they're doing, as opposed to being mentored by somebody who was made a Bishop yesterday and the day before didn't even know that there were seven sacraments. You have a very interesting and a fluid spiritual path. I find that fascinating. How do you incorporate your Buddhist practice into your Christian practice or do you?

PASZKIEWICZ: The point in my vocation is this ongoing search for integration. There's a lot of experiential points that are sometimes more intuitive to me than they are prone to being extrapolated and verbalize concretely. I go back and forth on this, but I look at Buddhist practice as primarily being a practice of introspection. It's a very humanistic tradition. It's a rational tradition, but it provides a real spiritual discipline of quieting down, settling down and paying attention. One of the gifts that I learned from doing this, going on a couple of decades now, is that our mind is what provides the power to sanctify our experience and that's what I find myself deriving now from our central sacrament of the Eucharist, is that when we consecrate the host on the altar it is our mind the power of our concentrated attention that is making those simple elements sacred and Holy. There's some notion of kenosis that comes up there, self-emptying to allow the mystery of grace to happen. We can't articulate exactly how this works in the whole mystic pursuit of actualizing the sacred on a day-to-day basis, but I look at the Eucharist as a concentrated practice in the experience of making our life meaningful, making our life sacred through the power of spiritual discipline and focused attention, if that makes sense.

KLING: That makes perfect sense. It sounds like Buddhism is almost like a philosophy and it can mesh well with Christianity. You had mentioned Paul Tillich, it would be like taking the existentialism within the philosophical tradition, as Tillich did, and combining it with Christianity.

PASZKIEWICZ: I think that's a good example. It's funny when you look at Buddhism in the Western world, there's a lot of synthesization that's going on. Look at Jewbu, some of the earliest Buddhist voices in America who came from the Jewish tradition and didn't renounce Judaism. My own Buddhist preceptor, my monastic father spent the first half of his life in a Roman Catholic Trappist monastery. He only came out to the world when Pope John XXIII had opened Vatican II and the encouraging of inter-religious contemplative dialogue. He was sent to India where he was supposed to do inter-religious dialogue with Buddhists and Hindus and discovered Buddhism and picked it up but never put Catholicism down. He did leave the Trappist monastery, but he considered himself to have a dual vocation and that's what's happening, right at the opening of Vatican II.

This is nothing new. We've had the mixing of Christianity and Buddhism, and Judaism and Buddhism, and Neopaganism and Buddhism, and Humanism within Buddhism tends to be the very genesis of the tradition on the Western shores. It's interesting how it's prone to being picked up and carried into other things. If you want to look at Buddhism as a philosophy, it really is a philosophy of rationality. It's a system of putting existentialism to work. I'm not just thinking about it, but learning to embody it in our day-to-day life, moving from head to heart adding the soma.

KLING: Thanks for sharing. I'm gonna switch gears a little bit. Let me share some backstory, I was involved at one time with a chapter of the College of Pastoral Supervision and Psychotherapy, and I was involved with them for a couple of years. The chapter that I was with disbanded before I was able to get certified. Can you talk a little bit about chaplaincy and your work in chaplaincy, the certification process, and your work with the College of Pastoral Supervision and Psychotherapy?

PASZKIEWICZ: I had a realization after I was ordained a priest, and after I was already a lineage holder in Buddhism, the equivalent to a Bishop. I realized that a lot of my colleagues had this thing called Clinical Pastoral Education. I was trying to find a way for my own students, and the Buddhist tradition I was in to be on a solid footing with our Western counterparts, so that we could do more work together and have a sufficiently common background to dialogue on the issues. One of my things has been, "I'll never put somebody through something that I myself have not done." On that basis, I enrolled in a unit of Clinical Pastoral Education (CPE), and I fell in love with it immediately. It just so happened that the organization that accepted my application first was accredited by College of Pastoral Supervision and Psychotherapy (CPSP) rather than the Association of Clinical Pastoral Education (ACPE). I took it up in full and it wasn't until much later that I realized there were some fundamental ideological differences between the two methods of clinical training, but they come from the same background. I was in love with the psychodynamic psychoanalytic emphasis of the CPSP. I continued with three more units of CPE and completed board certification as a pastoral counselor and clinical chaplain. The clinical process in clinical chaplaincy is the delineation that CPSP made to hold themselves out as being slightly different from other certifying organizations. The whole non-denominational inter-spiritual ethos of Clinical Pastoral Education really worked with my ongoing pursuit of integration. I was welcomed as an Independent Catholic priest and as a Buddhist teacher. I got to do clinical work with those folks and everybody in between.

Chaplaincy has influenced my practice of ministry substantially. I think Buddhism really helped support my entry into chaplaincy through concentrated attentiveness and learning to listen, but also Christian principles of self-emptying, those are important aspects of that work. It integrates well. I consider it a part of my ongoing formation. One of the unique parts of CPSP is that you mentioned chapters and we don't just certify somebody, and they're done. We really view collegiality and formation as an ongoing process. We require folks to be part of a local, or at least semi-local, or regularly meeting chapter of colleagues where they can continue building relationships and hone their pastoral skills and not just settling down into the laurels of having been ordained or endorsed for chaplaincy.

I think that speaks to your question and there are a lot of interesting analogies we can make between the Independent Sacramental Movement and formation and just probably counting the number of vocations that ISM priests and bishops doing chaplaincy as opposed to pastoral ministry is probably an interesting demographic. I think that you yourself, as a chaplain and a bishop, see lots of crossover in that world.

KLING: Indeed, I do. Can you describe the difference between the College of Pastoral Supervision and Psychotherapy model and the Association of Clinical Pastoral Education model?

PASZKIEWICZ: I should say that speaking of ACPE, as opposed to CPSP is difficult because ACPE is part of a trifecta of organizations. ACPE is an accrediting organization for Clinical Pastoral Education programs. They work with The Board of Chaplaincy Certification Inc (BCCI) to certify their chaplains. The professional membership organization where board-certified chaplains come from is the Association of Professional Chaplains (APC). CPSP has all three of these functions under one banner. We don't have separate organizations doing these things, we are a holistic organization. I would say that there are two main differences. One is that we really emphasize the local collegial aspect of the practice of pastoral ministry, pastoral counseling, and clinical chaplaincy that sets up in the chapter. Our clinicians are certified first at the chapter level and then ratified at a national level by a body of peers, that they may not be familiar with yet.

That's a unique part of our process and the other part is that when you really look at the nitty-gritty of the majority of training supervisors between the two movements, which is the ACPE movement and the CPSP movement, CPSP has a psychodynamic psychoanalytic, even Freudian sort of ethos, we work out of that philosophy, that pool of psychodynamics. ACPE when they do engage in psychodynamics really come from more of a Jungian perspective, which is interesting, but also on a practical level, a lot of ACP programs, and this goes back to the earliest time of the Clinical Training movement a hundred years ago with Anton Boisen and his one-time partner, Richard Cabot, between what is the function of a chaplain. Boisen was an occasional schizophrenic who was very familiar with psychoanalytic literature and he wanted to get toward the deeper levels of religious symbolism and what that means on a psychological level. Cabot, who was a physician, was much more interested in the religiosity of things, such as, "What prayer did you say with somebody" Whereas, Boisen might be concerned with, "Why did you pray at all? Why was that necessary? Did they want you to pray, or did you pray for yourself?" And of course, there's a crossover between the organizations and supervisors as CPSP has been around for 30 years. We did grow out of ACPE, but we're very much representative of that early division between Cabot and Boisen. We're concerned with the practice of religion as a psychological discipline, as a psychotherapeutic discipline. Whereas ACPE is looking at it in the terms of applying religion in a clinical context as you would expect religion to be applied, if that makes sense.

KLING: That makes Perfect sense. I appreciate that explanation. I got a lot out of my ACPE units. My four units of CPE were life-changing for me. It's funny, because when I go back and reread my application for CPE, I think the only reason why I got in was because they were short and needed people down in West Virginia. I read it and it's basically me trying to put my resume in an application and CPE allowed me to realize, "Hey, I have emotions. And these emotions inform my behavior." That's important.

PASZKIEWICZ: Absolutely, it's beautiful.

KLING: Because prior to CPE, I was very cerebral and still am but now I recognize that emotion does play a role and it plays an important role in the families and the patients that I provide care to. When a patient or a family member externalizes their emotions, I can see that because that's what I used to do all the time. CPE is so important for people who do ministry, and I can't preach that enough if you're doing any kind of ministry and you can get at least one unit, go do it.

PASZKIEWICZ: Well, it's accessible too, right. We know in the ISM; we all have interesting vocations. Very few of us are paid unless we're working in chaplaincy or psychotherapy for our vocation. So, there's no excuse for somebody to not get that formative experience. At best that costs about $300. We're not asking people to go and get a 72-credit hour master's degree and go into 30,000 or $70,000 worth of debt. We're asking you to dedicate some time, to undertake an industry standard of training. I think that all ISM priests should at least get a single unit as most mainline denominations require. It's accessible, available, and it's deeply meaningful.

KLING: Exactly, now I'm going to switch gears a little bit again and ask you what your greatest challenge in ministry has been, specifically within the Independent Sacramental Movement.

PASZKIEWICZ: I think the greatest challenge in ministry for me honestly, has been integration, not personally, but into a wider community. I find collegiality is sometimes a challenge within the Independent Sacramental Movement. My foray into the ISM was with this deep welcome of this weird Buddhist monk, wearing a funny dress that came to mass. It's not replicated everywhere, and it's not always replicated on the side of my Buddhist ecclesiastical superiors either. So many folks want you to be in one place or the other, "Hey, what are you? Are you a Christian? Are you a Buddhist or you're a Taoist, are you a Hindu?" And for me, "I'm a human being and I can speak multiple religious languages and claim them all as my informative background and culture." Being able to be in a wider community with that sense of authenticity, I have found to be a challenge, especially within some ISM jurisdictions that have more rigorous standards for training and formation, because the more standards we have, we tend to move toward exclusion, which is not necessarily a good thing all the time, but I see how it happens.

My biggest challenge is sometimes authenticity, with in my own vocation within a wider context; although, these days I'm shameless about just presenting myself. Maybe from my CPE training as to who I am emotionally, subconsciously, psychically spiritually, et cetera. That's been an issue. Of course, there's little issues of, I'm called to do this as a vocation. How do I make a living while dedicating most of my time to this as a vocation? Through chaplaincy and psychotherapy, I've been able to really do well with it in a way that's satisfactory to me, but the collegiality seems to be something that I always find a little bit missing from my participation in the ISM.

KLING: I wonder if this idea of "picking a team and sticking with it," and "are you Buddhist" or "are you Christian," I wonder if that's also a result of our times. Let me explain what I mean by that. If you look at the Esoteric or Occult community a hundred years or so ago you have the Theosophical Society, and they were pulling from different sources.

In my own tradition within the Liberal Catholic Church tradition all the Liberal Catholic Church founders, Wedgewood and Leadbeater, were also members of the Theosophical Society. Prior to that, you have the American Transcendentalist movement. I know Theodore Parker, Henry David Thoreau, Ralph Waldo Emerson, and Margaret Fuller, and several others were members of the American Transcendentalist Movement, which also draws from multiple sources. If you look at the mid-20th century, you have a several additional examples of Occultists who were also involved in multiple different paths. Gerald Gardner, for example, the founder of Gardnerian Wicca was also a Bishop in a Celtic Christian jurisdiction whereas, and you also have Ross Nichols, Violet Firth (Dion Fortune) and so on. Fast forward to our modern period and there seems to be this impetus on "picking a team" within these same esoteric circles. Does that make sense?

PASZKIEWICZ: Yeah, it does and, I agree with you. I think some of what we're dealing with is this rough and rocky transition from modernism to post-modernism. We look at the enlightenment construct of religion itself to see that how drawing a line and looking at this as a unique category of human endeavor created more synthesis and opportunities for dialogue. It was all new, fresh, and exciting and accentuated ever with Orientalism and poor translation. I think it was easier at the time. Especially when the Theosophical Society was burgeoning, along with the New Thought Movement, to take a creative transformative rendering, shall we say, and make analogies toward your own prevailing tradition and maybe lighten it up in a way that was more palatable, and you can mix it all together. And isn't the world friendly; whereas we went forward and started taking modernism apart and realizing that there's less lines drawn, than we wanted to do with the enlightenment, and modernism we've responded in an inverse way. Now, instead of blending things, we are trying to find a distinction. It's like the difference between Western culture and Eastern culture with collectivism versus individualism.

The psychological woes of collectivism are desired by those individualistic societies and vice versa. We always want what we can't have. When we draw lines, we want to mix everything together and when we start taking the lines apart, we have to put something arbitrary up again because after all, you've got to know where you stand, and it doesn't help that we've moved into a political milieu of tribalism in recent years. I think we're processing that on the grand scale with globalism and all these notions and questions are why I think movements like the ISM are so important. We're empowering people to ask these big questions within a sacred container and be able to process them. It's not always easy, but I think that's been a big part of my ministry anyway.

KLING: That's certainly a great challenge that a lot of us experience, which goes into my, last question of what has been your greatest blessing within ministry?

PASZKIEWICZ: Wow, greatest blessing within ministry? I would say the visibility and opportunity that ministry gives me to be present with other people in their most trying and most celebratory times, and to be able to reflect on that and integrate the wisdom arising from those experiences into my own life. That is the greatest blessing. Being able to genuinely connect with people and reflect on those experiences and grow through them, to hopefully help people as much as I am helped in helping them. That's the heart stuff of ministry for me.

KLING: And that's what makes it worth it, right?

PASZKIEWICZ: Yeah, absolutely.

KLING: My work with hospice, most of the nursing homes that I go to have closed their doors, they're on lockdown because of the COVID-19 pandemic. I have a couple of homes, about three or four home patients, that I can go see regularly. I'm glad for that, because now I'm seeing some of these folks twice a week instead of once a month because I don't have anybody else to go see. It's been good because I'm able to see the fruits of my labor, because I'm seeing them more often. Do you have any closing thoughts?

PASZKIEWICZ: Just that as far as disjointed and sometimes silly as the ISM can be it's a beautiful thing. I think I'm left with a feeling of gratitude for the movement and for people like you that are there doing things to give us all a wider perspective and a remembrance that we're part of something bigger. Not just these small, isolated communities, and that it's all valid and important, but most of all, very human work. I'm left with a closing thought of gratitude and just thanking you for this opportunity.

"The question now arises: What is the content of our ultimate concern? What does concern us unconditionally? The answer, obviously, cannot be a special object, not even God, for the first criterion of theology must remain formal and general. If more is to be said about the nature of our ultimate concern, it must be derived from an analysis of the concept ultimate concern. Our ultimate concern is that which determines our being or not-being. Only those statements are theological which deal with their object in so far as it can become a matter of being or not-being for us." – Paul Tillich

"Concluding Thoughts"

As I write these concluding thoughts, the effect of the pandemic is starting to cool down. I can get back into the nursing homes I had been locked out of, and now I can see my patients. Recently, I visited with a patient who used to be a schoolteacher. She struggled during the pandemic because of isolation her family could not visit. I spent a couple of hours with her, and we talked about many things because she was starving for conversation. We talked about all the taboo subjects, like religion and politics. As I was leaving, she said, "You turned a bad day into a great one. I needed this." She had been feeling isolated and needed some human interaction.

Life as a deacon, priest, or bishop within the Independent Sacramental Movement can be isolating. For those clergy that have a parish, the congregation can help to spiritually sustain them. In my work in hospice and with the Ohio Military Reserve, I have fellow chaplains to help keep me sustained; however, being surrounded by your own community is where one becomes truly sustained and spiritually fed.

It is my hope, through "Sacramental Whine: An Independent Sacramental Movement Podcast," and these books that mirror the podcast, to help people within the Movement to feel less isolated. To help tell our stories, to preserve our history. It is my hope that these series of books, "Sacramental Whine: Chronicling the Independent Sacramental Movement," will help us build connections and to sustain friendships.

The ISM is diverse, and I love it all. From the Traditionalist who thinks I'm a heretic, to the Gnostic who thinks I'm too conservative. To the progressive who loves Vatican II, to the Liberal Catholic who embraces Theosophy. The Independent Sacramental Movement is a family and as such does not always agree. The disagreements will hopefully be cordial, but often they are not. I still love this Movement and will continue to document and preserve the greatness within it. I will not paint a picture that it is perfect. Critical reflection is important, that is how a community grows and develops. I want this Movement to come of age and impact more people. This takes time and effort, and a lot of hard work. Let us do the work together.

For Reflection, Contemplation, & Prayer:

- What are some of the effects the pandemic has had upon your life?
- Each of us juggles several roles in our lives. What are some of the roles you have and how do you integrate all these roles into who you are as a person?
- What are your greatest blessings? What are the things in your life that bring you the greatest joy?

Our Sacred Advantage

"For when there is a change in the priesthood, there is necessarily a change in the law as well." — Hebrews 7:12

In this chapter, I examine the question of how to improve the Independent Sacramental Movement in ways that are more ontological than practical.

In my work as a hospice chaplain, I have the pleasure of teaching new employees about culture, religion, and spirituality. When I discuss the differences between religion and spirituality, attendees are usually divided in their opinions on religion, but they always unanimously view spirituality as a positive. This phenomenon is not unique to the new employees at the hospice where I work. It permeates our society. In her book, *Belief without Borders*, Linda Mercadante states, "The percentage of Americans claiming, 'no religion' has grown dramatically since religion's heyday in the 1950s."[1] I confirmed this in my work as a hospice chaplain: When I conduct new patient assessments, I find that most of my patients and their families have ceased attending a church. The growing trend seems to be a general distrust of organized religion.

When I wrestle with the question of how to improve our movement, my mind immediately goes to obvious ways of improvement, such as better education of and communication between clergy in various jurisdictions. While these subjects are important, I keep coming back to the dichotomy between religion and spirituality, and I believe there is something there that we, as a movement, should recognize and acknowledge. Our culture is changing, and society is morphing into something much different from the 1950s church experience.

When I ask new employees, who dislike religion why they feel the way they do, their responses often focus on how religion is perceived to be authoritarian, oppressive, legalistic, and impersonal. When I invite them to share their thoughts on spirituality, I get responses that illustrate feelings of connection, personal relationship with the Divine, and feeling loved by God. Reflecting on these views, many of us who end up in the Independent Sacramental Movement identify as "spiritual-but-not-religious." We are repelled by the legalistic and oppressive

---

[1] Mercadante, Linda A. (2014). *Belief without Borders: Inside the Minds of the Spiritual but Not Religious*. New York: Oxford University Press.

characteristics of organized religion, yet we feel drawn and compelled to live a spiritual life with those aspects of traditional religion that we find comforting. Whether or not we identify with the label "spiritual-but-not-religious," we seek a deeper connection with God in ways that go counter to mainstream, normalized society. We are not spiritual anarchists or loners. Instead, we ask, "Who am I and where do I belong?" We more effectively answer the question of who we are as members a spiritual movement that focuses on that ontological question, without being placed in a "box" we did not create.

In her book, *Christianity After Religion*, Diana Butler Bass argues that we are living in a new age: We have moved out of the "Age of Belief" and into the "Age of Spirit." She writes, "The Age of Spirit is non-dogmatic, non-institutional and non-hierarchical Christianity, based on a person's connection to the 'volatile expression' of God's Spirit through mystery, wonder, and awe."[2] Bass is articulating a theory based on the works of scholar Harvey Cox. My experience of talking to hospice patients and families validates what Bass argues. The religious climate of our world is changing, and people are becoming suspicious of the "institutional church." People have not abandoned belief and a commitment to spirituality, but they seek solace from the harshness of life in different places. This phenomenon creates an opportunity for ministry by jurisdictions in the Independent Sacramental Movement. If we recognize this, we can more quickly adapt to the changing times than larger, more-institutionalized churches.

In comparing the Independent Sacramental Movement to larger denominations, let's consider the places we go to eat. When you go to a chain restaurant, you are more likely eat food that is pre-packaged and locally reheated, whereas locally owned restaurants often make their food on site every day. When I was a teenager, I worked at Pizza Hut®: Back in the 80s, we made our own dough and prepared all the toppings, but now the toppings are pre-cut and shipped in plastic bags, and the dough is created at a central location, frozen, and shipped to local units for final production. The personal touch is gone, and pizza production now becomes an act of conformity. Personally, I prefer to eat at local places, where the food is fresh, and dishes are created on site — and not in a microwave.

---

[2] Bass, Diana Butler. (2012). *Christianity After Religion: The End of Church and the Birth of a New Spiritual Awakening.* New York: HarperOne.

I don't want to paint mainline churches as the enemy or as "artificial." I have friends who do great work as clergy in mainline denominations, but their systems push for conformity and prevent them from fully hearing the whispers of the Holy Spirit. Older, institutionalized churches are often slow to adapt to change, and, as their attendance shrinks, they ask, "How do we get more people?" In contrast, non-traditional, non-denominational churches are less concerned with conformity and are filled with people.

When I consider how to improve our movement, I'm compelled to ask follow-up questions: "Who are we, and what do we offer?" Jurisdictions within the Independent Sacramental Movement are often intimate communities, and ISM bishops are more akin to mentors and colleagues than distant hierarchs to be reverenced or feared. Priests within our movement are not cloistered or fully removed from the vicissitudes of life. They are not insulated inside a clerical culture that takes care of them. They are "in the trenches" every day, experiencing life as everyday people.

ISM clergy live in a spiritually liminal space. We do not have the financial alacrity of the Roman Catholic Church or any of the mainline Protestant denominations. We often work on a shoestring budget, doing the best we can to finance our ministries. This can be our most sacred advantage.

I'll take a stab at answering the question of how to improve our movement. We can improve our movement by recognizing who we are and the advantages we have in being able to accommodate the shifting sands of contemporary culture. Roman Catholic parishes are closing and consolidating, and the average age of the priests in your area is likely close to or past the retirement age. Many Protestant clergy are bi-vocational or leave ministry after a few years of serving a congregation. More than ever before, people identify as "spiritual-but-not-religious," and the religious landscape is changing. We can improve our movement by being aware of these changes and leaning into them. Rather than view these changes with anxiety, we, in the Independent Sacramental Movement, should embrace the changes and provide quarter for those who, like ourselves, ask "Who am I?" and "Where do I belong?" We should offer would-be seekers an opportunity to develop authentic and meaningful relationships with others, instead of with rusting institutions that feel distant and out-of-touch. We should provide the opportunity to connect with God in a way that focuses on religious experience in a non-judgmental forum. For years, many ISM jurisdictions have welcomed and affirmed diverse expressions of sexual orientation and gender, long before even the most progressive denominations began to do so. Most importantly, we should share the sacraments with confidence and the conviction that what we offer is a blessing from God and the work of the Holy Spirit. We are part of the Mystical Body of Christ. We have something to say, something to offer, and a message we wish to bring to the world. How we offer our message will determine if we, as a movement, can remain relevant in our changing world.

"We must be ourselves. We must decide where to go." — Paul Tillich

For Reflection, Contemplation, & Prayer:

- What does the Independent Sacramental Movement offer? Why would anyone want to be part of this movement?
- Many people have talked about problems they have had with "organized religion," mainly with large denominations. Do you think the ISM can help people? How?
- What are some ways we can be our truly authentic selves? How can we live authentic lives, and can the ISM help us be more authentic?

Black Lives Matter

"There is no fear in love. But perfect love drives out fear, because fear has to do with punishment. The one who fears is not made perfect in love. We love because he first loved us. Whoever claims to love God yet hates a brother or sister is a liar. For whoever does not love their brother and sister, whom they have seen, cannot love God, whom they have not seen. And he has given us this command: Anyone who loves God must also love their brother and sister." -- 1 John 4:18-21

In this chapter let's take a moment to reflect on recent events of 2020 in the United States surrounding the death of George Floyd and the Black Lives Matter movement.

Bishop David Strong, presiding bishop of the Apostolic Catholic Church in America, shared some thoughts on recent events with a statement which I will read in a moment; however, in the statement he refers to events of the last 24 hours.

The events of the last 24 hours, that Bishop Strong refers to is the death of George Floyd by a Minneapolis police officer while three other police officers watched as Officer Derek Chauvin rested his knee on George Floyd's neck causing his death. The other incident is the story of Amy Cooper, the women who called 911 on an African American man because he asked her to leash her dog in Central Park. Christian Cooper (no relation to Amy) was bird watching. Yes, he was legitimately bird watching – the New York Times reported that he is a board member of the New York City Audubon Society. It seems like she was trying to cause him at minimum a run in with police resulting in much frustration for him and at worse a similar fate that George Floyd suffered. The situation of Christian Cooper did not end tragically like that of George Floyd, but it could have.

Bishop David Strong passionately expressed,

"Much of the independent Catholic community will be silent on the events of the last 24 hours in our country. They are silent because it is a majority white movement who are not affected personally or collectively by racism. They are silent because too often black and brown people are not members or leaders in this movement. The movement will hide behind color blindness, theological

theories, and notions of apostolic succession while people die in the streets or suffer the daily indignities of racism in America. Let's be clear racism is a sin. Whether it is practice[d] individually or collectively it is a failure of living sanctified lives. We need something more than talk and prayers, we need to changed behaviors, change hearts and a commitment to end racism in our churches and lives. If you love Jesus, you got a love everybody with your actions."

Since Bishop Strong posted this statement there have been countless demonstrations around the country in support of Black Lives Matter. This has been the largest grass roots movement since I have been alive in support of equal treatment by law enforcement through the appeal of black Americans to law enforcement of "stop killing us." I am moved by the words of Bishop David Strong. The Independent Sacramental Movement is overwhelmingly white and male. It is my hope that the movement will become more diverse with more women and more people of color choosing to embrace our flavor of sacramental Christianity. In the meantime, those who are here have an obligation to speak the truth of the Gospel and echo the words of Bishop Strong and to share in his commitment for justice.

As I was putting this chapter together, I searched for statements by jurisdictions on the events within the USA and the ripple effect the death of George Floyd has had upon the world. I came up with a few statements. The first by the Advocates of St. Sebastian, then the Convergent Christian Communion, then the Reformed Catholic Church, and finally my own jurisdiction the Community of Saint George – a Young Rite Jurisdiction.

First, **The Advocates of St. Sebastian:**

The Advocates of St. Sebastian affirms, unequivocally and without reservation, that Black Lives Matter, and we stand, sometimes literally, with the protestors on the ground calling for an end to racism, police brutality, and injustice.

We add to our prayers the names George Floyd, Breonna Taylor, Ahmad Arbery, and Atatiana Jefferson, along with all those lives lost to police violence in recent years.

We call on all clergy and all persons of faith and good will to speak up, advocate, and act on behalf of those striving for justice.

"O Lord, you will hear the desire of the meek; you will strengthen their heart, you will incline your ear to do justice for the orphan and the oppressed, so that those from earth may strike terror no more." Psalm 10:17-18.

Second, **Convergent Christian Communion**:

From the Presiding Bishop:

We are grieved by the murder of George Floyd in Minneapolis. Sadly, this is just another tragic example of our failure as a nation to be truly Christian--as so many like to tout. Sure, many will point to the change in external conditions that have occurred over the past few decades, but the sad reality is that we have failed to make the necessary internal changes to make those external adjustments more than superficial. Sadder still, a portion of the church will remain silent today because they are unaffected by racism either personally or collectively. The C.C.C. will not be counted among the silent!

Each week, during our Sunday liturgy, we are reminded of Christ's commands: "You shall love the Lord your God with all your heart and with all your soul and with all your mind. This is the first and great commandment. And the second is like it. You shall love your neighbor as yourself." It is our responsibility, as the church, to be the change that this world needs. Before any change can happen in our nation, it must happen in our churches. That means that we need to wake up to the reality of racism, to stand up for those impacted by it, and to speak up when we see it. This is how we love our neighbor as ourselves. We cannot be silent or immobile; it is only through our action that we truly become the hands and feet of Jesus. This is how we do justice and love mercy (Micah 6:8).

To our brothers and sisters of color: we see you, we love you, we stand with you, and your lives matter.

+Kenny

Presiding Bishop, the Convergent Christian Communion

Let us pray: Wake me up Lord, so that the evil of racism finds no home within me. Keep watch over my heart Lord, and remove from me any barriers to your grace, that may oppress and offend my brothers and sisters. Fill my spirit Lord, so that I may give services of justice and peace. Clear my mind Lord, and use it for your glory. And finally, remind us

Lord that you said, "blessed are the peacemakers, for they shall be called children of God." Amen.

Third, Bishop Christopher Carpenter, of the **Reformed Catholic Church**, indicated they signed onto the following document of LGBTQ Organizations Unite to Combat Racial Violence:

"If you are neutral in situations of injustice, you have chosen the side of the oppressor." Those words, written over 30 years ago by Archbishop Desmond Tutu, remind us that indifference can never bridge the divide of hate. And, today, they should serve as a call to action to all of us, and to the Movement for LGBTQ equality.

This spring has been a stark and stinging reminder that racism, and its strategic objective, white supremacy, is as defining a characteristic of the American experience as those ideals upon which we claim to hold our democracy — justice, equality, liberty.

• We listened to the haunting pleas of George Floyd for the most basic of human needs — simply, breath — as a Minneapolis police officer kneeled with cruel indifference on his neck.

• We felt the pain of Breonna Taylor's boyfriend as he called 9-1-1 after plainclothes Louisville police kicked down the door of their home and shot her eight times as she slept in her bed.

• We watched the shooting death of Ahmaud Arbery by white vigilantes in Brunswick, GA, aware that they evaded the consequence of their actions until the video surfaced and sparked national outrage.

• We saw the weaponizing of race by a white woman who pantomimed fear in calling the police on Christian Cooper, a Black gay man birdwatching in Central Park.

• We have heard and read about the killings of transgender people -- Black transgender women in particular — with such regularity, it is no exaggeration to describe it as a epidemic of violence. This year alone, we have lost at least 12 members of our community: Dustin Parker, Neulisa Luciano Ruiz, Yampi Méndez Arocho, Monika Diamond, Lexi, Johanna Metzger, Serena Angelique Velázquez Ramos, Layla Pelaez Sánchez, Penélope Díaz Ramírez, Nina Pop, Helle Jae O'Regan, and Tony McDade.

All of these incidents are stark reminders of why we must speak out when hate, violence, and systemic racism claim — too often with impunity — Black Lives.

The LGBTQ Movement's work has earned significant victories in expanding the civil rights of LGBTQ people. But what good are civil rights without the freedom to enjoy them?

Many of our organizations have made progress in adopting intersectionality as a core value and have committed to be more diverse, equitable, and inclusive. But this moment requires that we go further — that we make explicit commitments to embrace anti-racism and end white supremacy, not as necessary corollaries to our mission, but as integral to the objective of full equality for LGBTQ people.

We, the undersigned, recognize we cannot remain neutral, nor will awareness substitute for action. The LGBTQ community knows about the work of resisting police brutality and violence. We celebrate June as Pride Month, because it commemorates, in part, our resisting police harassment and brutality at Stonewall in New York City, and earlier in California, when such violence was common and expected. We remember it as a breakthrough moment when we refused to accept humiliation and fear as the price of living fully, freely, and authentically.

We understand what it means to rise up and push back against a culture that tells us we are less than, that our lives don't matter. Today, we join together again to say #BlackLivesMatter and commit ourselves to the action those words require.

Finally, my own jurisdiction: **The Community of Saint George – a Young Rite Jurisdiction** – put out a statement:

Dear Brothers and Sisters,

Saint Isaac the Syrian wrote, "Conquer men by your gentle kindness, and make zealous men wonder at your goodness. Put the lover of justice to shame by your compassion. With the afflicted be afflicted in mind. Love all men but keep distant from all men."

Compassion begets wisdom and in these controversial times we must be called to be a people of compassion. The Church throughout the centuries has been a haven, a sanctuary for those mistreated and oppressed. Our country bleeds, suffers, and is in the throes of so much oppression both internally and externally. Because of this we are subject to many things, fear, and anger chief among them. Our clergy pray and seek justice through peace and only through radical change can we find solutions. The peaceful martyrs of the past, by their very nature, died for the cause and offered their lives for their convictions. They were opposed to violence and chaos which does not hurt those who are the enemy of the people but instead hurts our own brothers and sisters in the crossfire. All possible solutions are bloody and devastating. We are NOT here to judge anyone as this is not the work of men but of God.

We seek to embrace all people in a time where embracing is discouraged for our very lives are at stake. The notion that socio-economics and a pandemic hurt the same people at a greater rate and now on top of this we have violence from those who swear to serve and protect is an untenable position and the very idea of violence, though horrendous, should provide opportunity to reflect and pray. Violence also breeds hatred and people with an agenda try to create separateness and division. Bishop James I. Wedgwood taught that, "People often fail to realise what is involved in the doctrine of the unity of life. It means that the whole of creation is interdependent, linked together in one chain of being." We are all affected by the suffering of others and their pain is our pain and we must strive to overcome fear with compassion and stand with the oppressed and mistreated and provide them a sanctuary of peace.

We oppose all violence and terror; fear is overshadowing so much of our world:

- "So do not fear, for I am with you; do not be dismayed, for I am your God. I will strengthen you and help you; I will uphold you with my righteous hand." Isaiah 41:10
- "For God has not given us a spirit of fear, but a power and of love and of a sound mind." Timothy 1:7
- "There is no fear in love. But perfect love drives out fear, because fear has to do with punishment. The one who fears is not made perfect in love." 1 John 4:18
- "When anxiety was great within me, your consolation brought joy to my soul." Psalm 94:19
- "Have I not commanded you? Be strong and courageous. Do not be terrified; do not be discouraged, for the Lord your God will be with you wherever you go." Joshua 1:9
- "Therefore, do not worry about tomorrow, for tomorrow will worry about itself. Each day has enough trouble of its own." Matthew 6:34
- "The Lord is my light and my salvation - whom shall, I fear? The Lord is the stronghold of my life- of whom shall I be afraid?" Psalm 27:1

- "God is our refuge and strength, an ever-present help in trouble." Psalm 46:1
- "Fear of man will prove to be a snare, but whoever trusts in the Lord is kept safe." Proverbs 29:25.

Scripture teaches us how to navigate our fears. These may feel like platitudes or simple words that mean nothing in a world such as ours but reflect upon the harsh time and place in which they were written. Reflect upon how the Christians of the desert and throughout the history of Christianity often struggled with similar issues we face today. Our flesh fails us often, we are imperfect, we hurt each other, we kill each other, and we do not love as we should. We are all one humanity and as such we deserve dignity and liberty so many have fought to acquire.

We challenge ourselves to be better and to do better. We challenge justice to do better and be better and we challenge all leaders to look at what they are doing or failing to do. We must endure these things but not unscathed. We must learn and do better and let the scars of these events be worn as badges of how we learned from others and not what caused us to break apart as a country. Compassion begets wisdom.

May the Lord God bless all of you, bring his justice to this world and allow all people to see the humanity in anyone who stands before them.

In Solidarity,

Rt. Rev. David Oliver Kling, M.Div
Rt. Rev. Robert Lamoureux, OM
Rt. Rev. Kirk Jeffery, D.Min

Bishop David Strong said it succinctly, "Racism is a sin." Let us, together, combat injustice, and support what is just and right."

> *"I do not pretend to understand the moral universe; the arc is a long one, my eye reaches but little ways; I cannot calculate the curve and complete the figure by the experience of sight; I can divine it by conscience. And from what I see I am sure it bends towards justice."* — Theodore Parker

For Reflection, Contemplation, & Prayer:

- Racism is a sin, what are some ways we can fight racism in our communities and our churches?
- Our society seems to be much more polarized today than it has been in the past. What are some ways people can be brought together without partisanship overshadowing friendships and community building?
- What are some ways we can challenge one another to be better?

Clerical Celibacy: An Agenda of Power in Roman Catholicism.

"The bishop therefore must be without reproach, the husband of one wife, temperate, sober-minded, orderly, given to hospitality, apt to teach..." -- 1 Timothy 3:2

In my discussion with Bishop Jason Spadafore, he and I talked about clerical celibacy, let's take a closer look at the idea of clerical celibacy. Most Independent Sacramental jurisdictions allow married priests. There are some Traditionalist Catholic jurisdictions that work to maintain a snapshot of the Roman Catholic Church from the 1950s as experienced during the reign of Pope Pius XII, the last true pope according to the *sede vacantist* position. I thought it would be a good idea to discuss clerical celibacy because as a bishop within this movement when I say, "I'm a type of Catholic, just not Roman Catholic. I fall outside of the authority of the Vatican," I often get asked, "If you're Catholic then you can't get married right?" Independent Sacramental clergy often must justify their positions especially with those not specifically within our movement. Because of this it is good to reflect on practices that are done by the "Roman Church," and discern why we retain or reject a practice. In a previous episode I talked about women's ordination and concluded that I believe women should be ordained. In this episode I look at clerical celibacy and share why I think it should be rejected unless you are called to a monastic vocation.

The Second Vatican Council revolutionized the Roman Catholic Church. The liturgy of the Church, once a bastion of Catholicity, was replaced by a new order of mass that allowed for such innovations as Eucharistic ministers, concelebration, communion under both kinds, the use of the vernacular, and other new approaches that have now become Catholic custom well after the close of the Council. One of the documents of Vatican II, *CHRISTUS DOMINUS*[3], dealt with the collegial nature of the episcopate and moved the episcopate into a more collegial nature that has been enjoyed in the Byzantine and Orthodox Churches for centuries, thereby, removing the more monarchical nature of the Roman episcopate

---

[3] Vatican II Document – Christus Dominus.
http://www.vatican.va/archive/hist_councils/ii_vatican_council/documents/vat-ii_decree_19651028_christus-dominus_en.html

within the polity of the Church. Many, but not necessarily all, of the innovations at Vatican II were and are liturgical and ecclesiological practices of the Byzantine-Rite and Orthodox Churches, and this distinction is important. It is important because within the Orthodox Churches there is a fully functioning married priesthood, but during the time of the Second Vatican Council, as it is today, the priesthood was celibate. There was a hope by some within the Roman Church that the discipline of clerical celibacy would be modified to allow married men an opportunity to become priests. The Second Vatican Council never removed the discipline of clerical celibacy, and it has been the custom since Vatican II for the Bishop of Rome to insist that clerical celibacy is a matter of ecclesiastical law that is not going away.

After so much change in the Roman Catholic Church the question has to be asked why retain the antiquated custom of clerical celibacy. It doesn't seem to be a doctrinal issue of "liberal vs. conservative" because the conservative Orthodox Church retains a celibate episcopate, but the majority of their priests are married. The Churches of the Anglican Communion have a married clergy and range from very liberal to conservative "Anglo-Catholic." Clerical celibacy doesn't seem to be a Biblical requirement[4], so why the need to retain such a custom when vocations to the priesthood are down within the Roman Catholic Church? I hope to successfully argue that the reason for clerical celibacy within the Roman Catholic Church is the desire for power and control; what Michel Foucault would call "biopower."[5] I will argue that the means of exercising this power is two-fold using a system of rearranging norms and by isolation of the priesthood from the laity. I suspect there are additional reasons and factors leading and perpetuating the discipline of clerical celibacy, but the limitations of this podcast episode force me to look at the issue in specific terms. I don't have an unlimited amount of time to do research!

I mentioned Michel Foucault. For those who have never heard of him, he was a French philosopher who wrote on social theory and the

---

[4] 1 Timothy 3:1 – 3: This saying is trustworthy: whoever aspires to the office of bishop desires a noble task. Therefore, a bishop must be irreproachable, married only once, temperate, self-controlled, decent, hospitable, able to teach, not a drunkard, not aggressive, not gentle, not contentious, not a lover of money.

[5] Foucault, Michel. The History of Sexuality: An Introduction. Vol. 1. New York: Vintage Books, 1990. 3 vols. Page 140.

history of ideas. I am aware of two of his works, Discipline and Punish about incarceration and his The History of Sexuality in three volumes. My interpretation of his work is that he focuses a lot of attention on power and how power works. If you perceive a system as being dysfunctional, just ask the question, "Who benefits from the dysfunction." I have been a fan of his writings since I first read about Foucault while studying philosophy in college. Okay, back to clerical celibacy!

While still retaining the practice of clerical celibacy Vatican II did modify their position somewhat on the subject, perhaps instilling a false sense of hope for those who would advocate for married priests. Edward Shillebeeckx comments on the Vatican II document, "Decree on the Ministry and Life of Priests,"

This decree sees clerical celibacy in the light of "perfect and perpetual continence for the sake of the kingdom of heaven." It is explicitly stated that celibacy is not essentially bound up with priesthood. Therefore, the council evidently does not consider the eastern practice of having married priests as second rank. Nevertheless, the emphasis is placed on the "many-faceted suitability" of celibacy and priesthood.[6]

The Second Vatican Council was more amicable to Byzantine Rite Greek Catholics[7] than it had been in previous years, so this new way of looking at clerical celibacy didn't view celibacy and priesthood in an *a priori* fashion, but rather as more of an ideal than a necessity linked with the "kingdom of heaven" rather than as a preferred state of purity.

The Roman Catholic and Eastern Orthodox didn't formally sever ties with one another until 1054 CE, and except for a few tumultuous times the two branches of Christendom were united before that date. One aspect of this unity was the fact that both branches, East & West, had married and celibate priests. Monasticism had become a phenomenon within Christianity in the period of the early Church and it was an established norm that monks and nuns were by default celibate.

---

[6] Schillebeeckx, E. Celibacy. New York: Sheed and Ward, 1968. Page 111 – 112.
[7] The term Greek Catholics having been introduced into ecclesiastical usage in the 18th century to refer to Byzantine Rite Catholics in union with Rome, also known as Uniates. See Barriger, Lawrence. *Good Victory*. Brookline, Mass.: Holy Cross Orthodox Press, 1985

However, the celibacy of the monastic was not mandated upon the non-monastic clergy and it was the norm for priests to also be married and this practice was reinforced early at the Council of Nicea (325 CE) where celibate Bishop Paphnutius commented that, *"too heavy a yoke ought not to be laid upon the clergy ... marriage and married intercourse are of themselves honorable and undefiled."*[8] The norm of a married clergy was replaced by clerical celibacy through three primary stages, although there were minor victories for clerical celibacy along the way. The first being the various controversies in the early church with canons found from a Spanish council at Elvira in 306 forbidding priests from having sex with their wives.[9] The end of this first stage culminated with the actions of Pope Gregory VII advocating for clerical celibacy, the second being the First and Second Lateran Councils (1123 & 1129 CE), and finally the Council of Trent (1545 – 63 CE).[10] What resulted from these councils and the actions of the various Popes was a shift in the norms of the Church where clerical celibacy was exalted as superior to marriage and as a result of this the priesthood itself was exalted as a state higher than that of the married laity. With a fully celibate priesthood the priesthood became isolated from the laity, elevated above it as being free from the presumed impurity and burden that results from marriage. Additionally, without a married priesthood the hierarchy of the Church need not worry about what to do with the widows of priests or their orphaned children[11]. The elimination of inheritance issues further isolates the priesthood from the laity. In short it is cost effective to have celibate priests.

The case of biopower as a means of control by the Catholic hierarchy is overwhelming in an analysis of the Carpatho-Russian Greek Catholic problem of the 19th and 20th century in the United States. Uniate, or Greek Catholics, are very similar to their Orthodox cousins; however, they are in union with Rome and as such fall under the ultimate

[8] Maier. Page 24. Its important to note that Bishop Paphnutius was celibate.
[9] Hunter, David G. Marriage, Celibacy, and Heresy in Ancient Christianity: The Jovinianist Controvery. Oxford: Oxford University Press, 2007. Page 214.
[10] McBrien, Richard P. "Celibacy rule deviates from earliest tradition." National

Catholic Reporter

38.39 (2002): Page 16.
[11] O'Sullivan, Owen. "The silent schism." Cross Currents 44.4 ([YEAR]): 518.. Page 518.

jurisdiction of the Papacy as do all Catholics. These Uniate branches of Catholicism were a "non-issue" within Catholic ecclesiology because they were exclusively limited to parts of Eastern Europe and small enclaves in the Middle East; however, during large immigrations to the United States you had Greek Catholics mixing with Roman Catholics and it was unsettling when these immigrants brought over their priests who in turn brought their wives and children. Catholic married priests? Such was unthinkable, yet a cold reality for Roman Catholic hierarchs in the new world. Over several years the Vatican issued decrees attempting to enforce clerical celibacy upon these Byzantine Rite priests, often in violation of their agreements of unity.[12] A whole, rather unknown, branch of Catholicism has had an historical married priesthood, but their existence was considered threatening to Roman Catholic polity concerns; therefore, the only recourse was to attempt to restrain the use of sexuality amongst the Byzantine Rite clergy operating within the United States. It would seem that these Uniates were considered non-threatening as long as they remained in their Eastern European or Middle Eastern "ghettos" and stayed out of sight of their Roman Catholic brethren. Having had enough of the controlling arm of Rome a large faction of the Carpatho-Russian Greek Catholics, under the leadership of Fr. Orestes Chornock officially left the authority of Rome. The schism was sealed when Chornock was consecrated a bishop in Constantinople on September 18, 1938[13] establishing the Carpatho-Russian Orthodox Greek Catholic Church.

A very important catalyst in the development of clerical celibacy is the rise of monasticism. Monasticism rose as a movement of asceticism of the laity and a phenomenon orchestrated by lay people seeking a deeper spiritual life by fleeing to desert communities or seeking isolation as hermits. Most of the early monastic legislators were of the laity and were never priests, such as St. Benedict and St. Pachomius. What was inaugurated by Pope Gregory VII and promulgated at the various councils afterwards was a systematic change of norms taking the monastic chrism of celibacy and transferring it to the priesthood. Raymond J. Lawrence addresses the attitude of Gregory as,

---

[12] Berriger. Page 50.
[13] Ibid. Page 120.

For Gregory, any sort of sexual pleasure was culpable, and the penalty for sex outside of wedlock was eternal damnation. By anyone's measure, he drove a hard bargain. Gregory also promoted clerical celibacy, making de facto monks of all the clergy, but he lacked the power to impose such a rule on the whole church. His namesakes for hundred years later, the so-called Gregorian popes, implemented his vision.[14]

The priesthood was already separated from the laity because of the sacramental nature of the priesthood. With the addition of clerical celibacy, the contrast between priest and laity became even more distinct. With this insulation from the laity, it is easier for the priesthood to be monitored by their religious superiors, who are in turn monitored by their religious superiors who are monitored by the Bishop of Rome. Additionally, the isolation of the priesthood from the laity allows the priests to observe the laity in a superior to inferior relationship.

It is a clear historical fact that clerical celibacy was not mandated upon clergy either in the Western or Eastern branches of Christendom since apostolic times; but rather, a process of ecclesiological significance. In the Orthodox churches the compromise has been that married men can be priests, but bishops are drawn from the pool of unmarried priests – widowers in the case of Orestes Chornock or monks as is the case with most Orthodox bishops. In the West it has been the policy for almost a thousand years, as I have shown, for priests to be celibate; however, there are always exceptions to this general rule. I will address three exceptions to clerical celibacy in the Roman Catholic Church,[15] the cases of Father Richard McKnight, Father Tom McMichael, and Fathers Dominic Cosslett and Ron Cosslett.

Father Richard McKnight is a former Anglican priest, a father of two, and a married man and is currently a functioning priest in the Roman Catholic Church.[16] He was ordained an Anglican priest in 1980 but resigned from the priesthood in 1984, and "Since 1984 he has been a

[14] Lawrence, Jr, Raymond J. Sexual Liberation: The Scandal of Christendom. Westport, CT: Praeger, 2007. Page 47.
[15] In contrast to the situation of the Byzantine Rite, also known as Uniate or Greek Catholics, which are in union with Rome yet have a married priesthood.
[16] "A married Roman Catholic priest." Christian Century 104.35 (25 Nov. 1987): 1056-1057.

truck driver, a museum security guard and a construction worker."[17] Father McKnight approached an auxiliary bishop in Toronto Canada and was eventually ordained a priest in the Roman Catholic Church while still being married; with no known clauses to abstain from sexual practices with his wife.

The case of Father Tom McMichael is similar to that of McKnight; however, McMichael was a former Lutheran minister.[18] McMichael had formerly served as pastor at Lynden's Hope Lutheran Church until he resigned in 2005 and was ordained to the Roman Catholic priesthood on January 11th, 2009 to serve in the Seattle Washington diocese. Like Father McKnight, the situation with Father McMichael raises some paradoxical questions in the discipline of the Roman Catholic Church.

The third case is that of the father and son pair of Fathers Ron Cosslett and Dominic Cosslett. The elder Cosslet, Ron, is 70 years old whereas his son Dominic is 36. Both Cossletts reside in the United Kingdom and are former Anglican priests and the elder Cosslet joined the Roman Catholic Church and was ordained a priest in 2005 his son was ordained in 2008. Father Ron Cosslet is married, but his son Father Dominic is not; however, this could still be seen as a case of "hereditary priesthood." The case of these two men raise similar questions as posed by the other two men mentioned; what makes these men so special that they are permitted to keep their marriage and function as Catholic priests with full ecclesiastical faculties?

Foucault discusses the relationship of power and sexuality when he wrote, "…it is a power whose model is essentially juridical, centered on nothing more than the statement of the law and the operation of taboos."[19] It is not an issue of doctrine that clerical celibacy is the standard in the Roman Catholic Church, because if it was a doctrine then there could not be the exceptions mentioned earlier, or the many examples not covered in this podcast episode of active and fully functional married priests. What the notion of clerical celibacy has

---

[17] Ibid. Page 1056.
[18] Stark, John . Bellingham Catholic Church welcomes married priest. 2009. The Seatle Times. 23 May 2009
<http://seattletimes.nwsource.com/html/localnews/2008653832_webmarriedpriest21m.html>.
[19] Foucault. Page 85.

become is an issue of ecclesiology, and how the Roman Catholic Church wants to see itself. The power that the Church wields over its clergy is juridical, and the paradox remains that a vocabulary is used that attempts to showcase the superiority of the celibate life while reality shows that married priests, both Roman and Byzantine Rite, exist and function in a capacity that is equal to their celibate brothers in the priesthood. When exceptions are made, as the examples mentioned of the former Lutheran and Anglican clergy, they are made without pomp and circumstance; Rome has spoken and there is no further discussion necessary. On the contrary, if there are married priests within Roman Catholicism and until clerical celibacy becomes a doctrinal issue; then there will always be dialogue – even without the hope of change. While I argue that clerical celibacy is an issue of power, the Roman Catholic Church continues to advocate that power is not the reason for this discipline. There are several arguments in favor of clerical celibacy and I will address three of them.

It has been argued that sexuality creates a state of impurity and therefore clerical celibacy is important to ensure the purity of the priesthood. In the Jewish tradition there were several ways the priests could become unclean, such as being around corpses and/or unclean animals, or being near a menstruating woman or woman after childbirth; however, with all the means of making a priest impure there were means in which a priest could purify himself and therefore be able to perform his priestly duties. Additionally, the Levite priesthood was hereditary and passed down from father to son. Rabbi Mark Verman discusses the procreative nature of sexuality within Judaism as requiring desire and joy in order to be productive[20]; Judaism does not, in the normative sense, have the aversion to sexuality that Catholicism has infused into Judaism. The Jewish tradition, in which Christianity emerged, had a strong norm that priests were married and raised and trained their sons as new priests.[21] Anne Barstow comments on the adoption concepts of purity from ancient Judaism when she writes, *"The model for the new ascetic views was the Hebrew priesthood, that had abstained from sex for three days before*

---

[20] Verman, Mark. The History and Varieties of Jewish Meditation. Northvale, NJ: Jason Aronson Inc, 1996. Page 78, quoting from the *Keter Shem Tov*, no. 16:4a, based on *Ben Porat Yosef, Noah* 19d.

[21] Leviticus 11-15 address purity and impurity laws and Number 19 addresses how to become pure again.

sacrificing at the altar. If the priests of the old dispensation had thus disciplined themselves, should not then the servants of the final revelation do more?"[22] The idea that if the Levite priesthood could abstain from sexual relations for three days at a time then the Christian priesthood could do it indefinitely; this conclusion seems absurd in that it alludes to a sort of priesthood/religious Olympics with the winner being the most ascetic and disciplined – a concept that seems very close to the condemned heresy of Donatism. Furthermore, the Levite priesthood was set apart from the rest of Judaism, and it had a special place within Judaism of antiquity – there is no question about this. It was Ambrose, bishop of Milan, in the 4th century who equated the "set apart" status of the Levite priesthood upon the Christian ministerial priesthood[23]; therefore, laying the groundwork for future support of clerical celibacy.

The Jewish tradition aside, the argument that sexuality is impure is simply a value judgment that has changed over the years in the Roman Catholic Church. At the council of Nicea it was deemed that married sexuality was not impure and the evolution of the discipline of priestly celibacy was a process of changing norms by co-opting celibacy standards of the monastic culture. The notion that married sexuality brings about an impurity in the priesthood is arbitrary and using the purity argument only lends additional credence to the argument that celibacy is about power.

Another argument for clerical celibacy is that celibate priests can devote more time to ministry than married clergy. On the surface this might seem like a reasonable argument; however, it breaks down very quickly when looking at ministry as a profession. This argument could be used to justify celibacy within any profession claiming that doctors, attorneys, corporate executives, et al., would be better employees if they too were celibate. Additionally, a recent study surveying married Protestant clergy and celibate Catholic clergy indicated that celibate priests performed more private prayer but that both forms of clergy invested the same amount of time into parish ministry.[24] Therefore, a

---

[22] Barshow, Anne L. Married Priests and the Reforming Papacy: The Eleventh - Century Debates. New York: The Edwin Mellen Press, 1982. Page 22.

[23] Hunter. Page 223.

[24] Swenson. Page 43. "The results of this study are substantially consistent with the hypothesis that there are no significant differences in dimensions of religiosity and parochial commitments between celibate priests and married clergy. The exceptions to

celibate clergy does not necessarily have more time to invest into ministry.

The final argument in support of clerical celibacy that I will address is the argument that Jesus was celibate and therefore his priests should be celibate. My initial response to this argument for celibacy is that there is no Biblical evidence that Jesus was celibate; it is simply a tradition and opinion. That being the case I would like to tackle this argument using Biblical language itself. The Book of Matthew addresses this issue indirectly when it looks at discipleship. Jesus addresses his followers not to love "father or mother" or "son or daughter" more than him[25], but he is silent about the love a man should have for his wife in this context. Furthermore, later in the text Jesus talks about how a man will "leave his father and mother and be united to his wife."[26] Surely, if Jesus had mentioned the superiority of clerical celibacy it would probably have been recorded by the Gospel writers but in truth this is not the case. Jesus was actually in favor of marriage, but this is open to dispute. Furthermore, in evaluating the celibate Jesus narrative Barstow writes, "Given the silence of the early church concerning the sexuality of Jesus, it is not surprising that the church did not recommend celibacy for its ministers. There are no known references to Jesus' marital state before the third century, except for some Gnostic material."[27] If anything the inconclusive evidence that Jesus was celibate is enough to make the argument that a celibate priesthood is more like Jesus an argument impossible to support; simply using the excuse that tradition dictates such is not good enough. For example, at one time tradition indicated

---

this are that priests spend longer periods of time in prayer than do evangelicals. However, this does not make a difference on an important dimension of experiential religiosity, namely meditation."

[25] Matthew 10:37-39: "Anyone who loves his father or mother more than me is not worthy of me; anyone who loves his son or daughter more than me is not worthy of me; and anyone who does not take his cross and follow me is not worthy of me. Whoever finds his life will lose it, and whoever loses his life for my sake will find it."

[26] Matthew 19:4-6: " 'Haven't you read,' he replied, 'that at the beginning the Creator "made them male and female," and said, "For this reason a man will leave his father and mother and be united to his wife, and the two will become one flesh"? So they are no longer two, but one. Therefore what God has joined together, let man not separate.' "

[27] Barstow. Page 20.

that the world was flat or that evolution was condemnable – all later supported by the Vatican.

An important question needs to be asked, "Who benefits from priests being celibate?" I have addressed some of the reasons for the evolution of priestly celibacy. I argue that the Church itself, namely the clergy, benefit from celibacy. The laity needs the Church to administer the sacraments and the sacraments are only available, to most Roman Catholics, by a priesthood married only to the Church. The laity in all its forms is inferior in dignity to the priesthood, and this includes monks and nuns, since priests are by default pseudo-monks by their celibacy. There is no fear by the priesthood that nuns could ever be more pious because of their celibacy since a nun is similar to a priest only by her celibacy. Therefore, the priesthood wins the "battle of the sexes." The Second Vatican Council decreed that clerical celibacy is not essential to the priesthood[28], but affirms the discipline as good for the Church. Good for the Church or good for the clergy who administer the Church? In all the rhetoric supporting clerical celibacy nothing is mentioned about power, and this lack of acknowledgement raises a further question of, "Does the Church really believe the rhetoric or is the rhetoric a disguise of the power of clerical celibacy?" Many of the innovations at Vatican II were new approaches brought into the Roman Catholic Church from the Byzantine and Orthodox Churches and therefore did not require rewriting the justification for a change in policy. Clerical celibacy, however, is a practice that has been justified for over a thousand years as the ideal and has been so ingrained as a norm that it seems problematic to some hierarchs within the Church to reverse this rhetoric. So, I will not point fingers at the Vatican and shout, "Conspiracy," but I will argue that clerical celibacy is about power and not faith and whether or not the leaders of the Church acknowledge their true motivations for clinging to celibacy the power relationship of celibacy remains.

What is very important to consider in an analysis of clerical celibacy is that the policies of the Vatican, and therefore the laws of the church, have changed over the past (almost) two thousand years. With any change of policy comes a new set of justifications and a new rhetoric

---

[28] Vatican II Document – Presbyterorum Ordinis.
http://www.vatican.va/archive/hist_councils/ii_vatican_council/documents/vat-ii_decree_19651207_presbyterorum-ordinis_en.html

to promote the change. The momentum for clerical celibacy started early in the history of Christendom and was used to mold the perception of the clergy in such a way as to turn every priest into an ascetic and to invest within the priesthood a unique identity of elitism. The priesthood is called a vocation, as opposed to simply a profession. To be a priest is to be called, by God, to sacerdotal service; however, it seems counter-intuitive to ask a young man to make a commitment to celibacy for the rest of his life. It also seems counter-intuitive to require celibacy from Roman Catholic priests while allowing for married priests in the Byzantine Rite of the Greek Catholics; furthermore, it seems even more counter-intuitive to allow Protestant clergy the opportunity to embrace Catholicism and seek ordination as Catholic priests. Does the ordination of former Protestant clergy to the priesthood imply that their vocation to the priesthood was more loudly called out by God? Or is their priestly vocation solely in the hands of some office in the Vatican making decisions that will affect the lives of these men?

Finally, the issue of ordination within Catholicism and the sacramental character of the sacrament of Holy Orders cannot be ignored from my argument. If, as the Catholic Church teaches, the sacrament of Holy Orders instills grace upon the recipient of the sacrament then receiving this sacrament will assist the recipient in reaching salvation. The Catechism of the Catholic Church states, "The grace of the Holy Spirit proper to this sacrament is configuration to Christ as Priest, Teacher, and Pastor, of whom the ordained is made a minister."[29] Likewise, the Catechism instructs the following on the sacrament of Holy Matrimony, "This grace proper to the sacrament of Matrimony is intended to perfect the couple's love and to strengthen their indissoluble unity. By this grace they "help one another to attain holiness in their married life and in welcoming and educating children.'"[30] Who would be better qualified to educate his children a lay-father of said child or a priest and father of said child invested with the grace of the Holy Spirit in his capacity as Christ-Teacher? Does it not seem intuitively correct to assume that a married man, invested with the grace of the sacrament of Matrimony, would be better suited to the priesthood because a married Catholic has received more sacramentally bestowed grace? Monastic

---

[29] Ratzinger, Joseph Cardinal, ed. *Catechism of the Catholic Church.* Liguori, Mo.: Liguori Publications, 1994. Page 396.
[30] Ibid. Page 409.

profession is not a sacrament, but rather a sacramental and the Catechism teaches that "sacramentals do not confer grace of the Holy Spirit in the way that the sacraments do."[31] The conclusion to this reasoning is that marriage is a holy state of being, and to deny the priesthood to a married man because he is married is an illogical use of reason; the logical conclusion is that more grace is better and married life and clerical life are not incompatible – as I have shown throughout this discussion. The only logical reason for clerical celibacy that follows is the restriction of sexuality as a means of controlling the priesthood by setting them apart from the laity and making them dependent upon the church.

"Everyone agrees the celibacy rule is just a Church law dating from the 11th century, not a divine command." – Hans Kung

For Reflection, Contemplation, & Prayer:

- I argue that clerical celibacy is a power issue within the Roman Catholic Church. Do you agree or disagree?
- In the ISM the practice of clerical celibacy is almost non-existent. Is this a good practice or is "there something" about clerical celibacy that the ISM can learn?
- This essay argues, in part, that the idea of clerical celibacy was a means of making priests like monastics. What are your thoughts on monks maintaining celibacy, or can one live a monastic life while married?

---

[31] Ibid. page 416.

Freemasonry

"Now the Lord is the Spirit, and where the Spirit of the
Lord is, there is freedom." – 2 Corinthians 3:18

Let us explore Freemasonry. I had a conversation recently with a
friend from work. I've mentioned in previous episodes that I work as a
hospice chaplain. I was asked about my church affiliation and my
elevator speech on the Independent Sacramental Movement is, "I'm a
part of the Young Rite which is part of the Liberal Catholic Church
tradition which has roots in Old Catholicism, a Dutch branch of the
Church that split with Rome awhile ago." Then the topic of Freemasonry
came up and I was asked, "Can Catholics be Freemasons?" I then briefly
explained why Roman Catholics are forbidden to be Freemasons but
how that didn't apply to me. This episode will look deeper into that
conversation and I will be looking at Freemasonry from a few points of
view. First, I will look at the Roman Catholic position on the fraternity
and why Freemasonry is a problem for Roman Catholicism and the
Papacy. Then I will look at the intersection of Freemasonry and the
Liberal Catholic Church. Finally, I will share some recommendations for
those within the Independent Sacramental Movement who might want
to explore Freemasonry.

A simple definition of Freemasonry comes from the book, *The Other
Brotherhood: When Freemasonry Crossed the English Channel* where author
Darren Lorente-Bull writes,

> "Freemasonry is a fraternal society present in almost every
> nation on the globe which exists as such, officially, since 1717
> and has its origins in England. What differentiates
> Freemasonry from other fraternal and charitable societies such
> as the Rotaries or the Lions Club is the fact that Freemasonry
> makes use of ritual ceremonies to impart complex moral and
> philosophical teachings to its members. Freemasonry also
> differs from other organizations in one important respect: it has
> helped shape the modern world, at least in the west."

The teachings of Freemasonry are philosophical in nature and the
vibe of the fraternity IS somewhat religious. You might see candles and
incense burning during a lodge meeting. Ritual is important. There is
always an altar present and upon that altar is a volume of sacred law,

which is usually a Bible but can be any sacred text from any religion on Earth. Sometimes an altar will have multiple volumes of sacred law, a Bible and a Quran, for example.

Another brief definition of Freemasonry is "Masonry uses symbolism based upon the tools of stonemasons who built vast cathedrals and castles in medieval times: the construction of a building is symbolic for building our own individual character." This definition illustrates the work of Freemasonry being the building up of the individual character of its members. Self-improvement being an important hallmark of the Order.

Freemasonry is divided into two branches. One branch is Anglo-Freemasonry with the United Grand Lodge of England being the flagship jurisdictional authority along with several Grand Lodges throughout the world that show respect to England as the "first Grand Lodge among equals." The Grand Lodge of Ohio, for example, falls within Anglo-Freemasonry. The other branch of Freemasonry is Continental Freemasonry, having its origins in the European continent, with the Grand Orient of France as the "first Grand Obedience among equals." The International Order of Freemasonry for Men and Women – Le Droit Humain is an example of Continental Freemasonry. An easy way to differentiate the two branches is to see Anglo-Freemasonry as dogmatic. For example, they believe a Mason needs to believe in God and are opposed to women being Freemasons. While Continental Freemasonry values liberty and is non-dogmatic, allowing women and does not require members to have any specific religious beliefs. Continental Freemasonry tends to be more diverse and open to diversity; whereas, Anglo-Freemasonry tends to prefer homogeneity.

Freemasonry has been condemned by several Roman Catholic popes starting with Clement XII in 1738; followed by Benedict XIV in 1751; Pius VII in 1821; Leo XII in 1825; Pius VIII in 1829; Gregory XVI in 1832; Pius VIII in 1846, 1849, 1864, 1865, 1869, and 1873; and by Leo XIII in 1882, 1884, 1890, 1894, and 1902. That's a lot of condemnation!

Canon 2335 of the 1917 Code of Canon Law explicitly condemns Roman Catholics from becoming Freemasons and imposes excommunication upon any Catholic who becomes one. Canon 1374 of the 1983 Code of Canon Law implicitly condemns Roman Catholics from becoming Freemasons and imposes excommunication upon any Catholic who joins the Masonic fraternity.

Why did these Roman Pontiffs condemn Freemasonry and what is it about the Order that these Popes find so troubling? Let me break it down.

Freemasonry is non-sectarian. It is, in theory, open to anyone of any religion. Within Ango-Freemasonry a man simply needs to believe in God however he chooses to believe in God. In Continental Freemasonry the would-be Freemason, man or woman, need not necessarily believe in God. In the non-sectarian sense Freemasonry is a brotherhood of religious, spiritual, and philosophical diversity.

Freemasonry has secrets. A true secret society is hidden and isn't listed in the phone book (remember those things?) Masonic lodges are in the public view; however, Freemasonry utilizes rituals to teach a moral philosophy and those rituals are guarded. Church authorities were not and are not given free rein to evaluate and scrutinize Masonic rituals or teachings.

Freemasonry employs oaths. When a person is initiated into Freemasonry and when he or she progresses through the degrees of Freemasonry an oath is taken to keep the secrets of the order intact and abide by the judicial rulings of the order. Therefore, Grand bodies within Freemasonry are called obediences, such as The Grand Lodge of Ohio or the Grand Orient of France.

Freemasonry was considered a threat. In the United States many of our founding fathers were Freemasons, with George Washington and Benjamin Franklin being two examples. Freemasonry was linked to the French Revolution and the papal condemnations against Freemasonry were ignored by French Catholics. The papacy considered Freemasonry to be subversive in the sense that it operated with goals not always in synch with the Papacy. Freemasonry wants to promote equality, liberty, and justice and these traits were often interpreted differently by Roman Catholic authorities.

These four reasons why the Roman Catholic Church condemns Freemasonry have been expanded by anti-Masonic Catholic apologists and other points given. These, I believe, are the main reasons why the Roman Catholic Church has condemned Masonry. This will hopefully give you an idea of the historical reasons why the popes have acted as they have.

Yet, Freemasonry, at its core is about promoting "Brotherly Love, Relief, and Truth," and the teachings of the fraternity build upon these three concepts using symbols, stories, and allegory. Freemasonry tries to improve society and promote tolerance, equality, liberty and to promote the inner work of self-discovery and awakening potential.

While the Roman Catholic Church, and the papacy, have condemned Freemasonry there is a historical precedent of Freemasonry existing peacefully within the Independent Sacramental Movement. The founding bishops of the Liberal Catholic Church, Bishops James Wedgwood, and Charles Leadbeater, were involved in Continental Freemasonry. Wedgwood and Leadbeater worked with Annie Besant who founded the British Federation of the International Order of Co-Freemasonry, Le Droit Humain. The early history of the Liberal Catholic Church has been intertwined with Masonic principles. The difference between the Liberal Catholic Church's opinion of Freemasonry and that of the Roman Catholic Church helps to illustrate why churches within the Liberal Catholic Church Tradition need to exist. To promote liberty and personal growth without necessarily forcing its members into an easily controlled box.

Historically, the Roman Catholic Church has taught "No salvation outside of the Church," and maintained an exclusive monopoly on salvation. The Liberal Catholic Church tradition holds that there are truths in all religions and there is more that unites humanity than separates it. The Gospel truly is good news, but that Good News should not be used to oppress people, it is there to give life and is inviting rather than divisive.

The Freemasonry promoted by the early founders of the Liberal Catholic Church was, and is, focused on esotericism. What this means is that it introspective and intellectual in its approach to spiritual truths. The word esotericism often suggests unorthodoxy, but that is not the implication I wish to make. If exotericism is the public work of the church, then esoteric is the hidden work of the church. The mystic and the esotericist both seek union with God, and with spiritual ideals. The mystic will likely approach this process through contemplation and meditation; whereas the esotericist will use study and experience to achieve these goals – in reality there is often a combination of both practices by mystics and esotericists alike. The Roman Catholic Church does not want its people to use any means to achieve union with God, and this approach goes back to the exclusive claims held by the Vatican. The Liberal Catholic Church, and those jurisdictions within the Liberal Catholic Church tradition, are more open to allowing its adherents to seek union with God however the Holy Spirit speaks to you.

The Continental Freemasonry of the early Liberal Catholic Church movement was and still is liberal in nature. What this means is that it is non-dogmatic and allows both women and men free access to all aspects of the order and does not impose a requirement to believe in God or a higher power. It should be noted that the Masonic ritual, crafted by Annie Besant, and used by the British Federation of Le Droit Humain is very spiritual in nature and would likely be uncomfortable to a militant atheist. It is not that they allow atheists, it is that they do not require specific religious beliefs. In a conversation I had with Bishops Domen and Aristid, Continental Freemasons in Slovenia and members of my own Jurisdiction the Young Rite, it was said to me that while they allow atheists in their lodges, they have yet to encounter one. Anglo Masonic lodges require their members to believe in God, but my experience is that some members fake it because they want to join the lodge – for motivations that usually do not include self-improvement.

Continental Freemasonry was compatible with the Liberal Catholic Church of Wedgwood and Leadbeater's time because the principles of Freemasonry were compatible with the church they were trying to promote. The Roman Catholic Church, under the authority of the Pope and the Vatican Curia, wants an exclusive claim on truth and wishes to maintain power over everyone under their umbrella. This is the reason why the Independent Sacramental Movement exists; because we do not want to succumb to the power of Rome and in the more liberal branches of the movement we often see truth differently.

Thus far, I have shown how the Roman Catholic Church feels about Freemasonry. If you're a Roman Catholic and you become a Freemason you are excommunicated. Plain and simple; however, you are welcome to join us in the Independent Sacramental Movement, especially The Young Rite. I have also talked about how Continental Freemasonry was important to the founders of the Liberal Catholic Church movement.

I joined Freemasonry when I first petitioned Harmony Lodge #8 in Urbana, Ohio back in 1997, which is a part of the Grand Lodge of Ohio. Since then, I have been a member of four Masonic Lodges in two different states and several appendant bodies. Not all my experiences in Freemasonry have been good. I have encountered bigotry that has troubled me deeply; however, I have also encountered wonderful people and have learned a lot about myself as I seek to constantly chip away at my imperfections.

I would recommend joining a lodge to anyone who is interested in improving their character and becoming a better person. There are two branches of Freemasonry out there for the would-be seeker of its mysteries. I would recommend looking into both branches and communicating with their representatives – an Anglo-Masonic Grand Lodge near you or an organization like The International Order of Freemasonry for Men and Women – Le Droit Humain. Get to know the members and decide for yourself which branch of Freemasonry best suits you and your interests. Each individual lodge has its own culture and I know wonderful people within both branches. But remember this, Masons are people. You might encounter people in a lodge you do not like, and who may not share your values. Keep looking because not all lodges are the same and there are true gems out there within both branches of Freemasonry. Find the one that best suits you.

This discussion on Freemasonry will hopefully give you an understanding of why the Roman Catholic Church prohibits its members from joining Freemasonry, but also illustrate how Masonic affiliation can be a spiritual resource to those of us within the Independent Sacramental Movement. The Freemasonic ideal of working To the Glory of the Great Architect of The Universe and the Perfection of Humanity are perfectly compatible with Christian values. I believe bishops within the various jurisdictions of the Independent Sacramental Movement should seriously consider enriching their lives and those under their care by encouraging engagement with Freemasonry, like Bishops Wedgwood and Leadbeater.

While the Roman Catholic Church may be seeking control over its membership, I believe our experiences with God should be liberating, filled with joy, and reverence for the sacred seen in our world. The church should be a safe place that accepts you for who you are, and the lodge should be the same.

"Quick condemnation of all that is not ours, of views with which we disagree, of ideas that do not attract us, is the sign of a narrow mind, of an uncultivated intelligence. Bigotry is always ignorant, and the wise boy, who will become the wise man, tries to understand and to see the truth in ideas with which he does not agree." – Annie Besant

For Reflection, Contemplation, & Prayer:

- Was the Roman Catholic Church correct in condemning Freemasonry?
- Most Grand Lodges prohibit women from becoming Freemasons; however, Co-Freemasonry exists and allows men and women to become active within lodges. Most ISM jurisdictions permit women's ordination. What are your thoughts on gender and Freemasonry and the intersection of Freemasonry for men and women and ordination open to both genders?
- The Liberal Catholic Church tradition has had a connection to Freemasonry, especially Co-Freemasonry. Do you think it would benefit ISM clergy to take up membership in a Masonic Lodge?

Afterward

The Most Ven. Dr. Joshua R. Paszkiewicz

As Bishop David Oliver Kling is keen to observe in his recurring introduction to the Sacramental Whine podcast, the Independent Sacramental Movement (ISM) is likely one of, if not the best kept secret in Christianity. Casual observers might have a difficult time arriving at that conclusion, however. After all, a cursory survey of the ISM is likely to yield initial feelings of confusion and ambivalence at best, and impressions of outright Live Action Role Playing (LARPing) at worst. These are realities that longtime participants in the ISM are quite familiar with, and still, can-be goofiness aside, there is a sense of integrity and sincerity at the core of the Movement, and in the hearts of its persistent adherents. In this, I'm reminded that etymologically, the word integrity is related to the word integer, which the New Oxford American Dictionary defines in part as "a thing complete in itself."

Integrity and wholeness are essential elements of any authentic spiritual path, and to be whole or complete requires the presence and awareness of both light and shadow, of blessings and banes, of virtues and convictions. In this, the ISM perhaps has a foot ahead of most so-called mainline religious institutions as we plainly vest in our shadows alongside our virtues by means of our very existence. Participants in the ISM have no borrowed institutional legitimacy or cultural authority. Each adherent to the Movement, be they cleric or lay are, of necessity, in constant dialogue with their sense of calling, the realities of their qualifications, and the limitations intrinsic to ministry beyond the reach of the coffers of conventional denominations. As the late western spiritual luminary Swami Kriyananda Giri once wrote "a certain amount of ridicule is good for the soul, and for the freedom-seeking ego!"

Without a doubt, for some, the ISM offers but a pathway toward quick credentials, replete with lavish vestments, and often inflated styles and forms of address. For others, however, including some of those quick-credential seekers that have become longtime and sincere disciples of the way (if not by means of mere stubborn devotion to genuinely fulfilling the developmental and Maslovian needs that drove them here, oft unconsciously), the ISM offers a path of authentic introspection, devotional transformation, and kenotic service in the work of healing the hearts and minds of our ever-broken world.

In the global west we have been dealing with the decline of religious participation and valuation generally, and Christendom specifically, for a number of decades. Such a lackluster spiritual landscape has made justifying bowing to the dogmas and debts of formation and service in mainline churches an untenable enterprise. It seems likely that in the decades to come the arguments in support of religious legitimacy via congregational size, pulpit height, and pension contributions will become "utterly null," just as Anglican Holy Orders at large were once considered by the Roman Catholic hierarchy. Indeed, religious professionals, both inside and outside the ISM may soon find themselves more alike than not. As common devotees of increasingly obscure, and (seemingly) culturally irrelevant "systems of symbols," the line between LARPing and legitimate vocation draws ever more thin, and what remains of that line is certainly to be found nowhere else but in the arenas of integrity and authenticity.

What the ISM may lack in resources and cultural authority it makes up for in integrity, and authenticity. This is plainly obvious beyond the cursory surveys alluded to here previously, and highlighted, perhaps uniquely, in the variety of testimonies and accounts detailed in the Sacramental Whine podcast. The beating heart of this movement is comprised not of buildings and bank accounts, but of big questions, sincere concerns, and undeniable senses of call alive in the minds of the estimated one-million-plus participants said to currently constitute the movement. Among these are physicians and fast-food workers, military and healthcare chaplains and retirees, white collar managers and differently abled folks, college professors and GED holders – laity, deacons, priests, and bishops alike.

A recurring theme throughout the world of the ISM is that of sacramental justice, and even if such a thing is to be had among just us (the ISM and our mutual recognition of one another, that is), we have it. Our sacramental lives are not valid via the endorsement of bureaucracies and international communions, but rather via the actual experience of those electing to live them out within the context of a movement that offers little in the way of authority, but much in the way of wholeness via our invitation in myriad forms to show up exactly as you are, and to be both confirmed and transformed by the sacred in the near infinite ways in which it is made manifest, beyond the constructs and limitations of ever discriminating psyches.

The Most Ven. Dr. Joshua R. Paszkiewicz, BCPC, BCCC, CIC
Order of Contemplatives Ecumenical - The Ascension Alliance
December 9th, 2020 - Kansas City, MO USA

Acknowledgements

I would like to acknowledge the following:

Bishop Gregory Godsey for all the work you do to support the ISM, you are an inspiration.

Father Jayme Mathias for initiating this book project.

Bishop Alan Kemp for welcoming me into the Ascension Alliance as an affiliate member.

Bishop Kenneth von Folmar for welcoming me into the Convergent Christian Communion as an assisting bishop.

Bishop Robert Lamoureux & **Deacon Timothy Olivieri** for being such great colleagues and friends.

To my wife **Jacki Dietz**, for your continued support.

To my daughter, **Vivianne Leona Kling**, I strive to create a legacy that will make you proud.

All the members of the **Community of Saint George**, we have a great community and I love you all.

To all the **guests** I have had on the podcast, *Sacramental Whine: An Independent Sacramental Movement Podcast*, you folks are awesome.

Made in the USA
Monee, IL
18 January 2022